No Band of Brothers

SHADES OF BLUE AND GRAY SERIES

Edited by Herman Hattaway and Jon L. Wakelyn

THE SHADES OF Blue and Gray Series offers Civil War studies for the modern reader—Civil War buff and scholar alike. Military history today addresses the relationship between society and warfare. Thus biographies and thematic studies that deal with civilians, soldiers, and political leaders are increasingly important to a larger public. This series includes books that will appeal to Civil War Roundtable groups, individuals, libraries, and academics with a special interest in this era of American history.

No Band of Brothers

Problems in the Rebel High Command

Steven E. Woodworth

University of Missouri Press • Columbia and London

Copyright © 1999 by
The Curators of the University of Missouri
University of Missouri Press, Columbia, Missouri 65201
Printed and bound in the United States of America
All rights reserved
5 4 3 2 1   03 02 01 00 99

Library of Congress Cataloging-in-Publication Data

Woodworth, Steven E.
    No band of brothers : problems in the rebel high command /
Steven E. Woodworth.
        p.   cm.—(Shades of blue and gray series)
    Includes bibliographical references (p.   ) and index.
    ISBN 0-8262-1255-7 (alk. paper)
    1. Conferederate States of America—Military policy.   2. United
States—History—Civil War, 1861–1865—Campaigns.
    3. Conferederate States of America—Politics and government.
    4. Davis, Jefferson, 1808–1889—Military leadership.
    5. Generals—Confederate States of America.   6. Confederate
States of America. Army—History.   7. Command of troops-
–History—19th century.   8. Strategy—History—19th century.
    9. Leadership—History—19th century.
    I. Title.   II. Series.
    E487.W8   1999
    973.7'3—dc21   99-35480
                                                                CIP

∞™ This paper meets the requirements of the
American National Standard for Permanence of Paper
for Printed Library Materials, Z39.48, 1984.

Designer: Mindy Shouse
Typesetter: BookComp, Inc.
Printer and binder: Thomson-Shore, Inc.
Typefaces: Minion, Shelley

For My Son David

To God Alone be the Glory

Contents

Preface

"THE BONNIE Blue Flag" was second only to "Dixie" in its popularity as a Confederate marching song. Its opening words, "We are a band of brothers," expressed the unity and solidarity that Southerners claimed and for which they hoped in their new republic. While the sentiment may well have been reality for common soldiers—the regiments, brigades, and divisions that made up the Confederacy's armies—it was emphatically not the case with the Confederacy's high command. Among Jefferson Davis and his often rebellious generals, a far different spirit prevailed. Pride, jealousy, mistrust, and cross-purposes among those in high places hamstrung the South's war effort. Whatever the bond that linked Southern common soldiers, the men who sent them into battle were clearly no "band of brothers."

The Confederacy was not yet in its grave before the analysis of its cause of death began. Southerners first and other students of the war afterward began to examine the Confederate high command in search of the reason for the South's failure to gain its independence. More than a century later, we ought to see, at least, that no such single sufficient cause exists. Rather, the fall of the Confederacy, like practically anything else important that happens in the world, was the product of numerous and complex causes, the result of a great many human decisions, and ultimately, as its contemporaries North and South recognized, a manifestation of God's providential hand in history.

While a search for a single human cause of the Confederate defeat must ever be a fruitless errand, we can still profit from analyzing the actions of Southern leadership during the war. One may admire the fortitude displayed by the Southern people and the boldness and effectiveness of many of their leaders' decisions. One can even wonder that the Confederacy survived as long as it did, for that endurance was no more automatic than was its eventual demise. Yet the fact remains that the South lost a very winnable conflict, and among the many reasons for that loss was the performance of the Confederate high command. Jefferson Davis and his top brass were bound to make some mistakes; as events played out, they made a few more than the Confederacy could endure—all other circumstances (the many other contributing factors of Southern defeat) being just what they were. If one of the purposes of studying history is to learn from other people's mistakes, then studying the Confederate high command should have definite value.

The essays in this volume are aimed at doing just that, examining Jefferson Davis, several of his more important generals, the Confederacy's strategic plans, and the South's success in making useful officers out of numerous men with very little military preparation at the beginning of the war. Not surprisingly, such an examination reveals some weaknesses, many strengths, and much that should be instructive either to students of war or of human nature.

A unifying theme in these studies can be found in the personal nature of Civil War command. More than disputes about this or that strategy, defensive versus offensive operations, or allocation of troops to one front or another, the key questions in matters of high command during the Civil War were often ones pertaining to the personalities of those who exercised leadership and how those personalities interacted with each other. Such issues could take various forms, from matters of personal relationships, to an officer's natural tendencies to dodge or accept responsibility, to his ability to handle pressure, or his inclination to take aggressive action or remain passive.

Successful interaction of personalities was one of the chief factors that made the Davis-Lee collaboration so successful. Indeed, the fact that Lee knew how to handle Davis's sometimes difficult personality—and had the humility to do so—explains why Davis and Lee formed one of the most successful partnerships of the war despite their barely submerged but fundamental differences about the strategy the Confederacy should pursue. No doubt they could have been even more effective had they been of one mind about strategy, but the personal harmony between them was the most important factor. Lee's excellent personal-relations skills also stood him in good stead with such opposite personalities as Thomas J. "Stonewall" Jackson and James Longstreet. By contrast, Braxton Bragg, though he tried hard sometimes, possessed a prickly personality, and simply could not succeed in charming and motivating those with whom he had to serve. Likewise, the festering personal problems between Davis and such of his generals as Joseph E. Johnston and Pierre G. T. Beauregard had obvious effects on the performances of all concerned as well as on the outcome of the war. Had Joseph E. Johnston shared every one of Lee's ideas about offensive operations and the need to carry the war to the enemy, but yet suffered the same poor relationship that he did with Jefferson Davis, it is doubtful that his Confederate career would have been much more successful than it was. Personal factors ensured his ineffectiveness as a Confederate general.

An important point to note here is that military professionalism was not then what it is today. The entire revolution of professionalism in many facets of American society was a thing of the Progressive Era and was nearly half a century in the future when the leaders of the Civil War were internalizing their institutional culture. While there was such a thing as a "profession of arms" and military officers were professionally trained, to some extent, at West Point, the ethos of the professional—who behaves in certain ways and conforms to certain standards simply because he is a professional—was not in operation yet. Instead, members of the officer corps tended much more to think of themselves as high-toned gentlemen of sensitive honor. Thus dueling, though against regulations, nevertheless continued to take place in the Old Army. Other behavior that today would be considered highly unprofessional was then commonplace. Indeed, during the 1850s, U.S. Secretary of War Jefferson Davis and General-in-Chief Winfield Scott, though stopping short of physical violence, carried on a prolonged and unseemly exchange of letters and newspaper blasts that were the antithesis of the modern idea of professional behavior. Thus when considering the actions of Civil War generals and civilian leaders, it is misleading to ask oneself whether this or that course of action is one that a professional (as we now understand the concept) would adopt. Would a trained professional impair his efficiency, risk his command or the success of his cause, because of personal differences? Whether a modern-day professional would do such a thing is for others to answer, but I have no hesitance in asserting that a "professional" soldier of Civil War vintage might do just that.

Not surprisingly, the personality and personal style of Jefferson Davis molded the entire shape of Confederate war making. Davis was an intelligent man and a rigorous but conventional and uncreative thinker. He did not have much imagination, and he was not long on deep, fundamental consideration of first principles. Thus his selection of strategy for the Confederacy was conventional—defensive strategy with frequent and energetic but mostly rhetorical nods to the desire of the Southern public (or at least the noisy portion of it) for occasional offensive action. Conventional things do not always have to be bad, and Davis undeniably carried through his conventional approach to the war with vigor, determination, zeal (he literally worked himself almost to death), and much competence.

Davis's sound but unimaginative thought made him the polar opposite of one of his first famous generals, Pierre Gustave Toutant Beauregard. The Louisiana Creole, "hero" of Fort Sumter and Manassas, was given to thought that was highly imaginative but often not at all sound. In chapters one and eight of this book, I develop this contrast, showing how Davis's estimates of the military situation and what was possible to accomplish were far more realistic than those of Beauregard. The two situations presented in those two chapters, the first and fourth summers of the war, show that this difference was constant throughout the conflict. It tended to bring Davis into conflict with Beauregard, and that conflict affected the course of Confederate history mainly in the ammunition it gave to Davis's political enemies, adding to the rancor in the Confederate Congress.

"The evil men do lives after them," Shakespeare had the cunning Mark Antony say, "the good is oft interred with their bones." So it often is with the unfortunate Davis. The competent parts of his performance excite little comment and analysis, perhaps because so many of those competencies fell largely in mundane but indispensable administrative and support functions that lend themselves little to analysis. By contrast, Davis's shortcomings stand out. Analyzing them can be instructive, but it is well to remember that only a very talented and hardworking man could have achieved the opportunity to make such mistakes.

And mistakes he did make, often recognizable as features of his own personal style of command. Sometimes they were the result of his pride. Davis had reason to consider himself a man of high military attainments before the Civil War: he was West Point educated, a seven-year veteran of the regular U.S. Army, a celebrated commander of a volunteer regiment in the Mexican War, a successful U.S. secretary of war, and, finally, a member of the Senate committee on military affairs. During the war he occasionally showed an unfortunate and destructive tendency to overrate this strength and demand due—or perhaps undue—recognition of it. In chapter five I deal with one such occasion, probably the worst, wherein Davis's offended military pride led him to make a bad decision rather than be upstaged by his secretary of war.

Davis's pride in his military abilities also led him to take a very hands-on approach to the role of commander-in-chief. This was most evident during the Seven Days' battles, discussed in chapter four, wherein Davis was frequently on the battlefield and on at least one occasion even bypassed the chain of command and gave a direct order to a brigade commander. Davis's presence on the battlefield was clearly not appreciated by Lee, though the latter always handled the matter with tact. As also became apparent during the Seven Days, Davis's pride was not of the common sort—a desire to be recognized as a V.I.P. and honored with appropriate pomp and ceremony. In that sense Davis showed impressive and commendable humility, being, like Lincoln, ready to hold his general's horse if that would help produce victory. However, the Confederate president did desire to be acknowledged as a top military mind. This pride also contributed to his difficulties with Beauregard and Joseph Johnston, who each possessed the same characteristic in greater quantity.

Another aspect of Davis's personality that affected Confederate war-waging was his strong personal loyalty to those he considered his friends. That in itself was not necessarily a liability, if tempered by sober judgment of each friend's capabilities, but Davis carried it to the point of cronyism. Strangely enough, the man in whose favor Davis is most often and virulently accused of cronyism, Braxton Bragg, had been a personal enemy of Davis's before the war and certainly did not become a friend until at least well after the hue and cry had gone up against the president for maintaining Bragg solely from reasons of personal regard. On the other hand, Davis did practice disastrous cronyism in the case of his old West Point friend Leonidas Polk. Polk, in turn, demonstrated that the most disastrous aspect of his unwarranted appointment to general officer rank was not his ignorance of strategy and tactics (though these were profound), but rather his own considerable pride, self-will, and refusal to come under the authority of any superior not entirely of his own choosing. The problems he caused for the Confederacy, enabled by Jefferson Davis, form the subject of chapter two and part of chapter six of this volume.

Another problem general for Davis was Joseph E. Johnston. Oddly, Davis clung stubbornly to the idea that Johnston was a great general who could do much for the Confederacy if only he could be persuaded to apply his full powers. This conviction Davis held throughout most of the war despite mounting evidence to the contrary. Yet perhaps the president was right after all, at least to some degree. Johnston was an enigma and a prime example of the thesis that factors of personality, more than chessboard strategic or tactical abilities, determine a general's success. Johnston was proud and rank-conscious in ways that never occurred to Jefferson Davis, and he very quickly allowed his conceit to poison his relationship with the president. Beyond that, Johnston repeatedly showed what looks very like a dread of having his reputation tarnished by any appearance of failure. Certainly in Virginia in 1862, in Mississippi in 1863, and in Georgia in 1864, he refused to place his reputation on the line by taking timely aggressive action for the sake of what he called his country. It is difficult if not impossible to prove, but it is tempting to speculate that Johnston's commitment to the Confederacy was far less solid and intense than that of, say, Jefferson Davis. This would bear out a theme currently the subject of ongoing research by Professor Jon Wakelyn that the Confederacy suffered from a lack of complete support on the part of some of the Southern people. Clearly, it would be a mistake to conceive of a "solid South" in 1861, unified in its determination to fight to the last gasp for Confederate independence. If that had been the case, they would have won. Johnston's case is at least a study in the complex motivations that can influence a general's performance. It is not a simple matter of supporting the cause or opposing it: there are myriad shades of gray in between.

One manifestation of Johnston's reluctance to risk his reputation was a hesitancy to accept responsibility for anything if there was any possible way to dodge it. This appears in chapter three, a study of the Confederate command at the early 1862 battle of Williamsburg. Johnston should have commanded in person on that field but left it instead to his subordinate James Longstreet. Then when Longstreet bungled the affair, Johnston passed lightly over his subordinate's miscues, since they would have reflected poorly on his own reputation. Indeed, Johnston seems to have convinced himself that Longstreet's performance had been acceptable, since he accorded that general a key role in his subsequent attack at Seven Pines. Excessively loose supervision of subordinates and failure to examine their performances closely made it easier in some ways to avoid responsibility. In the long run, however, it was not a particularly successful behavior for Johnston, from any point of view.

Davis's prolonged confidence in Johnston, never justified by events, underscores another way in which the Confederacy's war was influenced by the president's personal outlook. Several times during the war, Davis turned to the consistently ineffective Johnston to take over key commands. Why did he not try other generals in those positions, once Johnston had proved irresolute? The answer lies once again in Davis's conventional, unimaginative, inflexible thinking. He would stick with those generals who had had strong reputations in the prewar U.S. Army, stubbornly clinging to the belief that someone like Johnston must, after all, be a good general. This, coupled with Davis's tendency to be hesitant and uncertain in his direction of the war, particularly in the western theater where he was not personally present, led him back to Johnston several times. He was not always enthused by the necessity of choosing him, but he did not make up his mind to take daring and decisive action in finding another commander. Chapter seven of this book deals with some of the options that were available to him. Chapter nine shows what could happen when Davis did, however hesitantly, choose another commander but did not exercise sufficient supervision over him.

Finally, the war was influenced by the personalities and personal choices of many men in positions of command high and low. Some of the most interesting of these were the nonprofessional officers who became generals. Both sides had to use a fair number of these generals in a war that mobilized numbers of troops vastly out of proportion to anything America had ever done before. The Confederacy, under the direction of Jefferson Davis, used many of them, often quite effectively. Chapter ten of this book analyzes the factors that made for success or failure in such generals, usually a combination of combativeness, humility, and teachability coupled with a driving personality and a reasonable opportunity to learn the trade of soldiering. These findings go far toward explaining why politicians and their ilk, appointed directly to high rank from civilian life, rarely made good generals, as borne out by the example of Leonidas Polk.

All of these factors, the subjects of the various chapters of this book, pertain to personal choices that people make entirely aside from decisions of whether to adopt the offensive or the defensive, whether to go around the enemy's left flank or his right. Yet they were of great importance to the course and outcome to the war. And last of all, for me (and I hope for others as well), personalities make very interesting stories.

That this book exists is largely thanks to Professor John Wakelyn of Kent State University and Professor Herman Hattaway of the University of Missouri–Kansas City, both of whom discussed with me the possibility of writing a book in this series. Professor Hattaway, an old and good friend who has greatly helped me on a number of occasions, suggested the concept of putting together a collection of essays, and gave much encouragement. Professor Wakelyn read the manuscript of this book and offered many helpful suggestions. For their assistance I am deeply grateful. Naturally, I am fully responsible for any shortcomings that remain.

Provenance of the Contents

C H A P T E R O N E appeared as "Capital Folly," in *America's Civil War*, May 1993.

Chapter two appeared as "'The Indeterminate Quantities': Jefferson Davis, Leonidas Polk, and the End of Kentucky Neutrality, September 1861," *Civil War History* 38 (December 1992): 289–97.

Chapter three appeared as "Dark Portents: Confederate Command at the Battle of Williamsburg," in William J. Miller, ed., vol. 3, *The Peninsula Campaign of 1862: Yorktown to the Seven Days* (Campbell, Calif.: Savas Woodbury, 1997). Reprinted with permission of Savas Publishing Company.

Chapter four was previously published as "Jefferson Davis and Robert E. Lee in the Seven Days," in Miller, ed., vol. 1, *The Peninsula Campaign of 1862: Yorktown to the Seven Days*. Reprinted with permission of Savas Publishing Company.

Chapter five was published as "'Dismembering the Confederacy': Jefferson Davis and the Trans-Mississippi West," *Military History of the Southwest* 20 (spring 1990): 1–22.

Chapter six is based on a talk given to the Chattanooga Civil War Round Table, September 1993.

A version of Chapter seven appeared as "Confederate Command Options, 1864" in *The Campaign for Atlanta* (Campbell, Calif.: Savas Woodbury, 1992). Reprinted with permission of Savas Publishing Company.

Chapter eight appeared as "Beauregard and Bermuda Hundred," in *Leadership and Command in the American Civil War* (Campbell, Calif.: Savas Woodbury, 1995). Reprinted with permission of Savas Publishing Company.

Chapter nine is based on a talk delivered to a Blue and Gray Education Society Symposium, Nashville, Tennessee, October 1995.

Chapter ten appeared as "Homespun Generals: The Confederate Use of Non-Professional Officers," in *North & South,* 1998.

No Band of Brothers

One

DAVIS, BEAUREGARD, AND WASHINGTON, D.C., 1861

O NE OF THE most striking aspects of the way the Civil War divided the country geographically was the fact that Washington, D.C., lay on the Potomac River, the same river that formed the dividing line— in the East—between the seceding states and those loyal to the Union. Here was the nation's capital, separated by only a few hundred yards of water from a state that claimed to be independent and with which the national forces were at war. This strange proximity was obviously not lost on the participants. Northern fears for the loss of the city dictated Federal operations in Virginia, to a greater or lesser extent, throughout most of the war, and Southern hopes for the capture of the District of Columbia at times burned very brightly indeed. In April 1861 the *Richmond Examiner* proclaimed, "There is one wild shout of fierce resolve to capture Washington."[1] The Confederate dream of seizing Washington and, perhaps, ending the war at a stroke, lived on into 1864, when Jubal Early's raid approached the city. But never did that dream seem as real as it did during the first year of the war.

Jefferson Davis and Pierre G. T. Beauregard were the two men to whom Southerners looked, above all others, to make that dream a reality. Davis, thanks to his Mexican War exploits, was the South's greatest prewar military hero, and now was its president and commander-in-chief. Beauregard, thanks to his easy victory at Fort Sumter, was the greatest hero early in the war. Both of these men were in Virginia during the summer and fall of 1861, and, together with other as yet lesser known

1

Confederate leaders such as Joseph E. Johnston and Robert E. Lee, they made the decisions by which the Confederacy fought its first and most hopeful campaign for the banks of the Potomac.

Jefferson Davis arrived in Richmond early on the morning of May 29, 1861, amid cheers and cannon salutes, and was escorted to his temporary quarters at the Spotswood Hotel by the governor of Virginia and the mayor of Richmond. Many rejoiced to see him there, as many had urged him to come, because of the widespread belief, especially among Virginians, that this was to be the crucial theater of the war, and that it was here that the South's greatest military leader, Davis, was most needed. Writing to urge the president to come to Virginia, one Old Dominion politician had gushed, "You are the man to whom all hearts turn."[2] At the time that was only a small exaggeration.

During the trip from Montgomery to Richmond, Davis, while passing through the Carolinas, had fired off a telegram to Beauregard, then still at Charleston, scene of his victory at Fort Sumter six weeks before. Davis had at least some acquaintance with Beauregard from prewar days, though the two were never close. Now he believed the Creole general from Louisiana was someone on whom he could rely in the defense of Virginia, and he ordered Beauregard to report to Richmond at once. The general arrived just the day after Davis did, to a similar ovation. On May 31, Davis and Beauregard met with General Robert E. Lee, commander of Virginia's state forces, for a lengthy discussion of the military situation. Beauregard thought Davis would have sent him to Norfolk had it not been for Lee's report on the seriousness of the situation at Manassas. A vital railroad junction for Confederate communications with the Shenandoah Valley, Manassas lay just thirty miles south of Washington, and was the logical next step for the Union forces that had just occupied Alexandria, on the south bank of the Potomac across from the capital. Davis decided it was at Manassas that Beauregard was needed.[3]

The general traveled up the Orange and Alexandria Railroad the next day and took command of the small Confederate force at the hitherto drowsy northern Virginia hamlet. President Davis, who seemed bent on directing the major operations in northern Virginia himself, bypassing the as-yet unproven Lee, apparently instructed Beauregard to write to him directly, without reference to any chain of command. And so it was that two days after his arrival at Manassas, Beauregard wrote the president with his first impressions. Offensive action was the furthest thing from his mind. He complained that the position was a weak one, that his force was too small, and that it was not adequately supplied. Several days after that, he was pestering Richmond with a request that the troops of General Theophilus Holmes, in a neighboring district, be made available to him.[4]

Yet even as he fretted about the weakness of his force and position, an officer of Beauregard's excitable—not to say downright flighty—temperament could be cooking up offensive schemes so optimistic as to be little short of fantasy. And no matter how fantastic his plans might be, the state of Southern public opinion was such that just then a good many people would have been prepared to believe he could carry them off. One piece of Beauregard mythology circulating at this time had it that the dapper Creole had assumed the disguise of an Irish laborer, entered the Federal lines around Washington, and inspected all of the fortifications there.[5] People who could believe this sort of thing would be unlikely to doubt the practicality of anything Beauregard might propose.

All of this made matters that much harder for Jefferson Davis, who was trying to fight the real war. During the first few days of June, Davis, in consultation with Lee and, sometimes, Adjutant and Inspector General Samuel Cooper, had worked out a basic strategy for the defense of northern Virginia. It keyed on the Manassas Gap Railroad, which connected Joseph E. Johnston's position near Harpers Ferry in the lower Shenandoah Valley to Beauregard's at Manassas. Other railroads connecting with the Manassas Gap line at the junction of that name would in turn allow rapid movement of troops between Beauregard's force and the other Confederate forces guarding the rivers of eastern Virginia. Davis hoped by the use of these railroads, particularly the Manassas Gap, to be able to shuttle troops rapidly in the face of any Federal advance.

It was not a bad system, given the circumstances, but it did not meet with the approval of Beauregard. On June 12 the general sent one of his aides to Richmond with a letter for the president. Far from believing now that his own position was about to be overrun, the Creole announced that Johnston's position at Harpers Ferry was the target of the enemy's immediate plans. That being the case, Beauregard suggested, would it not be better for Johnston to retreat at once, leaving a small detachment or two to guard the passes of the Blue Ridge, and join Beauregard for "a bold and rapid movement forward" that would "retake Arlington Heights and Alexandria," just across the river from Washington? Provided the Yankees would be foolish enough to leave those positions weakly fortified and garrisoned—a fact that he seemed to take for granted—Beauregard thought capturing them would present no problem. Since these heights on the south bank of the Potomac commanded Washington, Confederate possession of them would force the Federals to drop everything else in Virginia and rush all their forces to the defense of the capital.[6]

When the president wrote his remarkably courteous and patient reply the next day, he addressed Beauregard, "My dear General," and went on to concede generously that Beauregard possibly had access to information that Richmond did not, and so might just be on to something about the supposed threat to Johnston. Still, even allowing for that possibility, Davis could not see why Johnston would not be able to retreat *after* the enemy began his advance rather than saving the Federals the trouble of driving him back by abandoning his position now. As for the advance to the south bank of the Potomac, Davis allowed that it would indeed be pleasant to have possession of the high ground overlooking Washington. The problem was that having a large Union army to the rear, cutting off supply and retreat, would take a whole lot of the fun out the view of the capital from Arlington Heights. And to his rear was exactly where Beauregard was likely to find a Union army if he succeeded in taking the heights under his proposed plan. If, as Beauregard assumed, Johnston's entire force would be inadequate to stop a Federal advance up the valley, it followed logically that a small detachment of that force would be even less adequate to stop the Federals from crossing the Blue Ridge behind Beauregard and ruining his whole day.

To Beauregard's rather insulting request that "a concerted plan of operations be adopted at once by the government," Davis explained with amazing patience the necessity of maintaining flexibility in the face of the enemy's as yet undisclosed intentions. He closed by complimenting Beauregard's military abilities. Yet perhaps the most striking example of Davis's mildness toward the proud general was his ignoring completely the strong implication in Beauregard's letter that when his and Johnston's forces were combined, he, rather than his superior in rank Johnston, would command. Altogether, the president had treated his prima donna army commander with remarkable gentleness. That, however, did not prevent the growth of an attitude at Beauregard's headquarters that soon had his staff officers referring to the commander-in-chief as a "stupid fool."[7]

Beauregard was not daunted by the rebuff of his first grand design against Washington, but like other generals of overactive imagination— and few sane men were more given to fantasy than he—the Creole found that moral courage did not come easily. When a few days later intelligence reports revealed that Union General Irvin McDowell was poised to advance toward Manassas with a force of some forty thousand men, Beauregard's descent from heady heights of fantasy to the solid ground of reality took on the nature of free-fall. Early in July he wrote a letter addressed to Louis T. Wigfall but intended to influence Davis into sending reinforcements. Wigfall was a member of the Confederate Congress and at that time a close confidant of the president. "How can it be expected that I shall be able to maintain my ground unless reinforced immediately?" Beauregard moaned. "Is it right and proper to sacrifice so many valuable lives (and perhaps our cause) without the least prospect of success?" Clearly, the general was losing his nerve. Just as clearly, his plans were now wholly defensive, as he remarked, in the only optimistic note in the letter, "If I could only get the enemy to attack me, as I am trying to have him do, I would stake my reputation on the handsomest victory that could be hoped for." Three days later in a letter to Davis himself, Beauregard wrote, "I shall act with extreme caution."[8]

Yet such moods tended to be short-lived with Beauregard, especially when it came to drawing up grandiose plans. "A day or two" after his promise to "act with extreme caution," Beauregard had concocted another far-fetched scheme and dispatched a staff officer to Richmond to lay it before the president. At the same time, the Creole sketched his idea in a letter to Johnston.[9] "What a pity," he wrote, "we cannot carry into effect the following plan of operations," and thereupon described something very like the plan he had advanced the month before, except that this time the combined Confederate forces, instead of simply advancing to threaten Washington, would first defeat McDowell, then cross the Blue Ridge to deal with the Federal forces that had been threatening Johnston, before moving into western Virginia and dispatching the Union army there. Finally, after only fifteen to twenty-five days of campaigning, they would cross over into Maryland to threaten the national capital from the rear. As an operational plan, it had real possibilities—that is, if the Confederates had had twice as many men in Virginia as they did, if those troops had been seasoned veterans, well-equipped and provided with adequate transport, and if they had been led by experienced generals with efficient staffs, it might have been possible.[10] As it was, if the plan bore any resemblance to reality, such similarity appeared to be purely coincidental.

But Beauregard was not finished. No sooner had his first staff officer departed for Richmond than the general became so excited that he elaborated the plan still further and sent a second staff officer, Colonel James Chesnut, formerly of the U.S. Senate, to importune the president again. Beauregard, who had now swung to the extreme of feeling it "impossible to remain passively on the defensive," had given Chesnut written notes so that he would be sure to get every convoluted detail right in his presentation to Davis.

Chesnut left Beauregard's headquarters on Sunday morning, July 14, and arrived in Richmond around 3:30 that afternoon. Going immediately to the president's quarters, he found Davis sick in bed. Nevertheless, the president received him "with great kindness and cordiality," and learning the purpose of Chesnut's visit, made an appointment for the two of them to meet that evening along with Lee and Cooper. At the appointed time Chesnut and his fellow staff officer arrived and were ushered into the presence of the Confederacy's assembled brass. Chesnut laid out Beauregard's plan. Once again the Creole had assumed that when his and Johnston's forces combined, he, and not Johnston, would command. In other respects too the plan was like those that had gone before, except for a slight alteration to the grand finale. This time Johnston, with his own forces plus the Confederate troops then operating in West Virginia—including a good many soldiers existing solely in Beauregard's imagination—was to attack Washington from the rear while Beauregard threatened it from the Virginia side.

In response to this, Cooper seems to have remained silent, Davis showed surprising tact, and Lee displayed his accustomed diplomacy. "Earnest consideration was given by the President and the generals," Chesnut wrote to Beauregard two days later. In fact, he thought they had considered the scheme "brilliant and comprehensive, but, to its adoption at this time, two leading objections were urged by the President and by General Lee." Insofar as this plan was similar to Beauregard's previous design, the first objection was much the same. With Johnston's force gone from the Shenandoah, nothing would remain to stop the Federals he had been facing from coming down on Beauregard's left flank and rear. The other objection was more fundamental to the whole concept of trying to capture Washington. Even if Beauregard's plan should be a success up to the point of the approach to the national capital, the Northern forces would still be able to withdraw into powerful fortifications from which the Confederates could hardly hope to dislodge them, and the Federals would be able to draw massive reinforcements from the North. For these reasons the plan seemed impractical to Davis and Lee, but they generously allowed that it might be useful "at a later period."[11]

Once again the president's gentleness was lost on the haughty Beauregard. After the war he wrote that either his plan of June or that of July 14 would have had "the certain result" of "the taking of Washington," and that by declining to give him full authority over the Confederacy's armies in Virginia, Davis had lost the war for the South.[12]

One week to the day after Chesnut presented the second grand scheme in Richmond, Beauregard had his hour of glory at Manassas. Learning of the Federal movement on July 17, he telegraphed Davis, "Enemy is advancing." The moment had come for Davis to put into operation the system he and Lee had worked out. Orders went out to both Johnston and Holmes to reinforce Beauregard at once. The timing was crucial. Too late, and Beauregard would fight the battle alone and outnumbered. Too early, and disaster could result on the fronts that were thus left uncovered, much as Davis and Lee had foreseen in the case of Beauregard's grandiose schemes. As it turned out, the president got the timing exactly right, with the bulk of the troops reaching Manassas just before the battle and others arriving while the fighting was actually in progress, helping to turn the tide. Beauregard, of course, was not satisfied. He later wrote that he was "annoyed at the thought that it had been too long delayed to effect any substantial good," and at the time he wired the War Department with the gratuitous complaint, "I believe this proposed movement of General Johnston is too late." As the enemy approached, Beauregard alternated whining with pleading, begging the president, "Send forward any reinforcements, at the earliest possible instant, and by every possible means."[13]

But the troops arrived when they were needed and a great victory was won, more in spite of Beauregard's efforts than because of them. Davis had hoped to be present for the battle, probably not to take command, but most likely as an active adviser who would be far enough forward to come under enemy fire and be "in a position to assume command of at least portions of the army should the necessity arise."[14] As events developed, that proved to be impossible, and the president arrived on the field of battle after the fighting and just in time to get in on the controversy that followed. For months afterward a dispute would simmer in the Confederacy as to whether Washington could have been taken immediately after the battle of Manassas, and, if so, who was at fault that it had not been taken.

As the Union forces reeled backward in retreat that afternoon, both Beauregard and Johnston, each unbeknownst to the other, had given orders to separate units for pursuit of the beaten foe, but neither general had taken any pains to see to it that his orders were carried out. As a result, one of the movements was countermanded by a relatively junior staff officer. The other, the one ordered by Beauregard, died a slower death. By 6 P.M. the general who had of late been proposing grand sweeping movements north of the Potomac began to lose his stomach for aggressive pursuit north of Bull Run. Turning to a staff officer, he ordered, "Ride across the Stone Bridge and find Colonel Kershaw, who is conducting the pursuit along the pike. Order him to advance very carefully and not to attack."[15]

Apparently somewhat taken aback by this order, the staff officer asked, "Shall I tell him not to attack under *any circumstances,* no matter *what* the condition of the enemy in his front?" To which Beauregard replied, "Kemper's battery has been ordered to join him. Let him wait for it to come up. Then he can pursue, but cautiously, and he must not attack unless he has a decided advantage." What was left of the pursuit after this laming order was ended when Beauregard received an unsubstantiated report—which turned out to be false—that the Federals had broken his line on another part of the field. If a vigorous and thorough pursuit had been in progress, ample evidence would have been at hand to show the contrary. Instead, Beauregard, without checking on the validity of the report, canceled even the tentative pursuit he had previously ordered and began shifting troops to meet the nonexistent threat. When the truth was discovered it was about 7 P.M., and the sun was still half an hour high, but no effort was made to resume the pursuit.[16]

Meanwhile, Davis had arrived by railroad, procured a horse, and ridden toward the sound of the guns. At a field hospital to the rear of the fighting, a brigadier general who was having his wounded hand bandaged called out to the president, "Give me five thousand fresh men, and I will be in Washington City tomorrow morning."[17] The brigadier's name was Thomas J. Jackson, and he had just won his famous nickname, but Davis could hardly have known what to make of this strange and, as yet, little-known officer, even if he had had five thousand fresh troops to give him.

The president rode on, and, reaching the battlefield, actually got a glimpse of the fleeing enemy.[18] Caught up in the enthusiasm of the moment, Davis even joined the pursuit for a time, before finally reigning in and riding back to Beauregard's headquarters. There he found Johnston but not Beauregard, who was still wandering around the battlefield in response to the phantom Yankee offensive.

It was 10 P.M. before the general returned. When he came in, the president was engaged in writing a dispatch to the War Department, informing Richmond of the great victory. Beauregard now informed him for the first time of the false alarm that had scotched the pursuit. Davis seemed dismayed and asked if the pursuit could be renewed. At this point someone brought in news that an officer had been all the way to Centreville in pursuit of the foe and found nothing but abandoned equipment and supplies. If that was the case, Davis urged the generals, it was all the more reason to pursue immediately. An awkward silence followed.[19] Partially this was a result of the fact that both Johnston and Beauregard had used up their stock of moral courage for that day and were little inclined to press matters, especially with their exhausted and disorganized troops. The awkwardness, however, was also partially a result of the mistake Davis had made in coming to Manassas in the first place. His post of duty was Richmond; here in the field his presence only created confusion as to who was in command.

The situation was confused enough already. Johnston ranked Beauregard but was a weaker personality and had only just arrived on the field that day. Beauregard had been talking for weeks as if he would command their combined forces, and Johnston, when called to join the Creole a few days before, had actually felt uncertain enough to write the War Department for confirmation of his superior rank.[20] Davis, of course, ranked them both, but he was even more recently arrived and less familiar with the situation. He also seemed not quite aware that his mere presence there put him in command. He could either take up active command or order Johnston and Beauregard, as those familiar with the situation, to "carry on." Instead, he urged but did not order a course of action that his instincts told him was correct, but that his generals were not inclined to follow. And so the generals and their commander-in-chief sat in uneasy silence, each waiting for one of the others to speak first.

The silence was broken by neither general nor president but by Beauregard's chief-of-staff, who asked if Davis would like to dictate an order for such a pursuit. That was all the prodding the president needed. He eagerly agreed to give the order, and without saying so, took active command of the army. But, as Johnston or Beauregard could have told him (though they would not have dreamed of doing so), command was a very heavy load on a man's mind and emotions. And with his shaky knowledge of the situation, Davis's self-assured air began to falter almost immediately.

As the president worked out the precise wording of the order that Beauregard's staff officer was committing to paper for his signature, someone questioned the reliability of the officer who had reported the Yankees fleeing beyond Centreville. Davis paused. Someone else brought word that the officer had been confused, and had not been to Centreville but only as far as Cub Run, much closer to Confederate lines. The confidence with which the president had assumed command only a few minutes before now crumbled. Who could tell where the enemy was, or what his condition? Who could tell how much more the Confederate troops could take? Who wanted the responsibility for turning a great victory, incomplete though it might be, into a great defeat? Not Davis. He now entered into further discussion with the generals as to what should be done. The result was an unwritten and probably illusory consensus that seems to have been understood differently by each of participants. Davis thought he had left instructions for the pursuit to be renewed in the morning. Beauregard seems to have thought his duty fulfilled by the ordering of a tentative reconnaissance, which went forward the next morning and accomplished little besides scavenging the battlefield.[21]

In the weeks and months that followed, as increasing information came to light of the disarray in which the Federals had found themselves on the night of the battle of Manassas, many in the South began to ask why the victory had not been followed up, and Washington captured. As with most things that went wrong in the Confederacy, this was often blamed on President Davis. Beauregard was not above taking advantage of this by including in his Manassas report, which he allowed to be published contrary to regulations, a description of the plan he had submitted through Chesnut earlier in the month, thus setting off a long and bitter feud between himself and the president. To make matters worse, Beauregard was simultaneously claiming that a lack of supplies, for which the president was ultimately responsible, had prevented the army from taking Washington in the days and weeks after Manassas. By late September of that year he had cooked up another grand scheme for an offensive against Washington, and together with Johnston and Major General Gustavus W. Smith, presented it to Davis, who once again had to play the realist and decline to act on the Creole's pipe dreams. Beauregard's designs for taking Washington after Manassas were as impractical as his plans before the battle had been. Not one of them offered a realistic chance for success. The best chance the Confederacy had for capturing Washington during 1861 was in the hours immediately following the Federal rout at Manassas. Even then the possibility does not, in retrospect, appear to have been all that great. McDowell had a defensive line manned by unbroken troops at Centreville that night. The Confederates were tired, hungry, disorganized, and lacked an adequate supply system for a major advance. Before morning, rain began falling and continued throughout the next day, rendering movement on the dirt roads of northern Virginia all but impossible.[22]

Yet when the Confederate opportunity was greatest, Beauregard—who spent the summer and fall concocting schemes with far less promise and reproaching Davis for not allowing him to take Washington and win the war—had lost his nerve to the point of being unwilling even to try. In that moment it was Davis, the realist, who pressed most strongly for aggressive action. In the end his aggressive instincts were overcome not only by a certain natural indecisiveness that often plagued him during the war, but also by his growing appreciation of the realities of the situation he faced.

Two

Davis, Polk, and the End of Kentucky Neutrality

IN THE FALL of 1861, few issues were as vital to the Confederacy's ultimate survival as the status of Kentucky. That state's then declared neutrality was enormously favorable to the South. A neutral Kentucky, stretching from the Appalachians to the Mississippi and inviolable to the armies of either side, shielded the heartland of the South as no Confederate army ever would. Should Kentucky have ended its neutrality by declaring openly for the South, the result might have been even more significant. At least that seems to have been what Abraham Lincoln thought with regard to his native state when he remarked, "To Lose Kentucky is nearly the same as to lose the whole game."[1] Yet in September 1861 the Confederacy fumbled away its opportunities in Kentucky and actually helped drive that state into the arms of the Federal government. These facts have, of course, been well known to historians. However, documents that have come to light only in recent years have shaded this incident in a different color than previously and given new insights into the character of Confederate President Jefferson Davis and his relations with both his first secretary of war, Leroy Pope Walker, and his chief western general at that time, Leonidas Polk.

It is Polk who was primarily to blame for the Confederacy's blunder in Kentucky. Davis had appointed Polk to the Mississippi Valley command because of prior friendship. The two had been together at West Point and forged a bond of friendship that Davis, at least, carried with him to his deathbed more than half a century later. Yet in the quarter of a century that followed his graduation from the academy, Polk had neither served in the army nor so much as read a single book on military affairs, choosing instead a career as an Episcopal bishop. It seems likely, therefore, that aside from Davis's well-known blindness to the shortcomings of his friends, another reason for Polk's appointment may have been the president's hope that Polk's widespread familiarity with and popularity among the people of the Mississippi Valley would make him sensitive to the delicate political situation involving Kentucky.[2]

Certainly, Polk could hardly have been worse than his predecessor in the Mississippi Valley command. Davis had inherited General Gideon J. Pillow from the provisional army of the state of Tennessee.[3] A man of small intellect, Pillow had nevertheless made a fairly successful career for himself as a lawyer and a politician, with a brief and undistinguished military interlude during the Mexican War. Despite his primarily political background, or perhaps because leading a bold advance seemed the best way to gain political points with the electorate back home, Pillow seemed to know little and care less about the touchy political situation in Kentucky. In May 1861 Pillow had decided that the town of Columbus, Kentucky, situated on high bluffs overlooking the Mississippi River, represented a better position from which to defend that stretch of the river than anyplace in the northern part of Tennessee.[4]

Ignoring the political consequences, Pillow wrote to Kentucky governor Beriah Magoffin, requesting permission to occupy the town. At the same time he wrote Davis, informing him of his action and commenting that as he expected Magoffin to refuse permission, he then would "know of no alternative but to take the responsibility of acting on my own judgment."[5] Since the occupation of Columbus would have been exactly the sort of breach of neutrality that could have driven Kentucky to cast its lot with the opposing side, Davis had good reason to appoint someone, even Polk, to supersede Pillow before he should carry out his dangerous plans.

The problem, of course, was that Polk proved to be little better than Pillow. Throughout the summer of 1861 rumors circulated, some of them well-founded, of Federal plans to seize Columbus. In such a prospective case of Northern aggression, pro-Southern Kentuckians saw just the provocation they would need to drag the state out of the Union and into the Confederacy. Polk, on the other hand, saw in it only the necessity that it be Confederate, rather than Union, troops that first violated Kentucky neutrality and took possession of the strategic heights at Columbus.[6]

Meanwhile, Jefferson Davis was ignorant of Polk's line of thinking, and there is reason to suspect that this was no accident on Polk's part. The general had spent a good deal of time around the war office and the Confederate White House in Richmond before receiving his assignment to the Mississippi Valley command. It seems very unlikely, therefore, that he was ignorant of Pillow's plan or of Davis's failure to approve it, and his silence toward the president on so momentous an issue suggests that he had made up his mind what to do and did not want any direction from his commander-in-chief. Keeping the president in ignorance was made easier by the fact that Davis had been very sick for most of the summer and therefore was probably not as alert as he otherwise might have been. In a letter to Polk dated September 2, 1861, ironically the day before Polk's movement on Columbus, Davis explained, "I have been quite sick and have not before attempted to write a letter since my convalescence." Yet that the president had noticed Polk's lack of communication there can be no doubt. "Keep me better advised of your forces and purposes," he admonished the general in the same letter.[7]

Of course by the time that letter arrived, it would have been too late even had Polk been of a mind to comply. On the night of September 3, 1861, Pillow, acting now under Polk's orders, marched his troops into Kentucky, violating the state's neutrality and occupying Columbus. The move touched off a frenzied exchange of telegrams among Davis, Polk, Secretary of War Walker, and Tennessee governor Isham G. Harris. However, one of the documents generated in this exchange seems to have been unknown to historians until fairly recently, and another was apparently known only in a significantly inaccurate form. The result has been a long-standing misinterpretation of this important event and of the characters of the individuals involved. The whole matter is made more intriguing by the fact that these gaps in the documentary record were very possibly the result of deliberate falsification on the part of one of the participants.

Briefly, the accepted interpretation of the event has been that Davis immediately acquiesced in Polk's action, wiring the general, "The necessity justifies the action," as the *Official Records* have it. But Davis is supposed to have left Walker uninformed, with the result that the president and the secretary of war, both in Richmond but apparently completely ignorant of each other's actions and opinions, sent a series of more or less simultaneous and definitely contradictory dispatches to Polk. In fact, the course of events was not quite that simple.[8]

Tennessee Governor Isham G. Harris had been working hard to bring Kentucky into the Confederacy. Indeed, in setting up his state's army prior to its official entry into the Confederacy, Harris had staked Tennessee's defense on the existence of a Confederate or neutral Kentucky. Thus it was no doubt with horror that he learned, sometime on Wednesday, September 4, that Confederate troops had violated the state's neutrality. Harris had that very day dispatched three prominent Tennessee citizens to Frankfort as commissioners, in hopes that they might woo the wavering Kentucky government into siding with the Confederacy. Seeing in the previous night's movement the doom of all his efforts, Harris immediately telegraphed both Polk and Davis. To the president he wired, "Confederate troops, commanded by General Pillow, landed at Hickman, KY., last night. I regard the movement as unfortunate; calculated to injure our cause in the State. Unless absolutely necessary there, would it not be well to order their immediate withdrawal?"[9]

The message reached Richmond the following day, Thursday, September 5. Davis's immediate response was contained in an endorsement in his own handwriting on the telegram itself, dated that same day. Not appearing in the *Official Records*, this endorsement seems to have gone unnoticed by historians until discovered fairly recently by the editors of the Jefferson Davis papers. It states, "Sec[retary] of War—Telegraph promptly to Genl Polk to withdraw troops from K[entuck]y—& explain movement[.] Ans[wer]—Gov. Harris[,] inform him of action & that movement was unauthorized—Ask Gov. Harris to communicate to Gov. Magoffin." Walker seems to have done just as he was ordered and was not, as has previously been thought, working at cross-purposes with the president. The three telegrams with which he carried out Davis's orders are found in the *Official Records*. One was to Harris and informed the Tennessee governor that the move was unauthorized and the troops had been ordered back. It also called on him to inform Kentucky's Governor Magoffin of these facts. The other two telegrams Walker sent to Polk. Of these, one requests Polk to "give a reason for General Pillow's movement," and, like Walker's dispatch to Harris, is dated September 5. The other states simply: "News has reached here that General Pillow has landed his troops at Hickman, Ky. Order their prompt withdrawal from Kentucky."[10]

However, the *Official Records* give September 4 as the date for this wire.[11] If that is true, it could not have been a response either to Harris's telegram or to Davis's endorsement, but rather we would once again have Walker acting independently and without consulting the president.

There is good reason, however, to believe that the *Official Records* are mistaken in this case and that the message, like the other two, was actually sent on the fifth. First, Davis's September 5 endorsement on Harris's telegram seems to indicate that Polk's movement was previously unknown in Richmond. Second, the wording of Walker's message reflects that of Harris's, especially in describing the troops involved as Pillow's rather than Polk's and in identifying the town occupied as Hickman, which the troops had passed through en route, rather than Columbus. Third, this is just the sort of telegram Davis had ordered the secretary of war to send, and it is the only known message fitting that description. Finally, it seems unlikely that any other source for the news of Polk's movement could have reached Richmond ahead of Harris's telegram.

Had matters been allowed to rest as Davis had originally ordered, it is difficult to say whether Kentucky neutrality could still have been saved for the South. As it happened, things were not left that way, and the end of Kentucky neutrality was assured by the further actions of the Confederate high command. At the same time Harris had telegraphed Davis, he had also wired Polk, characterizing the movement as "unfortunate" since both Harris and President Davis were "pledged to respect Kentucky neutrality," and expressing the governor's hope that the troops would be "withdrawn instantly." The telegram reached Polk that same day, and the general replied at once. He was acting, he said, "under the plenary powers delegated to me by the President." The troops, he continued, would not be withdrawn, and he added, "I had never received official information that the President and yourself had determined upon any particular course in reference to the State of Kentucky."[12] It was not a particularly honest message. Aside from the fact that it is hard to imagine Jefferson Davis granting "plenary" powers to anyone, it is almost inconceivable that Polk did not know the Confederacy's long-standing policy toward Kentucky.

Having learned, perhaps, from the governor's message that the invasion of Kentucky was likely to have far-reaching repercussions, Polk apparently decided to cover the political front by belatedly notifying the president of his actions and at the same time presenting his own side of the story. On that same Wednesday, September 4, he got off a long telegram to Davis, presenting the movement as a military necessity welcomed by the local populace, and concluding, "It is my intention now to continue to occupy and keep this position."[13]

The president's response to Polk's invasion of Kentucky, if not specifically to this appeal, has long been thought to have been, "The necessity justifies the action," as his brief telegraphic reply is recorded in the *Official Records*. However, that dispatch is dated September 4, and for reasons already stated, it seems very unlikely that any of the various telegrams sent from West Tennessee that day could have reached Richmond before the fifth. If that raises suspicions as to the accuracy of the *Official Records'* version of the reply, those suspicions may well be considered as confirmed by a very similar—but significantly different—dispatch contained in the Polk Papers of the Library of Congress. Its date, September 5, seems more realistic, and it reads: "Your Telegram Rec[eived.] The necessity must justify the action."[14] This is undoubtedly the correct version of the telegram that appears, albeit in a corrupt form, in the *Official Records*. It is much less decisive and more equivocal, since its wording can be interpreted with equal ease to mean either, the necessity *does* justify the action, or, the necessity *had better* justify the action.

How, then, is Davis's role in these events to be reinterpreted in the light of these new sources? It would seem that on September 5, he received the telegram from Harris, notifying him of the invasion of Kentucky and urging its recall. Davis, who was indeed pledged to respect Kentucky neutrality, reacted immediately and correctly, ordering Walker to recall the troops and see that Governors Harris and Magoffin were so informed. Later in the day, Polk's telegram arrived and the president became irresolute, no longer insisting on the withdrawal he had already ordered and sending his almost cryptic telegram of acquiescence. Davis appears far more uncertain and indecisive in this version than in the conventional one, and his overreliance on personal friends seems even more destructive. Polk appears, if anything, even more manipulative and duplicitous. Walker, by contrast, comes off much better. He was not out of the loop in the Confederate decision-making process for this incident, nor did he make major decisions such as ordering the troops back from Kentucky on his own responsibility and without consulting the president. He carried out his orders quickly and efficiently, and if there was confusion in Richmond that day, as war department clerk John B. Jones seems to suggest, it was not the result of too strong a will in the secretary of war but of too weak a will in the commander-in-chief.[15] Taken as a whole, this new interpretation of the incident helps explain, in a way that has not previously been possible, how the Confederacy could err so grievously in its Kentucky policy.

All that remains, then, is to explain how incorrect versions of some of these documents found their way into the *Official Records*. Both of

the erroneous dispatches, the telegram from Walker to Polk falsely dated
September 4, as well as that from Davis to Polk also falsely dated the
fourth and somehow altered to make the president's approval seem more
emphatic and disguise the fact that such approval was elicited only by
Polk's own telegram of the fourth, were part of a set of recopied correspondence forwarded by Polk to the Confederate War Department later
in the month of September 1861.[16] Along with the rest of the Confederate
War Department files, they were taken over by the U.S. government at
the end of the war and eventually appeared in the *Official Records*. And
so, no doubt exceeding his fondest expectations, the general's deception
has lived on for more than a century after his own demise.

Three

Confederate Command in Microcosm

The Case of Williamsburg

O F A L L T H E forgotten events of the much neglected Peninsula campaign, none are more obscure than those of the Confederate retreat from Yorktown to the Chickahominy. As the Peninsula campaign itself is overshadowed by the more dramatic events of the latter half of 1862, so the retreat up the peninsula is dwarfed by the drama of the Yorktown siege on one side, and on the other by a whole succession of crises: the Davis-Johnston confrontations, the decision to defend Richmond, the massive but confused battle of Seven Pines, and finally the awesome finale in the Seven Days' battles. In the midst of these monumental events, the muddy miles of retreat from the Yorktown works to the banks of the flooded Chickahominy have attracted less notice than most other Civil War events of equal importance. Yet in the course of this dismal retreat, the Confederate army fought a battle that in other circumstances would have gained considerable attention, a battle that was all the more important because of what it revealed about the shortcomings of the officers of that army. The battle of Williamsburg foreshadowed in many ways the failures of Seven Pines and the frustrations Robert E. Lee would face during the Seven Days. Had the men responsible for the leadership been able—and willing—to assess and correct the problems revealed at Williamsburg, the course of the later battles—and the war—might have been changed.

On the evening of May 3, 1862, a heavy rain began to fall on the already none-too-dry armies, fortifications, and countryside around Yorktown,

Virginia. As the sheets of water coursed down from the blackened skies, the night was suddenly illuminated by the flash of cannon, the red glow of burning fuses tracing fiery arcs across the cloudy heavens, and the lurid bursts of the shells. In the Confederate fortifications, every gun had opened fire in what one observer called "a magnificent pyrotechnic display." The purpose of the bombardment was to cover the withdrawal of the Confederate army of General Joseph E. Johnston from the fortifications it had held for more than a month. Through the flash and thunder, cloud and rain of both the bombardment and the storm, Southern troops began filing out of their muddy trenches and onto the muddy roads leading back toward Richmond. By morning the Yorktown defenses were silent, the guns spiked, and the fortifications empty as the first Federal troops moved gingerly into the stronghold.[1]

At that moment, Johnston and his army were still only seven or eight miles away. For the Confederate commander and his men, the march had been a nightmare of rain, mud, mired horses, and hopelessly bogged wagons and guns, with the thought constantly present that McClellan's Union army would no doubt take up the pursuit in the morning. The tired troops continued their struggle with the elements and the wretched Virginia roads through at least part of the day on Sunday, May 4. By afternoon, Johnston's forces had reached the old colonial capital at Williamsburg. About two miles short of Williamsburg and roughly twelve from the lines around Yorktown, the two roads on which Johnston's army had been marching, the Yorktown Road on the north and the Lee's Mill Road on the South, converged into a single thoroughfare. At the intersection of the roads stood Fort Magruder, the centerpiece of a line of fortifications built by Major General John B. Magruder while he was commanding the peninsula before Johnston's arrival earlier that spring. The peninsula narrowed at Williamsburg, and this and other terrain features offered the Confederates an opportunity to make a stand there. Magruder had thus, with the approval and supervision of Confederate General-in-Chief Robert E. Lee, constructed a system of works here as a possible second position should Yorktown fall. When in March of that year Confederate President Jefferson Davis, after a lengthy conference with Lee, Johnston, Secretary of War George W. Randolph, and Generals Gustavus W. Smith and James Longstreet, had decided that the peninsula ought to be defended, he and Lee had almost certainly expected that Johnston, while his troops at least delayed McClellan at Yorktown, would improve the defenses at Williamsburg and occupy them for a determined stand against the advancing Federals. This would at least give Davis and Lee more time to prepare the Richmond defenses and to gather reinforcements and recruits from the rest of the Confederacy.[2]

Yet Johnston had no intention of doing anything of the sort. His attitude from the start had been one of going through the motions of defending the peninsula while actually planning to force the president into accepting his own strategic idea: rapid concentration of all the Confederacy's available forces for a showdown battle on the outskirts of Richmond.[3] It was not that Johnston was so very anxious to give battle—quite the contrary. He was the sort of general who could fearlessly expose his person to enemy fire but was paralyzed by fear at the thought of exposing his reputation to mishap in the ultimate test of an army commander's skill, pitched battle. For him, tomorrow was always a better day for fighting than today, and the day after was better still. Since defending the peninsula meant immediate confrontation with the hostile army, Johnston preferred retreat, staying well clear of the enemy for as long as possible and hoping in the shadow of Richmond to find more troops—and more nerve.

Johnston thus had neither the desire nor the intention of meeting the Federals at Williamsburg or anywhere in the vicinity. He planned to abandon the fortifications and continue his retreat. The first suggestion he got that this might not be entirely possible came when Union cavalry began skirmishing with his own mounted soldiers in front of Fort Magruder on the afternoon of the fourth. The Northern riders were successfully brushed off, but their infantry support could not be far behind. An encounter with infantry would be another matter entirely, and it would take a good deal more than Brigadier General J. E. B. Stuart's brigade of graycoat cavalry to keep them at bay.[4] This was significant since the army's wagon trains were making very poor time on the muddy roads. By the evening of May 4, Johnston seems to have realized that he was going to have to hold the road junction at Williamsburg for at least part of the next day. Currently stationed there in support of Stuart's cavalry were two brigades of infantry under Brigadier General Lafayette McLaws. McLaws's brigades were part of Magruder's division. They had helped build these fortifications, and they knew them well. The natural course would have been to let them man the works, reinforced perhaps by another brigade or two, until the army's trains were safely out of the way. Instead, Johnston ordered McLaws's troops to march at the head of the army's column the next day, while other troops assumed the duties of rear guard. The reason for this strange decision probably had something to do with the man to whom Johnston entrusted these duties. The division now called on to provide a rear guard was that of Major General James Longstreet.[5]

Longstreet was a man of imposing physique and even larger self-confidence, a fact that was all the more surprising since he had graduated fifty-fourth out of the fifty-six men in his West Point class of 1842 and had done little to distinguish himself since then. Yet the sense of self-assurance he exuded could be well nigh overpowering. In battle this made him an encouragement to those around him. Yet in those and other times of stress, it could make him a temptation to a weaker-willed superior who might seek emotional relief by leaning on the decisions of Longstreet's feeble intellect—delivered, as always, with the greatest of confidence.

Johnston was almost neurotic in his fear of risking his reputation by undertaking any endeavor in which all of the arrangements were not absolutely perfect. The story was told that in prewar days he had returned empty-handed from quail hunts rather than risk his reputation for marksmanship by taking a less-than-perfect shot.[6] His heart was now set on the perfect shot he planned to take at McClellan once he received massive reinforcements near Richmond, and he desperately wished to avoid battle for the present, especially with his army tired, wet, hungry, and stretched out along several miles of muddy roads. Yet in view of the fact that he obviously could not avoid at least some sort of battle at Williamsburg on May 5, the actions he took that morning were strange. Having turned responsibility for the rear guard over to Longstreet, he rode off with the army's leading units, abandoning the scene of likely battle and placing as many miles of muddy road as possible between himself and the enemy. In Longstreet's air of self-assurance, he had found a way to put an unpleasant circumstance out of his head for at least the time being.

Longstreet, for all his confidence, had very little idea what to do. Throughout the war he would demonstrate himself to be skillful in the mechanics of moving his brigades around the battlefield but hopelessly inept in devising strategy or tactics. Skill in handling troops was a very important asset, and one lacked by many an officer of greater intellect and even greater strategic insight than Longstreet. That ability, along with the steadiness he could impart to those around him and those under his command, would eventually make him a valuable lieutenant to any general who could induce him to use his skills in accordance with a wise plan of his superior's devising. Unfortunately for the Confederacy, Robert E. Lee was the only general who ever succeeded in doing that. Left to his own devices, Longstreet had pride enough to get himself into trouble and not brains enough to get himself out. Left by Johnston to cover the army's retreat, Longstreet made no effort to reconnoiter the ground he was to defend, but virtually turned over command of the operation to Brigadier General Richard Anderson, with two brigades posted in and around Fort Magruder.[7]

The rain, which had stopped during the day on the fourth, started again during the night, and continued throughout the day of the battle and the night after that. The morning of May 5 had just dawned cold, gray, and dripping under a leaden sky and a steady soaking rain, when Federal skirmishers began to press forward along either side of the Lee's Mill Road, exchanging fire with the Confederates around Fort Magruder and the nearby redoubts. Union artillery was brought up and joined in the long-range firing. The Confederates answered in kind, but for some time the contest remained low-key.[8] These Union troops were part of Joseph Hooker's division of the Army of the Potomac's III Corps. By advancing toward Williamsburg over the Lee's Mill Road, they were approaching the right of the Confederate line. Opposite the Rebel left, the Yorktown Road angled down toward the intersection in front of Fort Magruder. On that road another Federal division was approaching, W. F. Smith's of the IV Corps. McClellan had been a prewar friend of Johnston's, and was a man after the Virginian's own heart. He, too, had found other ways to occupy himself than be present for a battle his army was certain to fight that day. Commanding in his stead on the field of battle was sixty-five-year-old Major General E. V. Sumner. Whatever the old general's strengths—and they may have been considerable—he did not seem to have a very clear head on this day. The result was that he allowed Hooker to go forward unsupported, while Smith, for most of the day, was kept chafing in inactivity.[9]

Meanwhile, Longstreet, still not having visited the battlefield himself, began making the other brigades of his division available to Anderson. Around 7 A.M., the brigade of Cadmus M. Wilcox, which had already taken up its march through town behind the rest of the retreating army, was countermarched back to the vicinity of Fort Magruder to be ready if Anderson needed it. About an hour later, A. P. Hill was ordered to get his brigade up and moving toward the battlefield. George Pickett's regiments had gotten an early start from their camp at the College of

William and Mary, and about the same time Hill got orders for the front, Pickett too was directed to countermarch and await further orders at William and Mary. At about 10 A.M. the word came for this brigade as well to proceed to the scene of the fighting.[10] Longstreet's remaining brigade, under Raleigh Colston, was farthest from the battlefield, but turned back toward the action by midmorning.

Anderson, who had started the day with his own and Roger A. Pryor's brigades, was not slow to flex the extra muscle Longstreet had given him. He ordered Wilcox to cross a field to the right and enter the woods leading down to the James River to see what was in there. Seeing was no easy matter in this forest so dense a colonel could not see the whole of his regimental front at one time, but as he pushed forward a line of skirmishers, Wilcox found out soon enough what he was up against. Hooker had all three of his brigades off on this side of the road now, probing for a way around the daunting bulk of Fort Magruder. Realizing he could not cover the entire enemy front and that the Federals overlapped him badly on his right, Wilcox sent an urgent summons for aid not to Anderson but directly to A. P. Hill. Hill was not sure that his orders from Longstreet authorized this; after all, he had been directed to move up and support Anderson. The result was delay while Hill sent a courier dashing off to find Longstreet and get permission to make the move.[11]

Anderson, who was actually responsible for directing the action, was not consulted by anyone. At some point as the fighting was heating up that morning, he left the fort and rode down toward the right to take command in person. Apparently, messages missed him during the transition. Unable to exercise effective command from his advanced position, he may have returned to the vicinity of Fort Magruder. Wherever he was, he did little to coordinate the division's fighting on this day. Brave and talented, Anderson had nevertheless been dogged for many years by rumors of a bent to drunkenness. His ineffectiveness on this day—indeed, even his whereabouts during most of the fight—remain a mystery.[12]

Wilcox, however, needed reinforcements and quickly. He mentioned his plight to Stuart, who happened along at that time, and Stuart carried the request to Pryor, whose brigade held the redoubts near Fort Magruder. By this time it was still only about 9 A.M., and the rest of the reinforcements Longstreet had ordered had not yet come up. In response to Wilcox's dilemma, Pryor marched into the woods with half of his brigade, though by whose order this occurred remains in some obscurity. Anderson later reported having ordered the movement, while

Wilcox reported that Pryor had received his request intended for Hill and acted on his own responsibility. Pryor recounted that he had "received verbal orders from several sources," some of which apparently involved abandoning the redoubts altogether and taking his whole command into the woods. Feeling bound by his previous orders from Anderson to hold the redoubts "at every hazard," and believing it was actually Hill who was supposed to go to Wilcox's support, Pryor took only one under-strength regiment and three companies of another.[13]

Strangely, when Hill and Pickett came up around 10 A.M., Anderson still did not make use of their brigades. He may have been out of touch someplace between fort and front. Or he may have had only the sketchiest of ideas of what was going on in the underbrush, as the other brigade commanders, particularly Wilcox, seem not to have realized they were to continue reporting to him. Both Hill and Pickett had sent aides to inform him of their arrival. Both of them had returned to their respective commanders with the report that he needed no support. The men of the two brigades had thus been waiting as peacefully as their nerves would allow them to do as they listened to the thump and rattle of the simmering exchange of fire between the fort and the enemy lines a few hundred yards away. Yet within half an hour Anderson seems to have changed his mind, for around 10:30 he gave orders to both Hill and Pickett to advance to the support of the comrades in the timber.[14]

Meanwhile, Wilcox, upon receiving Pryor's reinforced regiment, immediately threw the entire force at Hooker's division. The Federals had something less than three brigades with which to meet this thrust, since Hooker was continuing to use some of his troops to engage the Confederates at Fort Magruder and the nearby redoubts. They still enjoyed a better than two-to-one advantage over Wilcox's short gray line, overlapping him substantially on the right. The Confederate attack made little headway beyond driving in the enemy skirmishers. As the battle lines collided, this advantage told on Pryor's command and on the right regiment of Wilcox's brigade, the Ninth Alabama, both of which reeled backward in confused retreat. Wilcox's center regiment, the Tenth Alabama, on the initiative of its colonel, swung the left side of its line forward to bring the regiment up to a rail fence that ran through the woods, then side-stepped along the fence to the right rear until it could confront the enemy head-on. A deadlock then developed as the two sides poured fire into each other, often at very close range in the dense, now smoke-filled woods.[15]

How long Wilcox's men could have stood this uneven exchange is an open question. They were required to stand it perhaps half an hour, as shortly after 10:30 Hill's brigade wheeled into position on the right. By this time it was no use trying to link up with Pryor's right, or even the right of Wilcox's brigade—the broken Ninth Alabama. Instead, Hill moved into position on the flank of the Tenth Alabama, helping it to break the impetus of the Federal pressure it had been resisting along its conveniently angled rail fence and covered the battered Ninth, along with Pryor's units, as they attempted to regroup. The cheering of Hill's men as they stopped the advancing Yankees and turned them back could be heard the whole length of the Rebel line. Ambrose Powell Hill was nothing if not aggressive and needed no one to urge him to follow up his advantage. Completing the deployment of his regiments with some difficulty in the dense woods, he now turned the left flank of the Federals who had been destroying Wilcox's right. Swinging his right-flank regiment forward on the rest of his line like a gate on a hinge, he broke the Union line and drove the bluecoats back through the woods in disorder.[16]

That he was able to enjoy this degree of success was probably due to the fact that one of Pickett's regiments was just then going in even farther to the right, fully occupying Federals who might have turned the tables on Hill yet again as he swung his flank across their front in the process of crushing the exposed left of the Union troops that had defeated Wilcox. Pickett had originally been ordered by Anderson to send in his other three regiments at the same place, in hopes of completely overlapping and rolling up the Federal line. Before he could comply, however, he was called back, probably by an urgent summons from Wilcox or from one or more of the latter's regimental commanders, whose situation was still dire. Pickett's other three regiments thus went into action in support of these already hard-pressed units. Wilcox, who had previously borrowed a regiment from Hill to bolster the shaky Ninth Alabama, now directed at least one of Pickett's regiments to move up and support his left-flank regiment, the Nineteenth Mississippi.[17]

With his own front now shored up by reinforcements from both Pickett and Hill, and with the remainder of those generals' brigades rolling forward on his right, Wilcox again ordered his line to advance. The Tenth Alabama swarmed over its rail fence, the regimental right swinging forward to get the line squared off once again toward the enemy. The Nineteenth Mississippi rushed forward with bayonets fixed, and the various companies of the Ninth Alabama, now acting independently or in small battalions, joined the advance. Still, on this end of the front where no advantage could be gained by flanking, Northern resistance proved to be stubborn. The Nineteenth Mississippi got into a furious firefight at a range of less than thirty yards with a line of Federals behind a log barricade, losing its colonel but finally driving the bluecoats from their cover. The Tenth Alabama fared worse, being thrown back in disorder from its attempted assault. The impetus of Hill's thrust, however, served to carry the fragmented Confederate line forward. Anderson had sent forward the remainder of Pryor's brigade, spreading his own regiments to cover both fort and redoubts. Thus, the Confederates now had four brigades committed in the woods, while Hooker had only three Union brigades, and at least some of his forces were still confronting Fort Magruder. The Rebel advance carried their battle lines forward to the edge of a large clearing covered with felled pine trees, and here the Federals dug in their heels and would give no more ground.[18]

By this time Longstreet's division was approaching a state of almost complete disorganization. Wilcox was exercising a general sort of leadership on the left part of the line, but he no longer commanded anything like a brigade. Under his direction was a collection of regiments from Hill's and Pickett's brigades. Of his own troops, the Tenth Alabama had rallied but was now fighting under Hill. The Nineteenth Mississippi had come apart after its ordeal in front of the log barricade. Half the regiment was still fighting, but now as part of Pryor's command. The other half had become entangled in the felled timber, then drifted off to the right to take possession of several abandoned Federal guns from two batteries that had been engaging Fort Magruder. Seizing the guns simultaneously with elements of at least two other Confederate regiments, they unfortunately came under the fire that the gunners in Fort Magruder had been directing toward the batteries when they were still in Yankee hands. Thereafter, that half of the Nineteenth Mississippi drifted out of the fight like a derelict ship that finally runs aground and stays there. Companies of the Ninth Alabama were all over the battlefield. Independent of Wilcox and apparently unknown to him, Pickett, with two of his regiments and a fragment of one of Pryor's, was operating along more or less the same stretch of the Confederate line. Pryor himself had only one of his own regiments and one of Wilcox's, while Hill's command was the most nearly intact brigade left on the battlefield. At least three regiments, two of Pryor's and one of Pickett's, seem to have fought entirely independent of any brigade command. Ominously, by this time virtually everyone was

getting low on ammunition. The division's supply wagons had already
been started on their way to the rear, and there was no reserve supply
of ammunition. Regimental and brigade commanders were reduced to
ordering their men to scavenge the cartridge boxes of the killed and
wounded Federals they had just overrun.[19]

It was about noon now, and listening to the sound of the fighting
from a point well to the rear, Longstreet noticed a sudden change in
the combination of sounds reaching his ears. A new set of notes, deep,
hammering, and insistent, had been added to the symphony of battle that
had been swelling through the misty rain for more than five hours already.
Longstreet would have recognized it as field artillery. That was nothing
new—each side had employed several batteries so far in the battle. It was
not the nature but rather the direction and the proximity of the source
of this sound that would have been startling, for the booming of these
guns was issuing from a point well to the left and somewhat to the rear of
Fort Magruder, the adjacent redoubts, or any Confederate units. It could
not have been a welcome sound to Longstreet, for it could only mean
one thing: his division was flanked. "From the swelling noise of battle,"
Longstreet blandly noted in his memoirs years later, "I concluded that it
would be well to ride to the front."[20] It would have been well to have done
so a good deal earlier. By this point, five of Longstreet's six brigades, all
the infantry then within reach, had become fully committed and largely
disorganized in a vicious dogfight in a pine thicket. Nothing but Stuart's
cavalry was available as a reserve, yet until now Longstreet had not so
much as observed the action or taken stock of the situation. Riding out
on the field a little after noon, he found a situation bad enough to have
shocked even a man of his own near-legendary imperturbability.

Somehow, as Anderson's two brigades had relieved McLaws's men the
previous evening, at least four of the redoubts on the far left of the line
had simply been missed. No one in Longstreet's division seemed to be
aware of their existence, and neither Longstreet nor Anderson had taken
the trouble to find out. By midmorning the Federals had found out, and
they also knew that the position was readily accessible from the Yorktown
Road, up which W. F. Smith's as yet unengaged division was advancing.
The ground around the unoccupied left redoubts, which looked down a
long, open, gradually sloping farm field toward Fort Magruder, enfiladed
the fort and the entire left of the Confederate position around Williamsburg. The Federals had but to walk in and take possession, and Longstreet
would be checkmated. His entire division would likely have been cut off

and captured or dispersed. The Confederates were saved by Sumner's bull-headed obtuseness. The crusty old general was letting Hooker's outnumbered division fight on unsupported while enough Northern troops waited within call to flatten Longstreet's whole division and walk straight over the thinly held Williamsburg works. Now he did the Rebels another unwitting favor by allowing Smith to send into the key position only a force too small to have a really decisive effect.

Brigadier General Winfield S. Hancock, with a reinforced brigade and two batteries of artillery, seized two of the undefended redoubts and then, unable to effect more with his small force, unlimbered his artillery and began to shell Fort Magruder and the other redoubts from the left rear. Incredibly, his thirty-four hundred men and ten guns, maneuvering in the open within plain view of the fort, had not been noticed by a single high-ranking Confederate officer up to this time.[21] Colonel Micah Jenkins, the highly competent young officer left in command of the fort when Anderson left, was understandably preoccupied with the troops of Hooker's division engaging his position from the front. Longstreet had not yet deigned to visit the scene of his division's struggle, and where Anderson was and what he was about remains an open question. However he had arrived, there was Hancock like a ghastly apparition squarely on the Confederate flank. For the time being, he held his position and continued his shelling of the Confederate fortifications.

The situation was bad enough for all that. The rear-enfilade artillery fire by itself was proving so hard to take that it appeared for some time Fort Magruder might have to be abandoned—with disastrous results. The possibility also existed that the Federals would reinforce Hancock, which was exactly what he and his division commander were hoping Sumner would finally allow. Longstreet knew at once that he was in trouble. Ordering his remaining brigade, Colston's, to hasten its march to the field, he sent an order to Major General D. H. Hill, whose division was next up the column from his own, to countermarch to his support.[22] Though he would not have shown it, Longstreet must have endured an uneasy couple of hours as he waited for the additional troops to come up and hoped the Yankees would not press their advantage.

By 3 P.M. he might have breathed a little easier, as Colston's troops and the leading brigade of D. H. Hill's division marched through Williamsburg and came sloshing down the muddy road toward the battlefield. He would at last have some sort of a force available to try to avert disaster on his badly exposed left. By this time, however, trouble was brewing again on the right. While Sumner continued to keep most of the Union troops in the area inactive, Union Brigadier General Phil Kearny had brought his division of the III Corps marching up the Mill Road in Hooker's wake. Kearny was the most experienced combat officer and one of the toughest fighters in the Army of the Potomac, and since he was not under Sumner's command, he wasted no time in throwing his troops into action in support of Hooker. His troops hit the tired and disorganized Confederates hard, rolling their line back into the woods. The ammunition situation became critical, as the troops frantically searched the knapsacks and pockets of the fallen for extra rounds. Some regiments were forced to pull out of the line entirely for want of cartridges. A. P. Hill reported that upon the exhaustion of his ammunition he led his troops in a successful bayonet charge. Wilcox was still senior officer on the field—Anderson again being curiously absent—and sent Longstreet an urgent appeal for reinforcements. In response, Longstreet dispatched Colston's brigade and two regiments of Early's oversize brigade. With these troops Wilcox was able to mount a small-scale counterattack, and the situation was stabilized.[23]

With D. H. Hill's fresh troops had come someone who must have been far less welcome to Longstreet. Army commander Joseph E. Johnston had ridden away from Williamsburg that morning hoping that nothing would happen there and that if something did, Longstreet would somehow deal with it. The distant thunder of battle to the rear had given the lie to such delusions, and Longstreet's call for help from D. H. Hill, explained as it was with the report that "the enemy was threatening to turn his left," would have removed all doubt as to the seriousness of the situation.[24] No longer able to ignore Williamsburg, Johnston turned back toward the battlefield himself, arriving about midafternoon. Incredibly, in view of the fact that his entire division was engaged in a hot fight with major enemy forces and that he had called on a neighboring division for aid, Longstreet had not communicated with Johnston in any way. This omission was too bizarre to have been an oversight. Clearly, Longstreet, who would spend much of the war conniving to gain independent command and who was currently campaigning for a corps command, had not wanted his commanding general present. He was also probably unenthusiastic about the prospect of Johnston's viewing what even Longstreet must have realized by this time was his highly questionable use of his division.

If he was worried about facing Johnston's disapproval, or even having Johnston take over direction of a battle that was now threatening to involve close to half the army, Longstreet's mind was soon put at rest. Johnston was content, as he related in his report a few days later, to be "a mere spectator, for General Longstreet's clear head and brave heart left me no apology for interference." The fact was that Johnston did not want to touch this mess with a ten-foot pole, and as he was to demonstrate after Seven Pines a month later, Johnston was not above falsifying the historical record in order to cover Longstreet's clumsy tracks, since admission of Longstreet's failures would for Johnston be a form a self-indictment, demonstrating the foolishness of granting Longstreet so much responsibility and autonomy.[25] Thus the army commander stood quietly by and allowed his subordinate to extricate himself as best he could from the predicament into which he gotten himself.

If Johnston was unwilling to take the unpleasant situation off of Longstreet's hands, Sumner was far more accommodating. Having stead-fastly refused to send reinforcements to Hancock to allow the exploitation of his incredibly advantageous position, he now ordered the Federal brigade to pull back and rejoin the rest of Smith's division. Hancock prepared to do so, and had the Confederates simply left well enough alone—as they had left him alone to their own great discomfiture all day long—he would, without further ado, have withdrawn himself from his threatening position and alleviated Longstreet's embarrassment. At this point, however, Brigadier General Jubal A. Early entered the equation of Confederate command. Early's was the lead brigade of D. H. Hill's division. Even after two of his battalions had been detached to blunt Kearny's counterattack on the Confederate right, he still had four excellent regiments in his command. Thankful to have at last some sort of force to cover the nakedness of his left flank, Longstreet posted Early some distance to the left and rear of Fort Magruder.[26]

Most of the Confederate brigade commanders so far this day had proven to be remarkably aggressive. Now Early would surpass them all. He was posted, as he later described in his report, "on the crest of a ridge in a wheat field, and near a barn and some houses, with a wood some 200 or 300 yards in front, in which position we were not in view of any body of the enemy."[27] The situation seemed to offer little enough chance for Early to emulate the reputedly successful efforts of Longstreet's brigadiers in driving the Federals back on the right, and the ambitious Virginian may well have reflected on this as Hill's other three brigades took up reserve positions behind his line. All the while he listened to the thumping of what must have been at least a full battery of artillery firing away steadily someplace just the other side of the woods his men were facing across the empty wheat field. Clearly that sound had to be coming from a Union battery, undoubtedly the one that had been shelling Fort Magruder all afternoon from near the location of the far-left redoubts now in Federal hands. Thus it was that Early conceived the idea of an attack through the woods to take the Union battery in flank and win easy laurels with the capture of these guns the Federals had so obligingly set down on his doorstep. Riding off to get permission for this attack, he found Johnston, Longstreet, and D. H. Hill together, and directed his request at first directly to Johnston. The army commander deferred to Longstreet, who agreed but ordered Hill to accompany the assault in person since he did not trust Early.[28]

What Hill did not know at the time was that Early had made absolutely no reconnaissance at all of the situation into which he proposed to hurl his brigade. His information was limited to the sounds he could perceive coming from the other side of the dense woods to his front. Early's mind was apparently already occupied with counting the guns he was going to capture—it sounded as if there might be a dozen of them—and thinking how good all this would look in his report. Whatever occupied his thoughts, taking a look on the other side of the woods before sending his troops there seems not to have entered his mind. By now it was about 5 P.M., and hurrying lest darkness close in on this already gray and gloomy day before they could launch their attack, Hill and Early got the brigade moving forward. Hill rode with the right flank, where two regiments from his native North Carolina were in line. Early took the two Virginia regiments on the left, and a certain degree of competition seems to have developed between the troops of the two states and their commanders as to which state would have the honor of capturing those guns. By the sound of things, if they pushed straight ahead, they ought to come out of the woods right on the flank of the Federal battery. The gunners might not even be able to swing their cannon around in time for a single shot. Eagerly, they pushed across the wheat field and plunged into the woods.[29]

Here things began to go wrong. Visibility was virtually nil in the dense underbrush. The regiments lost sight of each other and soon lost contact. A small stream had to be crossed, and in this weather it was more of a swamp. Hill's North Carolinians had just dragged themselves through the thicket and waded the stream when the general stopped them in order to reestablish contact with Early's two regiments. He sent an aide down the line to locate him, but not five minutes had passed before Hill was shocked to hear shouting and firing in front of them and just to the left, "and a voice, which I took to be General Early's above all the uproar, crying, 'Follow me.'"[30]

It was indeed Early. In his eagerness to capture the guns, he had raced ahead without thought of alignment or the security of his flanks. His men had burst out of the wood full tilt and straight ahead toward a wide open field of mud—just plowed whenever last the weather had permitted such an activity. In front of them was nothing else—all the way to the woods on the far side of the Yorktown Road. To their right the sodden furrows of the plowed field stretched down in a long gentle slope to where Early could see Fort Magruder in the distance through the misty rain. On their left a more interesting scene presented itself. Early's guess about the location of the sounds he had been hearing had been a little off. There, just about four hundred yards away and smack across his left flank was not one but two batteries of artillery, ten guns in all, and supporting them was Hancock's reinforced infantry brigade with some thirty-four hundred Yankees and Midwesterners.[31]

Early's reaction was characteristic. He ordered his regiments to wheel to the left and charge, and the accompanying shouting and opening shots were the sounds that had so shocked Hill down in the woods. The only thing Early had going for him was that Hancock's men were just in the process of obeying the order to retreat. Another few minutes and they would have been gone altogether. Now, they had just limbered up their guns and started for the rear when the Virginians burst into the open behind them. Early interpreted what he saw as flight, and was all the more encouraged to pursue. The time needed by the Federals to get their infantry back into line and their guns back into battery, coupled with the relatively short distance he had to cover, gave him a chance. In the stiff firefight that followed, however, the Virginians had much the worst of it. Early was wounded in the shoulder and, weak from loss of blood, had to relinquish command and go to the rear. His troops were not far behind, retreating diagonally toward the woods to seek the cover of the underbrush as quickly as possible.

Meanwhile, Hill had hurried his troops forward to join the fray and emerged into the open field to view the near hopeless tactical situation. To make matters worse, he had only one regiment still with him, the Fifth

North Carolina. His other regiment, the Twenty-third North Carolina, had gotten lost some time after they had crossed the creek and was still wandering around the woods. Hill heartily wished the Fifth was still there too, and that Early's troops had never entered the open field, but it was too late now, and since something might perhaps be accomplished by joining the attack he now saw the Virginians making, he reluctantly gave his consent to the eager colonel of the Fifth to wheel to the left and advance across the open field, angling farther out into the field all the while, so as to get around Early's regiments, now directly between them and the enemy.[32]

The result was an unmitigated disaster. Because their position on the right of the original brigade line put them farther away from the Union position, the men of the Fifth had to slog their way across more than half a mile of muddy field under the fire of Hancock's entire brigade and both batteries, now free to concentrate on the Carolinians as the Virginians fled for the cover of the woods. Hill's men got to within about a hundred yards of the Federal line, where they sought shelter—such as it was—behind a rail fence. They could go no farther, and Hill, who could see as much, sent the order for them to fall back. The retreat proved to be another ordeal of the nightmarish attempt to run through the soft mud while shells and bullets continued to tear through their ranks. In all, the Fifth North Carolina lost 302 men in the assault, 68 percent of those it had taken into battle that day. While this disaster was unfolding, Hill endeavored to get the other three regiments of the brigade into line and into the fight. It was no use. With the exception of the Thirty-eighth Virginia, which accidentally emerged into the open and just as quickly hustled back to the protection of the forest, none of them so much as got out of the woods.[33]

As the survivors of the Fifth North Carolina regained the relative safety of the thicket, Hancock's men once again took up their withdrawal. As darkness settled over the field a couple of hours later, Longstreet's division disengaged and pulled back toward Williamsburg and, beyond it, Richmond. Fort Magruder was abandoned. The battle of Williamsburg was over. Each side was quick to claim victory. For as much as it might be worth, the Confederates had at least accomplished what they set out to do. Their supply trains had escaped unmolested. Johnston himself was not a bit behind others in claiming victory and praising those of his subordinates who had directed the fighting. Those higher up the Confederate chain of command were not inclined to question the matter, especially as more pressing problems were at hand. Officially, it was a battle with which every Southerner could be satisfied.

Yet future events might possibly have been different, had Joseph E. Johnston observed more closely and pondered more deeply the events of May 5, 1862. The troops had performed well at Williamsburg, and regimental officers had led them with dash and vigor. The higher one moves up the Confederate chain of command, however, the more questions arise about the quality of leadership exhibited. Confederate brigade leadership at Williamsburg was at best uneven. Among the brigadiers engaged in the battle were men whose names were to become well known within the Army of Northern Virginia: A. P. Hill, Cadmus Wilcox, Jubal Early, Richard H. Anderson, and George Pickett. Some of these turned in performances that foreshadowed their future successes. Wilcox had performed about as well as could be expected of a brigadier who is ordered to conduct a battle in a dense woodland and is left in charge of several other brigades without much help or direction from his division commander. That he essentially lost control of the fight is less surprising than that he was able to accomplish as much as he did. His greatest fault— indeed, the greatest fault of all the Confederate brigadiers on this day— was an overaggressiveness that led him to advance without adequate reconnaissance and even when he should have realized his forces were badly outnumbered.

A. P. Hill did even better. Having perhaps less opportunity than his brethren to display overaggressiveness, he made no major errors and turned in the best performance of any of the brigade commanders.

Pryor, a political general pure and simple, had held that rank less than three weeks on the day of the battle. He had performed about as such qualifications gave cause to expect, courageously but unskillfully. Pickett, a West Pointer, had done little better. He would eventually rise to division command, not through his merits but rather through the favoritism of Longstreet.

Anderson is the enigma of the battle. He did not reenter Fort Magruder after leaving it in midmorning until at least sometime after Early's brigade came up late in the afternoon. He was supposed during that time to have been directing the battle on the right, but it is clear from the reports of the officers engaged there that after sending in Hill and Pickett, he was doing nothing of the sort. Where he was and how he occupied his time remains a mystery. His own report of the battle is curiously short and vague.[34] He would eventually rise to corps command. He was undeniably skillful, and sometimes he could be an excellent commander. Yet throughout the war there remained questions about him. Lee essentially relieved him of command the day before Appomattox. At Williamsburg, Anderson had shown the darker side of his generalship.

Early's was by far the worst performance of the Confederate brigadiers at Williamsburg. His overeagerness and carelessness in a business that was very intolerant of human error led to the butchery of his brigade.

As a group, the brigade commanders had had their flaws—they would require good division leaders over them in order for the army to function smoothly—but they had shown much promise, and there was good reason to believe they would grow into their jobs very nicely.

It was in the area of division leadership that the most glaring faults were displayed at Williamsburg. In D. H. Hill's defense, it can at least be said that he probably thought that either Early or Longstreet had dealt with the matter of a reconnaissance of the ground over which Early's brigade would be attacking and the Federal position it was to assault. Yet he ought to have made sure. His oversight was a costly mistake for the men of the Fifth North Carolina and the rest of the brigade. It was one of the least impressive days in the career of an otherwise usually competent combat commander.

Longstreet had displayed some tendencies that should have been alarming to his commander. He had essentially abdicated the leadership of his division to his brigadiers. Five of his six brigades were sucked into a vicious fight in a dense tangle of thicket, disorganized and almost out of ammunition in the face of potentially crushing Union numerical superiority before he even came on the battlefield. He completely lost control of his division not because he lacked the technical skill to manipulate his brigades but simply because he had no idea what to do with them. The five brigades thus fought without division command in an at least partially uncoordinated manner. Even more incredibly glaring was Longstreet's neglect in failing to watch the Yorktown Road, to reconnoiter the approaches to his position, and to see that all of the prepared defensive positions were occupied. Well might D. H. Hill have failed to imagine that any division commander—much less Johnston's favorite—could commit such a stupendous dereliction of duty. Had Longstreet effectively performed the most basic functions of a division commander, Early's debacle could never have happened. Indeed, even at this early stage of the war, no excuse existed for the overall Confederate conduct of the battle of Williamsburg. For a division commander to allow his brigades to advance into dense woods to meet a potentially superior enemy, when he could instead have accomplished his mission by holding prepared defensive works and forcing the enemy to advance toward him across open muddy ground, through an abatis of felled trees, displayed an ignorance of the art of war worthy of a man who had been just two places removed from being the "goat" of his large West Point class and who had learned little since then. Yet Johnston, eager to make himself look good and virtually enthralled by Longstreet's glib self-assurance, had high praise for that general in his report. From that day to this, historians have generally echoed his praises, without a closer examination of what actually took place on the field of Williamsburg.[35]

From all this, Johnston might have learned, had he studied the matter closely and with an open mind, that Longstreet, while he could be very useful to a commander who knew how to take advantage of his strengths and suppress his weaknesses, could also be a dangerous subordinate. His deliberate failure to notify Johnston of the serious situation at Williamsburg betrayed a lust for independent command that would—twenty-six days later—lead him to demolish Johnston's clever plan for the battle of Seven Pines by disobeying orders so that he could get himself command of one wing of the army. Longstreet's tactical blundering should have warned Johnston that here was a division commander who would require close supervision. Lee learned this lesson early, and almost invariably kept his headquarters close to Longstreet's. If Johnston ever learned it, he did so too late. At Seven Pines he gave Longstreet oral instructions only and a good deal of latitude. It was a mistake for which he was to pay in defeat at the only Civil War battle he stood a fair chance of winning at the outset.

The small action at Williamsburg, with its few hundred casualties on each side, was soon relegated to the status of "skirmish" and then all but forgotten as it passed into the shadows of the momentous events of the weeks that followed it. Yet this test of new commanders had lessons to teach, if it had found a ready learner in the man whose success depended on the wise use of these men. Had Joseph E. Johnston rightly assessed the strengths and weaknesses of his subordinates at Williamsburg, particularly Longstreet, he might have adjusted his employment of these men in such a way as to have improved his chances for victory at the only major offensive battle he would ever conduct as an army commander. That he did not was a flaw in his own generalship, and thus Williamsburg, insignificant as its fighting might have been to the course of the war, finally measured him as well.

Four

DAVIS AND LEE IN THE SEVEN DAYS

DARKNESS WAS SETTLING over the landscape of eastern Virginia as two riders urged their horses along the muddy roads leading to Richmond. Ahead of them, the spires of the young Confederacy's capital rose in silhouette against the fading light of the last day of May 1862. The two men had just witnessed the unraveling of a promising plan in the bungled battle of Seven Pines. In an appalling finale, they had seen the commander of their army, General Joseph E. Johnston, from whom much had been hoped but little gained, carried to the rear gravely wounded. The military outlook was dismal, and if it was to be brightened, these two riders, Confederate President Jefferson Davis and his senior military adviser General Robert E. Lee, would have to make the crucial decisions. Most of what passed between them on that ride is unknown, but one thing is certain. At some point Davis informed his companion that he was appointing him to take over the bloodied Confederate army defending Richmond.[1]

Thus began what would become one of the more successful civilian-military partnerships in the history of warfare. Rarely has the chief executive of a republic at war worked as closely and effectively with his top general as Davis did with Lee. Rarely has a commanding general shown the wisdom and tact in dealing with his civilian superiors that Lee did with Davis. And rarely has such a team had the successes that Davis and Lee enjoyed. Yet, in the end, after almost four years of working together, they failed, and defeat tested and measured their skills as no triumph ever

38

could. The mistakes of Davis and Lee loom larger for the consequences that followed them. The patterns of cooperation between these two men were hammered out during the first five tension-filled weeks of Lee's command of the Army of Northern Virginia, and particularly during the climactic fifth week, the Seven Days.

Lee had not been Jefferson Davis's favorite general at the outset of hostilities. That honor had belonged to the president's old friend, Albert Sidney Johnston, who had at one time been Lee's commanding officer in the Second U.S. Cavalry of the Old Army. Davis also had great respect for the abilities of Joseph E. Johnston and Pierre G. T. Beauregard, giving them important posts in the new Confederate army. Lee, on the other hand, seems to have enjoyed the president's respect, but more as a staff officer than as a field commander. Lee had been a favorite of General Winfield Scott during the Mexican War, and Davis and Scott were inveterate enemies. The Confederate president probably did not hold this against Lee, but it was a fact that would have made previous familiarity between them less likely. In addition, Lee was an engineer officer, and Davis, whose low grades at West Point had precluded his entry into that branch of the service, seems to have considered engineers bookish and timid and of little value as practical soldiers.[2]

During the first thirteen months of the war, Lee had held high rank but had not held the positions of key responsibility within the Confederacy's system of defense. The enormously important trans-Appalachian command had gone to Sidney Johnston, the Shenandoah Valley to Joseph Johnston, and Richmond's direct overland approaches to Beauregard. Of the Confederacy's original five full generals, only Lee and the decrepit old Samuel Cooper—for whom field service was out of the question—did not receive important field commands. In the fall of 1861 Lee was dispatched to the mountains of what was to become West Virginia to command a handful of troops and their fractious officers in a forlorn attempt to hold the area for the Confederacy. He spent the early months of 1862 directing the defense of the Georgian and South Carolinian coasts. Relegated to these secondary commands, Lee had served quietly while others had held the more important posts.

By June 1862, however, the situation had changed considerably. Albert Sidney Johnston was dead, killed at Shiloh. Beauregard was discredited in Davis's eyes, both by the unruly temperament that had led to his transfer to the West and by his actions since succeeding Albert Sidney Johnston in command there. Joseph Johnston, while still retaining a fair amount of the president's confidence as a commander, had been wounded at Seven Pines (May 31, 1862) and would be out of action for some months. Major General Gustavus W. Smith, Johnston's successor at Seven Pines, did not inspire confidence and could not be considered for permanent command in Johnston's absence. That left Lee, and Davis, perhaps with some reservations, gave him the command of the South's largest and most important army. Davis stressed that the appointment was temporary.[3] Lee was still to be the president's military adviser—in theory, commanding general of all the Confederate armies—and his appointment to command of a particular army was merely a stop-gap measure not unlike his brief assignments in the mountains of western Virginia and on the southern coast.

Nor was Lee particularly popular with the army or the public. "Officers of the line," loyal Johnston supporter James Longstreet later wrote, "are not apt to look to the staff in choosing leaders of soldiers, either in tactics or strategy. There were, therefore, some misgivings as to the power and skill for field service of the new commander." The Richmond press was less gentle. "Evacuating Lee," sneered the *Examiner*, "who has never yet risked a single battle with the invader." Others dubbed him "the king of spades" for his insistence that the troops entrench, while still others called him simply "Granny Lee." His opponent, Federal Major General George B. McClellan, expressed satisfaction that he would now be opposing Lee rather than Johnston, since Lee, as McClellan observed, was "cautious and weak under grave responsibility . . . wanting in moral firmness when pressed by heavy responsibility, and is likely to be timid and irresolute in action."[4]

Whence, then, came Davis's confidence, limited as it appears to have been, in this untried general? It may have come at least in part from one of the president's own military aides. Colonel Joseph C. Ives had been a member of the West Point class of 1852. Though a New Yorker, Ives had married a Southerner and had remained in the Confederacy when war came. About two weeks after Lee's assumption of command, Ives rode along the Confederate lines with artillery officer E. P. Alexander. The two men fell to discussing the recent newspaper criticisms of Lee. "Ives, tell me this," Alexander said at last. "We are here fortifying our lines, but apparently leaving the enemy all the time he needs to accumulate his superior forces, and then to move on us in the way he thinks best. Has General Lee the audacity that is going to be required for our inferior force to meet the enemy's superior force—to take the aggressive, and to run risks and stand chances?"

Ives drew up his horse in the middle of the road and, looking his fellow officer in the eye, replied: "Alexander, if there is one man in either army, Confederate or Federal, head and shoulders above every other in audacity, it is General Lee! His name might be Audacity. He will take more desperate chances and take them quicker than any other general in this country, North or South; and you will live to see it, too."[5] Where Ives had gained his insight into Lee's character is unclear, but it was manifestly correct. Whether Ives impressed his insight on the president or gained it from him, it is clear that Lee's qualities were recognized by Davis's staff.

Whatever the degree of confidence Davis might have placed in Lee during those early days, there can be no question that he liked the courtly Virginian. The two had worked together closely in Richmond since March, and Lee had shown marked skill in getting along with the proud and opinionated president. This alone meant that relations between headquarters and capital would be vastly better than they had been during the tenure of Joseph E. Johnston, whose pride, resentment of authority, and fear of responsibility had continually taxed Davis's patience. When Lee was appointed to command, Davis immediately showed his eagerness to keep relations with Lee strong and cordial. Davis met the general's request for the appointment of new officers to replace the losses of Seven Pines with less delay and more generosity than Johnston had encountered in similar situations. The president also showed his confidence in Lee's administrative ability by giving him complete discretion in the assignment of the newly promoted generals. "You will know best how to dispose of these officers," he wrote. "I give you the material to be used at your discretion."[6] Johnston might have had that sort of relationship with his commander-in-chief had he more of Lee's tact and humility.

Davis's kindness to his new army commander extended even to something as minor as the general's horse. Lee's favorite mount, Traveler, had a jolting gait that would have exhausted a less accomplished rider than the general. Davis had apparently noticed the animal's difficult habits during rides with Lee. Now, with Lee in command of the army and required to spend much time in the saddle, Davis thoughtfully offered to lend him his own horse. Lee was flattered but gracefully declined.[7]

No sooner had Lee taken command than he began to show both his skill in handling the president and his military aggressiveness. The day after formally assigning Lee to command the army before Richmond, Davis rode out to check on things at the front. Seeing a number of horses, including Lee's, hitched in front of a house, Davis dismounted and went inside. Lee was in the midst of a council of war with his senior officers. The tone of the conversation at that moment was not at all to Davis's liking. Lee's subordinates were speaking despondently of the inevitability of McClellan's victory by the slow but sure methods of siege. Showing no reticence as a visitor, Davis waded into the discussion, expressing "in marked terms," as he later described it, his "disappointment at hearing such views." Lee spoke up and said he had been saying the same thing before the president came in. Not long afterward Davis left the meeting and rode on to the front, where Lee joined him a short time later. The general respectfully asked the president "what, under the circumstances, [he] felt it most advisable to do." Davis replied that he still believed in the plan they had worked out together with Johnston before the battle of Seven Pines and that Johnston had failed to carry out, that is, by flank and frontal attack to destroy one wing of the enemy's army as it lay straddled across the Chickahominy River. However, Davis believed it would be necessary to modify the original plan. Because Johnston's botched movement had alerted the Federals and presumably allowed them to improve their preparations, it would now be necessary that the flanking force be larger and more powerful, and that could only be accomplished by bringing in Major General Thomas J. "Stonewall" Jackson's army from the Shenandoah Valley.[8] Lee concurred.

And so with Lee and Davis of much the same mind, the general began laying plans for his offensive. Lee knew of the bad feelings that arose from Johnston's failure to confide in his civilian superior, so he kept Davis fully informed of his preparations. The president remained in complete agreement with the general's views. Meanwhile, Davis sought to find what reinforcements he could for Lee in other parts of the Confederacy.[9]

The president's attitude remained ambivalent. "I have much confidence," he wrote with some exaggeration, "in our ability to give [the enemy] a complete defeat." But he went on to add, "The issues of campaigns can never be safely foretold." In a letter to his wife about the same time Davis again expressed his misgivings but also revealed the degree to which he considered the plan for the campaign his own. "We must find if possible the means to get at him without putting the breasts of our men in antagonism to his heaps of earth," the president wrote. "I will endeavor by movements which are not without great hazard to countervail the enemy's policy" by forcing McClellan into the open for a stand-up fight. Several days later, he wrote his wife that the time for the climactic battle was drawing near. "I am hopeful of success," he said, but confided that "the stake is too high to permit the pulse to keep its even beat."[10]

His worry came in part, no doubt, from his knowledge of just how much audacity Lee was already planning to display in the coming battle. By June 16, Lee had finalized his plans for the coming attack on McClellan, deciding to strengthen his blow against the Federal right by weakening the defenses of his own right, the section of his line immediately covering Richmond.[11] Not long thereafter Lee presented the plan to Davis, and the president would have been a cool man indeed if his pulse kept an even beat upon contemplation of the risk Lee was taking. The president pointed out to Lee that the Confederate right, that part of the line south of the Chickahominy, was too weak to stand up for long against a determined assault. Davis believed McClellan would not let such an opportunity pass. The president had a high opinion of the Federal commander. As secretary of war in the 1850s, Davis had honored the young McClellan by putting him up for promotion and assignment to one of two new cavalry regiments. He had also assigned McClellan to the highly responsible role of military observer for the Crimean War. If McClellan was the man he had taken him for back then, Davis warned Lee, "as soon as be found that the bulk of our army was on the north side of the Chickahominy, he would not stop to try conclusions with it there, but would immediately move upon his objective point, the city of Richmond."

Davis was not the risk taker that Lee was, and the plan troubled him. Still, perhaps to avoid offending the ever-courteous Lee, he conceded, "If, on the other hand, [McClellan] should behave like an engineer officer, and deem it his first duty to protect his line of communication," the plan would be excellent. If the intent was to avoid offending Lee, the words were ill chosen. Lee had been an engineer officer. As Davis later wrote, "Something of his old esprit de corps manifested itself" in his first response. He was not aware, he told the president, that engineers were any more given to such mistakes than other officers. Then, his self-control reasserting itself, Lee got to the main point: "If you will hold him as long as you can at the entrenchment, and then fall back on the detached works around the city," he told Davis, "I will be upon the enemy's heels before he gets there."[12] Lee's statement appeased Davis, and also indicated a measure of the mental dominance the general was already gaining over the president.

Yet Davis remained uneasy out of Lee's presence. On June 23, he wrote his wife, "Genl. J. E. Johnston is steadily and rapidly improving. I wish he was able to take the field. . . . He is a good soldier . . . and could at this time render most valuable service."[13] This was not quite the opinion Davis would have expressed a month earlier, and it would seem that Lee's heady risks were already making Davis wistful for the timid caution of Joe Johnston.

Davis was a man much given to nervousness, to the great detriment of his health. He always handled his nerves better when he could take some action connected with the source of his worries, so it was natural that he rode often to see the army defending the capital. He rode out on June 24, but missed seeing Lee, who had ridden to another part of the line to check on some skirmishing there. Lee's attack two days later brought the president a new opportunity for activity and also ended the long period of suspense. Davis felt so relieved from the effects of his nervous illness that he told his wife he felt "almost well again."[14]

Besides the nervous desire to do something, Davis was also driven by his perception of his role as commander-in-chief. He took his responsibility in this capacity very seriously. Throughout the first year and a half of the war, he showed a desire to lead his armies in person when they went into action. He had hurried to the field of Manassas but arrived too late to take part. He had frequently visited Johnston's headquarters near Richmond in hopes of being present for the crucial battle. The president had actually arrived in time for Seven Pines (much to the annoyance of Johnston) and had come under fire and issued orders. He saw no reason to alter his battlefield activity now that the army was under Lee. What role, if any, a commander-in-chief had on the battlefield was one of the issues Davis and Lee would address in the coming days.

Lee began his offensive by sending a copy of the day's general order to the president, as well as a notice that his headquarters would that day be on the Mechanicsville Turnpike. Later in the day, when the assault was delayed due to Jackson's failure to get his command into position, Lee took the time to send Davis a note explaining the situation. Lee probably did not intend his revelation of the location of his headquarters as a request for a visit, but the dispatch was the invitation the president needed. By about 2 P.M., Davis had joined Lee on the Mechanicsville Turnpike on the south side of the Chickahominy a little more than a mile west of the Federal-held hamlet that gave the road its name. With the president had come the secretary of war and a number of other men. One observer, at least, thought Davis gave the impression of one who had come not to watch but to take part.[15]

Late in the afternoon, Confederate forces opened the battle with a headlong and ill-coordinated assault on the Federal positions north of the river. As Southern forces surged across the Chickahominy, Davis, still followed by his excited cavalcade of staff officers, cabinet members, and other politicians, galloped across the rickety bridges spanning the river's two channels. So closely was Davis following the front lines that he got across just behind the infantry of the leading Confederate brigade, and before that unit's artillery could go over.[16]

Confederate infantry quickly drove the opposition out of Mechanicsville but found the Federal main line of resistance behind Beaver Dam Creek, a small watercourse beyond Mechanicsville. The position was a strong one, and waves of Confederate troops surged against it only to break and roll back again. From the shell-swept open ground around Mechanicsville, Lee watched in frustration as his plan went awry. Intent on achieving success, he was oblivious to the heavy and accurate fire of the Union artillery batteries on the other side of the creek. He soon became aware, however, of the presence of someone else. Not far off, and under the same hot fire, Davis and his entourage sat their horses, anxiously watching the progress of the battle.

Whether moved by fear of Davis being killed or wounded, by apprehension for the muddling of the command structure created by the commander-in-chief's presence on the field, or by frustration at having the president see the less-than-perfect progress of this battle, Lee reacted quickly. Riding over to Davis, he saluted stiffly and, before the president could get a word out, said sternly, "Mr. President, who is all this army and what is it doing here?" This was not the way Davis was accustomed to being spoken to by an equal, much less a subordinate. By this time, though, Davis was not quite thinking of Lee as a subordinate or even an equal. During the lifetime of Jefferson Davis there were a few men to whom he looked as father figures. To them and them alone he inwardly deferred. In his youth it had been his brother Joseph, twenty-three years his senior. Later, Albert Sidney Johnston, now almost three months in his grave, had held that place in Davis's esteem. Lee would never quite exert Johnston's power over the Confederate president, but he was beginning to come close. Despite the doubts Davis had entertained about Lee and his daring plans, he seems to have been increasingly prone to respond to the Virginian with an almost instinctive deferential respect.

Receiving this shocking rebuke from the normally mild-spoken Lee, Davis seemed uncomfortable. "It is not my army, General," he replied.

The other civilians had, of course, come of their own volition, and Davis hoped Lee would not blame him for their presence. He was not to be let off so easily. "It is certainly not my army, Mr. President," Lee continued sternly, "and this is no place for it."

"Well, General," the president replied meekly, "if I withdraw, perhaps they will follow me." With that he tipped his hat to his imperious subordinate, turned his horse, and rode down the hill away from the enemy. His entourage, some of them no doubt relieved to be able to do so without losing face, followed. Once out of sight of Lee, however, the president turned and stole back onto the battlefield. Again he came under artillery fire, and a Confederate soldier was killed by an exploding shell within a few feet of him.[17]

As the battle of Mechanicsville neared its climax, the confused system of command that had to result from having an active commander-in-chief on the battlefield became apparent. Davis could not resist becoming directly involved in the conduct of the battle. Seeing the assaulting columns of A. P. Hill falter in their efforts to breach the Beaver Dam Creek line, Davis decided that D. H. Hill must send over a brigade in support, and, accordingly, the president wrote out the order and sent it off in the hands of a courier to Brigadier General Roswell S. Ripley of D. H. Hill's division. If an infantry assault was to be made, Davis's order for the advance of Ripley's brigade made excellent sense. In fact, it was precisely the move that Lee himself, unbeknownst to Davis, had ordered a few minutes before. In ordering it, however, Davis had bypassed two links in the chain of command, including that of army commander. If the president had a legitimate role on the battlefield, this was not it. The confusion caused by Davis's duplication of Lee's order did not help matters during the closing hours of the already muddled battle of Mechanicsville.[18]

As the week-long struggle continued, Davis could not stay away. He may have been on the field with Lee on June 27 as Confederate troops went into action at the battle of Gaines Mill. The following evening he inspected the lines of Generals Benjamin Huger, Lafayette McLaws, and John B. Magruder on the south side of the Chickahominy. Lee had, in some of his communications, implied for Davis a more direct supervisory role in this sector, almost suggesting that he considered the president—or that the president considered himself—a sort of informal commander for the three divisions holding the line south of the river. As Davis visited these commands that night, he gave the officers there his opinion "that the enemy would commence a retreat before morning" and "gave special instructions as to the precautions necessary in order certainly to hear when the movement commenced." If the enemy could be attacked while withdrawing, the Confederates would gain a large advantage. Satisfied, Davis returned to Richmond, but during the night the Federals did indeed make good their retreat undetected by the Confederates opposite them.[19]

Lee faithfully informed Davis of the army's progress throughout the week, and the president carried on his more conventional role of forwarding reinforcements to the front.[20] At Frayser's Farm, however, the president was back in the thick of the action. Coming into a forest clearing about 2:30 P.M. on that last day of June, Lee discovered Davis in conversation with Major General James Longstreet, a senior division commander. The president was ready for Lee this time and not about to be caught off guard as he had been at Mechanicsville. "Why, General," he exclaimed, "what are you doing here? You are in too dangerous a position for the commander of the army."

Lee, who was exasperated almost to the limits of his considerable patience by the failures of his staff and subordinate generals to carry out his plans, replied, "I'm trying to find out something about the movements and plans of those people," meaning the Federals. "But you must excuse me, Mr. President," he continued, "for asking what you are doing here, and for suggesting that this is no proper place for the commander-in-chief." Of course, Davis could have answered that as commander-in-chief he would go wherever he pleased, but this was Lee to whom he spoke, a man to whom he inwardly deferred as his superior morally if not legally. Instead, he was able to dodge Lee's suggestion. "Oh," he answered, "I am here on the same mission that you are." With that Lee could do nothing, and the president stayed. Within minutes, however, the clearing came under heavy bombardment. A courier was wounded and several horses killed. The Confederates, generals, president, and all, quickly vacated the area.[21]

Later that same day, when Brigadier General Theophilus Holmes's green division broke under the fire of Federal artillery, Davis endeavored to rally the fleeing troops. He had just succeeded in stopping them when, as he described it, "Another shell fell and exploded near us in the top of a wide-spreading tree, giving a shower of metal and limbs, which soon after caused them to resume their flight in a manner that plainly showed no moral power could stop them within the range of those shells." Still within that range, Davis again encountered Lee, who at considerable personal risk was surveying the ground in search of a less exposed position for Holmes's battered division. Again the president remonstrated with his top general for exposing himself to the enemy's fire. It may have been another ploy of the president's to avoid being sent away himself, but it was probably sincere at the same time. Davis had lost Sidney Johnston, killed by enemy fire at Shiloh, and Joe Johnston, wounded at Seven Pines. He could not afford to lose Lee, but, besides, he was also coming to feel a genuine affection for the reserved and respectful Virginian.

This time Lee made no effort to shoo the president off the battlefield. The frustrated general merely explained that going to look the ground over for himself was the only way he could get the information he needed.[22]

The next day—July 1, 1862—saw the disastrous assault on Malvern Hill. Again Davis seems to have been lurking in the area.[23] The morning after the failed attack, the president, accompanied by his nephew Colonel Joseph Davis, paid a call to Lee's headquarters at the Poindexter house. Lee was present along with Jackson and a number of staff officers. Curiously, the general seems to have been surprised to see Davis, perhaps because of the cool temperatures and incessant rain. Dr. Hunter McGuire, Jackson's medical director, noticed that the apparently startled Lee addressed Davis not as "Mr. President," but rather as simply "President."

"President," Lee said, "I am delighted to see you." Davis greeted Lee and his aide, Major Walter Taylor, before turning with a questioning look toward the ungainly but obviously high-ranking officer who stood stiffly nearby. Davis and Jackson had never met, and their official relations had not been happy. The president's meddling had driven Jackson to submit his resignation six months before. Jackson had felt that his authority had been usurped when a subordinate had convinced Richmond authorities to overrule one of Jackson's orders. The government ultimately reversed itself and supported Jackson, and he had retracted his resignation, but the general's feelings remained bruised. When Davis had come in, McGuire had whispered to Jackson the identity of the visitor and Jackson, ever mindful of his duty to a military superior—even one he disliked—came to attention, as McGuire put it, "as if a corporal on guard, his head erect, his little fingers touching the seams of his pants."

"Why President," Lee interjected, apparently still trying to regain his mental equilibrium, "don't you know General Jackson? This is our Stonewall Jackson." Davis bowed. Stonewall saluted. With that unpleasant preliminary out of the way, Davis and Lee got down to the business at hand. Spreading their maps on the dining room table, they began to discuss the tactical situation. Lee explained the previous day's action and the subsequent withdrawal of McClellan's army. As the discussion continued, Dr. McGuire noticed something. "Every now and then," he later wrote, "Davis would make some suggestion; in a polite way, General Lee would receive it and reject it. It was plain to everybody who was there that Lee's was the dominant brain."[24]

As the Seven Days' battles ended, the basic boundaries of the working relationship between Jefferson Davis and Robert E. Lee had been set. Lee had established that he, not Davis, would fill the role of field commander. Davis had made it plain that he would continue to take a close interest in the army and, when possible, would endeavor to view its operations in person. Each had won a large measure of respect from the other. Davis must have impressed Lee with his battlefield courage as well as his often sound tactical and strategic advice, despite the frequency with which the general had to reject his less practical suggestions. The president had come to a level of deference to Lee that he felt for only a handful of other individuals in his life. On such persons he tended to rely with almost childlike trust, and this was no doubt the basis—along with Lee's superior military abilities—for the mental ascendancy the general had gained over the president.

The results of this relationship were both good and bad for the Confederacy. Lee, a general of brilliant abilities, was allowed free reign and given full support through the rest of the war in Virginia. No setback could shake Davis's confidence in him, nor could personal problems arise of the sort that had strained civil-military relations and hampered Confederate operations during the commands of Beauregard and Joe Johnston. If Lee failed to conquer a peace, it would not be for any failure by Davis to exert his considerable organizational talents in his support.

Yet if Lee had a fault as a general, it was an excess of the very audacity that made him effective. Left to his own devices, he would gamble too often and for very high stakes. He gambled with soldiers the South could ill afford to lose. Caught up in the events and emotions of campaigning, with final victory beckoning to him—his to be had for one more infantry assault, for one more daring thrust—Lee was often too close to the action to see the fine line that separated daring from madness, at least within the context of Davis's overall defensive strategy. A firm and wise hand was needed, a leader removed from the immediate turmoil of battle and able to judge the South's prospects against its dwindling resources. That hand should have been Jefferson Davis's, but the president was unable to fulfill the role, first because he desired the role of field commander for himself and second because he made his field commander an alter ego. He would, in the end, give Lee everything the president of the Confederacy could have given except the strategic guidance of a wise commander-in-chief.

"DISMEMBERING THE CONFEDERACY"

Jefferson Davis and the Trans-Mississippi West

T HE UNCOUPLING OF the Trans-Mississippi West from the rest of the Confederacy—and the negative effect this had on the Southern war effort—has been frequently noted by students of the Civil War. Certainly, after the fall of the Mississippi River bastions of Vicksburg and Port Hudson in July 1863, the Trans-Mississippi portion of the Confederacy was of necessity left to carry on its own war independent of, and with little bearing on, the military operations east of the river. When a somewhat halfhearted effort was made in 1864 to shift troops from the Trans-Mississippi to the theaters of the war that had by that time become more critical to the Confederacy's survival, stepped-up patrols by Union gunboats on the Mississippi made the operation so problematical that Trans-Mississippi cavalry chief John A. Wharton was prompted to remark, "A bird, if dressed in Confederate gray, would find it difficult to fly across the river."[1]

Yet the severing of the Trans-Mississippi from the rest of the Confederacy, at least as far as military operations were concerned, predated the point at which the Confederate loss of Vicksburg and Port Hudson allowed Union gunboats to prowl the Mississippi throughout all of its winding length. This curious circumstance—what amounted to self-amputation, on the part of the hard-pressed Confederacy, of a portion of its military strength—is alluded to by Thomas L. Connelly in his 1970 article "Vicksburg: Strategic Point or Propaganda Device?"[2] In that piece Connelly argued that the fall of Vicksburg was actually a much less

51

important event in real material terms than had often been represented up to that time. Rather, he suggested, its significance was much more in its impact as a symbol for propaganda purposes—both in reassuring the Northwest that the Mississippi would once again be open as a highway of commerce and in demoralizing the South by the loss of a fortified point that its leadership had declared vital and had committed itself to hold at all costs. To strengthen his argument that Vicksburg was less important militarily than had theretofore been asserted, Connelly pointed out that even before the fall of Vicksburg, the Confederacy did not take advantage of the capability its possession had provided of shifting troops from one side of the Father of Waters to the other.

In that much, at least, Connelly would seem to be completely correct. By the time Vicksburg fell, no major Confederate force had crossed the Mississippi in either direction in more than fifteen months. Nor had the Confederate forces on either side of the river engaged in any significant military cooperation, what Jefferson Davis called "cointelligent action on both sides of the river. "[3] Indeed, well before Lincoln could note with satisfaction that "the Father of Waters again goes unvexed to the sea," the Confederacy's two unequal parts had been, at least for purposes of military operations, as cleanly and completely severed as any foe could have wished them. Yet such was not the work of an enemy, but rather the consequence, albeit unintended, of certain decisions—and nondecisions—made by the Confederacy's own leaders.

To the extent that this has been recognized, much of the blame has been laid at the feet of Confederate General Edmund Kirby Smith; certainly there has been some reason for this perception. Assigned to command of all Confederate forces west of the Mississippi in early February 1863 and actually assuming that command just under a month later, Smith was fresh from the unsuccessful Kentucky campaign of the late summer and fall of 1862. There, his ego apparently inflated from the lavish praise that had been heaped on him as a result of his fortuitous appearance at precisely the right time and place on the battlefield of First Manassas (Bull Run), he had proved willful and headstrong; his stubborn refusal to cooperate with fellow Southerner Braxton Bragg had hamstrung Confederate operations and played a major part in the failure of the campaign.[4]

As commander of the Trans-Mississippi, Smith showed ability and imagination in going far to make the vast, undermanned, underequipped, and shockingly disorganized region self-sufficient and surprisingly successful in fending off Union thrusts, such as Union Major General Nathaniel P. Banks's hapless Red River expedition. Yet here, too, his self-will was evident; if he increased the region's strength, he did little to make that strength work for the larger cause of the Confederacy as a whole, except in simply surviving as a department (admittedly no mean task in itself). Despite being told by both the president and the secretary of war before he left Richmond that his most important efforts out west "would be directed to aiding in the defense of the Lower Mississippi, and keeping that great artery of the West effectually closed to Northern occupation or trade," Smith soon became caught up in the affairs of his own department and showed little enthusiasm for aiding in the defense of the Mississippi. When pressed by Richmond to undertake something for the aid of Vicksburg during the critical weeks of its siege, Smith's action was hesitant, halfhearted, and ineffectual.[5] By the end of the war the impression that the Trans-Mississippi had become completely the creature of its commander and that that commander answered—by this time mostly of necessity—to no one but himself, had grown so strong that people referred to the region simply as "Kirby-Smithdom."

Yet in Smith's defense, it can and should be pointed out that in failing to cooperate with the rest of the Confederacy, he was doing nothing new. By the time he took command, it had been nearly a year since a major body of Confederate troops had crossed the Mississippi, and not once had the Confederacy employed "cointelligent action on both sides of the river." In this aspect Smith's failings were merely those of his predecessors, who had far less excuse in the military exigencies they faced. Nor can the other various officers who commanded this region be made to take complete responsibility for policies that often originated in Richmond (although for some of them there is blame enough and to spare for their own policies). Indeed, much of the responsibility for the Confederacy's self-amputation of its Trans-Mississippi portion, at least as pertains to military operations, must rest with the Confederacy's commander-in-chief, President Jefferson Davis. It was his responsibility to see that cooperation took place across the river and that the Trans-Mississippi West was fully integrated into Confederate strategy. As a study of Davis's decisions and nondecisions during the first two years of the war will reveal, effective control of and cooperation with the Trans-Mississippi department had already been fumbled away even before Edmund Kirby Smith was appointed to that command.

It did not begin that way, nor was there reason at the outset to suppose that Jefferson Davis, who as a young army officer had served in the Indian Territory and whose own plantation was on the banks of the Mississippi, would allow the West's potential to remain partially unexploited by the Confederacy. During the early months of the war, Davis authorized Brigadier General Henry H. Sibley's unsuccessful New Mexico expedition, assigned the colorful Texan Ben McCulloch to command Confederate forces in northwestern Arkansas, and wisely, if not in his choice of man at least in his definition of the command, appointed Major General Leonidas Polk to oversee an area that embraced the Mississippi Valley and straddled the river itself.[6] This latter was the most important part of Davis's arrangements for the Trans-Mississippi, for it showed a readiness to integrate the military operations of the Trans-Mississippi with those of the rest of the Confederacy, at least in the defense of the river itself and thus of the Confederacy's connection with the West.

This readiness was continued and Davis's original arrangements improved when in September 1861 the president assigned General Albert Sidney Johnston to command of Confederate forces on the land front that stretched from the Appalachians in the East to the Ozarks—and beyond—in the West.[7] This meant that Johnston could not only arrange cooperation between the defenders on both banks of the Mississippi but could also, in theory at least, integrate the defense of the Confederate heartland with that of the Trans-Mississippi. Davis may very well have had this arrangement in mind for some time and simply been waiting for the arrival of a man fit for the position. Johnston, in whom Davis had enormous confidence, had not been available up to that point, having been forced to make his way from California, where he had been stationed in the prewar U.S. Army, across the deserts of the Southwest to join the Confederacy. One of Johnston's first moves as the Confederacy's western theater commander was to transfer a small force under General William J. Hardee from northeastern Arkansas across the Mississippi to join the more seriously threatened Confederate forces on the Kentucky front.[8] Of Jefferson Davis it can at least be said that he allowed this early cross-river shifting of troops.

Yet already some ominous signs were beginning to show up in Davis's handling of the western front. During the early summer of 1861 the Confederacy's capital had been shifted from sweltering, cramped, uncomfortable, but centrally located Montgomery, Alabama, to large, sophisticated, but far eastern Richmond, Virginia. Hundreds of miles from Johnston's headquarters in Bowling Green, Kentucky, and hundreds more from the lands beyond the Mississippi River, Davis, it seemed, began to lose touch with the events and situations there. To make matters worse, Davis had the nearby Virginia fighting front to distract him and in addition was coming to suffer increasingly wretched health, being confined to bed and attempting to run the war from his sickroom.[9] As a result, the resources, both in men and material, that he allocated to Johnston were so woefully inadequate as to be almost laughable. In this desperate situation, Johnston directed most of his energy to trying to contrive some sort of defense for Kentucky and Tennessee and paid relatively little attention to affairs in the Trans-Mississippi.

Some attention was needed there, for Confederate forces in that part of the country were in disarray, and their leaders were squabbling among themselves. Ben McCulloch, a former Texas Ranger and veteran of the Mexican War and much Indian fighting, held a Confederate command in northwestern Arkansas with the Confederate rank of brigadier general. Sterling Price, another Mexican War veteran and a popular Missouri politician, commanded a force of pro-Southern Missourians in the southwestern portion of that state with the rank of major general conferred on him by the governor of Missouri. Missouri was not officially a part of the Confederacy—even as far as Southerners were concerned— but the necessity for Price's and McCulloch's nearby forces to work together was manifestly obvious—obvious, that is, to all except Price and McCulloch. McCulloch hesitated to enter Missouri since it was not part of the Confederacy. He also insisted that his Confederate brigadier's commission made him superior in rank to Price, a Missouri major general. Price, a man of enormous person and even more enormous ego, was almost equally determined that he should command McCulloch. That Price's determination did not extend quite as far as McCulloch's probably had much to do with the fact that Price was a good deal closer to the enemy and in more immediate need of cooperation. He thus conceded the point long enough to achieve such cooperation and win the battle of Wilson's Creek. After that the bickering went on.

It did not escape the notice of Jefferson Davis, and he determined to do something about it. His proposed solution, however, nearly became a grave error and demonstrated one of the most important of the unfortunate tendencies that would eventually lead him to preside— inadvertently, of course—over the severing of the Confederacy's military operations on the two sides of the Mississippi River.

After conferring with Secretary of War Judah P. Benjamin, Davis decided to separate the Trans-Mississippi from Johnston's command, making the Mississippi River a dividing line between two independent Confederate departments. To command the proposed new Trans-Mississippi department, the president decided on Major General Braxton Bragg, then stationed at Pensacola, Florida, and much respected for the job he had done in training and organizing the Confederate troops there. Secretary of War Benjamin, whose military knowledge was virtually nil, could have been little help to Davis in either of these decisions; but, perhaps seeking reassurance in a second opinion or for some other reason, Davis preferred to hold long and extensive discussions with the secretary of war before making a major military move. In this case Davis still did not feel sure enough of his decision simply to order it done. Instead, he decided to see what Bragg thought and to let the general decide whether he wanted to go west. Apparently unwilling to write such a letter himself, Davis had Benjamin do it.

The letter was written December 27, 1861, and reached Bragg on January 4. In it Benjamin described in terms of "we" decisions that had obviously been Davis's, indeed, decisions made before Benjamin even became secretary of war. His explanation of matters in the Trans-Mississippi is thus an indication of how the Confederate president saw and reacted to that part of the war. The appointment of Albert Sidney Johnston to overall command in the West, Benjamin explained, was made in the belief "that he would proceed at once to the Mississippi and conduct the campaign in Arkansas and Missouri." Taking Missouri was seen as being of "supreme importance" to the Confederacy, equal in significance to holding Kentucky. Naturally, before Johnston had been able to concern himself with affairs in Missouri, he had been distracted by more pressing matters in Kentucky and Tennessee. This was troubling to Jefferson Davis, who apparently still wanted to see Confederate action in Missouri and was somewhat out of touch with reality about the possibility of such action, or any other aggressive Confederate operations in the West, with the meager resources he had provided to Johnston.

A further source of concern to the Confederate president was a switch in Union commanders for the area. Several months earlier, Northern forces in the region had been under the command of the flashy, bombastic, and ineffective Major General John C. Frémont, "whose incompetency, well known to us," by which Benjamin meant Davis, "was guarantee against immediate peril." Now, however, "all this is . . .

changed." Frémont's duties had been taken over by Major General Henry W. Halleck. West Point trained, nicknamed "Old Brains," and highly respected for his writings and translations of French books on strategy, Halleck was the sort of officer about whom Jefferson Davis, as U.S. secretary of war during the 1850s, would have heard much. The Confederate president, like Halleck's Union mentor and Davis's prewar nemesis Winfield Scott, doubtless expected much from the bookish Northern general and was equally surprised when Halleck turned out to be a plodding and ineffective leader. In any case, Davis was disturbed by the change of Northern commanders and was further influenced to take steps he felt would increase the strength of the Confederate defenses west of the Mississippi.

Finally, there was the wretched business between Price and McCulloch. "Dissensions exist between General Price and General McCulloch," as the smooth and polished Benjamin euphemistically put it, "which prevent their cordial cooperation." Davis was never anxious to deal personally with squabbles among his generals, and he was never very good at it. Now he hoped his plan to create a separate Trans-Mississippi commander would solve this problem along with the others. "We are threatened with grievous disaster," Benjamin continued. "Price has advanced alone, and we fear with fatal rashness." President Davis also feared that Price would not know how to discipline and organize his force. West Point trained himself, Davis set great store by military professionalism and, at least at this point in the war, had little use for such upstart amateur generals as Price. The Missouri general's army, Davis suspected, was "a mere gathering of brave but undisciplined partisan troops."

What was needed, therefore, was "a master mind to control and reduce [the troops] into order and to convert [them] into a real army." That was where Bragg came in. "After long and anxious consultation with the president we can find no one but yourself on whom we feel we could rely with confidence as commander-in-chief of the Trans-Mississippi Department." Yet the purpose of the letter was not to order Bragg there, but "to ask you if you would consent to go to the West." Apparently, Davis had some hesitance about the move.

The serious strategic error of Davis's new concept was contained near the end of Benjamin's letter. In the event that Bragg should accept the Trans-Mississippi post, "General Johnston's command would be limited by the Mississippi River. . . . Your command would embrace everything west of the Mississippi except the coast defenses." Bragg's command was to be "entirely independent" except when the "tide of battle should turn toward the Mississippi River," in which case joint operations with Johnston's neighboring army would be in order and Johnston, with his higher rank, would command. Such joint operations, however, could take place only with Bragg's consent or "by special order of the President."[10]

This first step toward the uncoupling of the Confederate forces on opposite sides of the Father of Waters was averted not by any change of mind on the part of Davis but by his chronic reluctance to make an officer do anything he seemed the least bit reluctant to do. In this case it was Bragg who had misgivings about the transfer. Bragg wasted no time in responding to the letter the secretary of war had written on behalf of the president. On January 6, 1862, he wrote that had Davis ordered him to the Trans-Mississippi command, he would have gone without a murmur, but, given a choice in the matter, he was uncertain at best. He felt he was needed at his present post in Pensacola; more to the point, he believed that the Trans-Mississippi was, "under present aspects, not enticing." Bragg feared he would be able to accomplish little or nothing with troops already accustomed to the sort of poor discipline Benjamin had described in his letter. "But should the President decide on it, after knowing the state of affairs here, I will bend all my energies and faculties to the task, and offer myself (as a sacrifice, if necessary) to the great cause in which we are engaged." He then finished up with a discussion of the particular units and staff officers he would want if he were given the Trans-Mississippi job.[11]

This was hardly a stubborn refusal or even determined foot-dragging, but Davis chose to take it as final. Thus, a first step toward the strategic separation of the Trans-Mississippi was avoided, but Davis's tendency in that direction had been displayed. As the war progressed, he showed little inclination to improve the faulty concept on which it was based.

With Bragg passed over for command of the Trans-Mississippi, the problem remained of what to do about Price and McCulloch. While Benjamin's and Bragg's letters had passed between Richmond and Pensacola, reports had continued to come in noting the failure of the two western individualists to cooperate. On January 3, Polk had written directly to Davis, warning of this situation and pointing out that it could have an effect on Confederate operations east of the Mississippi as well.[12] Davis therefore felt something had to be done and immediately. If Bragg would not go, someone else must. The Confederate president had apparently been sincere when he had stated, through Benjamin, that Bragg was the only man he trusted to command the Trans-Mississippi independently, at least at that point. Rather than select another officer to fill the position Bragg had found "not enticing," Davis instead tapped Major General Earl Van Dorn to assume a similar, but not independent, position.

Van Dorn was a Mississippian, a West Point graduate, and well acquainted with Davis. Bragg's reply to Benjamin's query had hardly arrived in Richmond before Van Dorn was on his way west to command the Trans-Mississippi, subject to the overall command of Albert Sidney Johnston.[13] Van Dorn's career in the Confederacy's westernmost theater of action more or less confirmed the misgivings Bragg had harbored. Gathering Price's and McCulloch's forces under his command, Van Dorn led them into battle at Elkhorn Tavern (Pea Ridge) in northwestern Arkansas. Poor discipline, organization, and coherence had plagued these forces before, and Van Dorn was not the man to cure such ills. Now they combined with Van Dorn's questionable planning to produce a decisive Confederate defeat. McCulloch was killed, hope of a Confederate Missouri faded, and Southern forces lost the initiative west of the Mississippi.

Yet if Van Dorn's service west of the Mississippi was something less than a striking success, at least his tenure there saw continued integration of the Confederate defenses on either side of the river. It was to be the last such cross-river cooperation the Confederacy would achieve.

Van Dorn himself desired cooperation, but only such as would maintain him in his command west of the river. A few days after his defeat at Pea Ridge, he wrote Johnston to say that it was his intention "to fall upon the forces of the enemy in the vicinity of New Madrid or Cape Girardeau and attempt to relieve General Beauregard," who then commanded the portion of Johnston's department immediately east of the Mississippi. Failing that, he proposed to march on St. Louis.[14]

Johnston did not share his subordinate's exuberant optimism regarding the prospects west of the river and correctly judged that the greatest threat to the Confederacy's continued possession of the Mississippi Valley lay in U. S. Grant's move up the Tennessee River. He therefore ordered Van Dorn to bring his force across the Mississippi to join the grand concentration Johnston was planning in hopes of defeating Grant.[15] As it turned out, however, Van Dorn's army arrived too late to take part in the subsequent battle of Shiloh.

Shiloh marked a distinct downward turn for the Confederate command system in the West. Albert Sidney Johnston, whatever his strengths or weaknesses as a general, possessed the complete confidence of Jefferson Davis.[16] After Johnston's death at Shiloh, problems between Davis and his western commanders began to multiply. More important, Davis, who had doubted Johnston's ability to handle the entire western theater of the war including the Trans-Mississippi, was now unlikely to believe that any other general would even come close to equaling the task.

This was soon manifested. On May 26, 1862, just seven weeks to the day after the battle of Shiloh had ended, general orders were sent out from Richmond redefining the Confederate departmental system in the West and constituting the Trans-Mississippi as a separate department answering directly to Richmond.[17] Thus the step had been taken, and organizational unity had been broken between the Confederate forces in the Trans-Mississippi and the rest of the South's defenses. The danger now was that the separate commands on either side of the river might go their own ways, failing to cooperate and being defeated in detail by superior and more unified Federal forces. Now that the Trans-Mississippi reported directly to Richmond, it was the responsibility of Jefferson Davis to prevent this from happening. Under the circumstances it was an almost impossible task, but that the uncoupling of the Confederacy's Mississippi Valley defenses followed so quickly and completely was one of the Confederate president's most costly mistakes.

Having created an independent department of the Trans-Mississippi, Davis set out to find a suitable commander for it. Van Dorn, who had commanded the Trans-Mississippi under the umbrella of Johnston's command, was now playing a vital role in the defense of his home state of Mississippi and could not be spared for service west of the river. Accordingly, President Davis looked elsewhere. The man he finally chose was Major General (soon to be promoted to lieutenant general) Theophilus H. Holmes.[18] Holmes was a graduate of West Point and a professional soldier, but though about the same age as Davis and such Southern generals as Robert E. Lee and the two Johnstons, he seemed to he suffering from hardening of the arteries. He was also nearly deaf and was possessed of a mediocre intellect and a sour disposition. As a general he was almost completely ineffective, but he was a personal friend of Davis, who tended to be overly generous in his judgment of those he knew well.

Even at that, Holmes had not been the president's first choice for the Trans-Mississippi command. Original plans had been to send Major General John B. Magruder, but questions about Magruder's performance in the just-concluded Peninsula campaign in Virginia led to his being recalled before he could even reach what was to have been his new command. In his place Holmes was sent. In fact, Holmes's record in the peninsula was at least as bad as Magruder's, and Magruder was almost certainly the better general of the two.[19]

That anyone was sent at all was much against the wishes and the advice of Earl Van Dorn. Undoubtedly, this was partially the result of Van Dorn's pride and ambition, as he probably desired such an independent command for himself, but there were other reasons as well. The man Van Dorn had left in charge when he had crossed the Mississippi that spring, Major General Thomas C. Hindman, was a colorful and eccentric former Helena, Arkansas, lawyer. A resourceful and determined man who had gotten his wife by climbing a convent wall, Hindman was proving to be equally resourceful and determined in raising (through vigorous conscription), training, and equipping a substantial force in an area that had supposedly already been stripped of military material, both human and otherwise. Though headstrong and impetuous, Hindman had some of the makings of a good soldier and was already familiar with the situation in the Trans-Mississippi as well as with Van Dorn, who would be commanding the Confederate forces on the opposite bank of the river. Van Dorn urged that Hindman be allowed to continue in his present capacity as de facto Trans-Mississippi commander, but Davis would hardly have considered such a possibility since Hindman was not West Point trained and still relatively inexperienced. Hindman's test of battle, when it came, would prove the president correct.[20]

During the summer and early fall of 1862, Davis, in his correspondence with Holmes and the other generals commanding in the Mississippi Valley region, spoke vaguely from time to time of the importance of cooperation across the river; but little came of such nebulous urgings. When Major General Richard Taylor, the president's brother-in-law, was sent to command, under Holmes, the Confederate forces operating in Louisiana west of the Mississippi River, his orders included the admonition, "As circumstances will permit, you will . . . endeavor to maintain cointelligence with General Van Dorn commanding the military district from which yours is divided by the Mississippi River." The orders also included, among a list of things Davis hoped Taylor might accomplish, the statement, "You will . . . embarrass the enemy in the navigation of the Mississippi River." In a letter to Van Dorn written on August 4, Davis urged the general to "confer with [Holmes and Taylor] as to their ability to aid you."[21]

Taylor, at least, made some gesture toward cross-river cooperation, writing to Brigadier General Daniel Ruggles, Van Dorn's subordinate commanding Louisiana east of the river, to promise to see if any heavy guns could be spared west of the river to aid Ruggles in the defense of the strategic Mississippi River bastion of Port Hudson. Communication was poor, however, and six weeks after Taylor wrote his letter, Ruggles wrote to Richmond to complain that he had not known up to that moment of "Major-General Taylor having been assigned to the Trans-Mississippi command," and then to state incongruously that he had had "no personal and but little official intercourse with" Taylor. In any case, he had made no effort to consult with Taylor about his military plans.[22] Cross-river cooperation was no better between Van Dorn and Taylor or Van Dorn and Holmes.

This was the state of the Confederate command system in the Mississippi Valley when Grant's fall and early winter campaign of 1862 made the issue of unity in the region's defense especially pressing. As early as October 9, 1862, pleas from the east bank were going out for reinforcement from Holmes. Ruggles suggested in a letter to Holmes of that date that the Trans-Mississippi commander cross the river with a part of his force to join Van Dorn in opposing Grant.[23] Though Ruggles seems to have made the suggestion hastily and without proper authority, there was some sense in it. The purpose of Grant's offensive was to take control of the Mississippi River. He happened to be operating on the east bank of the river, but if he were successful, the west bank forces would be almost as completely lost to the Confederacy as if they had been captured or annihilated in battle.

Not surprisingly, nothing came of Ruggles's hasty suggestion, but the idea that the Trans-Mississippi forces should join in the battle to help prevent themselves from being cut off was too obvious to go away. Seven days later, Van Dorn wrote his newly appointed superior, Lieutenant General John C. Pemberton, "You had better get some of Holmes's troops, if you would save Mississippi."[24]

In reaction to this the Richmond authorities in general, and Davis in particular, stepped up their urging that all three generals now commanding independent departments west of the Appalachians—General Braxton Bragg (then in Kentucky), Pemberton, and Holmes—work together. On October 20, Adjutant and Inspector General Samuel Cooper telegraphed Bragg, who was then just returning from his Kentucky campaign, "Cooperation between your command and that of Generals Holmes and Pemberton is indicated. This is from the President."[25] The same day, Secretary of War George W. Randolph, who had replaced Benjamin, wrote Holmes: "Your next object should be speedy and effective cooperation with General Pemberton for the protection of the Mississippi Valley and the conquest of West Tennessee." Randolph went on to mention Bragg's return from Kentucky and then hinted, "An opportunity offers, therefore, of converging three armies (Generals Bragg's, Pemberton's, and your own) upon some central point, and regaining Tennessee and the Mississippi Valley." He concluded by suggesting that Holmes should seize Helena, Arkansas, on the Mississippi River, as a "first step necessary to secure Arkansas and the Mississippi Valley and to put you in position for entering Tennessee."[26]

The next day Davis wrote personally to Holmes, stating in part, "A conjoint movement by Pemberton, Bragg and yourself may enable our forces while the rivers are low to drive the enemy from Tennessee and Arkansas. . . . The concentration of two or when practicable of all the columns in the attack upon one of the enemy's armies is so obviously desirable that it is needless even to state it."[27]

Still the desired cooperation did not take place. Grant's forces moved forward, and Pemberton grew more desperate. On October 25 he telegraphed Richmond, "More troops are greatly needed. Cannot some of Holmes's be spared?"[28] Holmes was indeed the natural source of reinforcements for Pemberton, whose forces stood in the path of the only major Union offensive under way at this time. Bragg, still retiring from Kentucky to Tennessee by way of far-off Knoxville, was (for the moment at least) out of the picture. Yet Holmes seemed little inclined to take notice of Pemberton's dilemma.

It was very likely in hopes of getting Holmes to take action that Secretary of War Randolph wrote to the Trans-Mississippi commander on October 27, two days after Pemberton's request for more troops. As a motivation, Randolph apparently intended to appeal to Holmes's vanity, the driving force in a good many Civil War generals. He began by informing Holmes of his promotion to lieutenant general. Then, after relating a glowing report of Bragg's recently concluded Kentucky campaign, he proceeded to state, "Cooperation between General Pemberton and yourself is indispensable to the preservation of our connection with your department. We regard this as an object of the first importance, and when necessary you can cross the Mississippi with such part of your forces as you may select, and by virtue of your rank direct the combined operations on the eastern bank. "[29]

There was nothing really new in this. Davis had told Holmes less than a week earlier that the concentration of his army with that of Pemberton or Bragg (or both) against a single enemy army was "so obviously desirable that it is needless even to state it."[30] Unless Davis envisioned an attack on a Union army situated in the middle of the Mississippi River or unless he was contemplating equally ridiculous ideas of moving one or both of the armies covering the Confederacy's heartland into the Trans-Mississippi, it is obvious that Davis meant that Holmes should cross the river. Since Holmes ranked Pemberton, and Bragg was, at the moment of Davis's writing, on his way to Richmond to report on the Kentucky campaign, it is equally obvious that no special orders from Richmond were necessary to give Holmes command of his and Pemberton's combined armies once he did cross the river. It is likely that Randolph merely intended to dangle this attractive arrangement in front of Holmes's eyes in hopes that the general might find it more enticing to enlarge the size of his command by *taking* troops to Pemberton's aid than to decrease its size by *sending* troops.

Randolph, however, made the mistake of failing to clear the letter with Davis before sending it—apparently the first breach of this sort on his part.[31] It might not have been true, as his enemies then and later claimed, that Davis dictated to the secretary of war every detail of the War Department's business, but he was excessively touchy about anything that seemed to bypass him. With the air of a man not quite secure in his powerful position, Davis occasionally seemed to fear that others might forget he was in command. In the case of Randolph's letter, this touchiness led to an unfortunate lapse. Though throughout the war the Confederate president used his enormous force of will to suppress his pride and drive his body nearly to the point of collapse for the good of his cause—and for his trouble was rewarded with the howls of his political enemies that he was proud and self-willed—this was perhaps the only occasion on which he allowed his pride and self-will to get out of check to the detriment of the Confederacy. Sadly for Davis, this, like most of his other failings, seemed to come at the time and place it could do the most damage.

By November 12 a copy of Randolph's letter to Holmes had reached the president's desk. Davis now did an about-face from the position he had taken in his own letter to Holmes just three weeks earlier. In a letter he immediately penned to Randolph, Davis expressed his "regret" that the Secretary of War had suggested

> the propriety of [Holmes's] crossing the Mississippi and assuming command on the east side of the river. His presence on the west side is not less necessary now than heretofore, and will probably soon be more so.
>
> The co-operation designed by me was in co-intelligent action on both sides of the river. . . . The withdrawal of the commander of the Trans-Mississippi Department for temporary duty elsewhere would have a disastrous effect, and was not contemplated by me.[32]

It is not easy to credit the truthfulness of this statement. Nor is it made any easier by the fact that Davis concluded by stating that "it was rather hoped" that Holmes would take Helena, something urged on the Trans-Mississippi commander in the letter of Randolph's that Davis had before him as he wrote.[33]

Randolph himself was not without his pride, and rather than send a letter of his own to Holmes, taking back what he had previously written, he simply forwarded a copy of Davis's November 11 letter. Once again Davis was quick to reply. "Confusion and embarrassment will inevitably result," Davis wrote to Randolph, "unless all orders, and directions in relation to movements and stations of troops and officers, be sent through the established channel, the bureau of orders and correspondence."[34]

"Confusion and embarrassment" would indeed be the result—confusion for Holmes, who would have two letters written by the president within three weeks of each other expressing opposite opinions with regard to the strategy Holmes should follow—and embarrassment for Davis, whose abrupt and less-than-candid change of mind would thus be fully exposed to the Trans-Mississippi commander. There followed in Richmond an exchange of stiff and unfriendly letters between the president and the secretary of war, culminating in Randolph's resignation, which Davis promptly accepted.[35]

This unfortunate affair probably made it a matter of personal pride with Davis not to order Holmes or any substantial portion of his command across the Mississippi in the future. This, along with Davis's preexisting friendship with Holmes and his reluctance to force any general to carry out a course of action of which the general disapproved, probably goes far toward explaining the Confederate president's failure to act decisively to prevent the final unraveling of cross-river cooperation and the resultant "dismembering of the Confederacy."

Pemberton's pleas for reinforcements continued. In response, Adjutant and Inspector General Cooper telegraphed Holmes to suggest that a part of that general's force, perhaps ten thousand men, be sent "to operate either opposite to Vicksburg or to cross the river." He pointed out as well that a successful defense of Vicksburg would be conducive to the defense of Arkansas, but stopped short of giving a direct order. To Pemberton, however, Cooper reassuringly stated, "General Holmes has been ordered . . . to send 10,000 men to Vicksburg."[36]

That satisfied the seriously threatened Mississippi commander for a time, but it soon became apparent that Holmes had no intention of sending the troops. Pemberton's subordinates stressed that obtaining reinforcements from Holmes was Vicksburg's only hope. "It is my opinion," wrote Van Dorn, "that if Holmes does not send troops to this side [of the] river soon the opportunity will be lost." Major General M. L. Smith at Vicksburg informed Pemberton that Holmes apparently objected to sending the troops and that "another order from the War Department is necessary." Even one of Holmes's subordinates, Richard Taylor, wrote Pemberton, "You ought to have 25,000 men from Holmes." While this was not quite accurate as to the number of men available to Holmes, there should have been no question as to the propriety of some reinforcements. After a week of anxious waiting and the news that Holmes objected to sending troops, Pemberton once again began to bombard Richmond with requests for aid.[37]

Holmes did indeed object to sending troops to the defense of the Mississippi Valley and the connection it provided between his department and the rest of the Confederacy. In fact, he raised a lengthy list of objections. "I could not get to Vicksburg in less than two weeks," he wrote. Besides, he lacked supplies and was threatened by the enemy.[38] Instead, he wrote to Pemberton to offer to send Sibley's cavalry brigade from Texas. This would have been of little help to Pemberton in his circumstances, and in frustration the Mississippi commander wrote directly to President Davis. Davis, who had been monitoring the affair and, very likely, giving his approval to each one of Cooper's dispatches, was displeased, though not enough to issue direct orders. "Has General Holmes replied to your dispatch?" he penned in a note to Cooper at the bottom of Pemberton's telegram. "I am disappointed by a renewed attempt to withdraw Sibley's brigade from the special service for which it was designed." He was also disturbed that Holmes had refused to send troops at the same time he was requesting rifles to arm twenty thousand new recruits. His instructions, however, were merely that Cooper "attend to this dispatch."[39]

Cooper had telegraphed Holmes the previous day, at Davis's behest, arguing against Holmes's objections and pleading, "Is not your force sufficient under these circumstances to make a detachment, as heretofore proposed, to re-enforce General Pemberton . . . ? Whatever can be done should be executed with the utmost rapidity." Now Cooper sent a stronger dispatch: "Sibley's brigade is not wanted at Vicksburg." Keep it in the Trans-Mississippi. "Send to Vicksburg without delay the infantry force which you have been twice telegraphed for. The case is urgent and will not admit of delay."[40]

This was still insufficient to stir the lethargic Holmes to action, and so matters stood when General Joseph E. Johnston assumed overall command of Confederate forces between the Appalachians and the Mississippi several days later. Davis had created such an overall command and appointed Johnston to exercise it in hopes of avoiding the sort of disjointed operations that had hampered Confederate efforts that fall in campaigns in Kentucky and northeastern Mississippi. Now Johnston, as Pemberton's supervisor, was faced with the growing crisis in the Mississippi Valley.

Davis had Cooper assure Johnston that Holmes had "been peremptorily ordered to re-enforce" Pemberton (a considerable exaggeration, since Davis almost never gave orders he considered truly peremptory) but urged the new commander to draw troops from Bragg to reinforce Pemberton in case Holmes's troops did not arrive in time. In a series of dispatches, Johnston objected that it would be far quicker and more practical to reinforce Pemberton from Holmes than from Bragg.[41] For once, Joseph E. Johnston's strategic judgment was superior to that of his commander-in-chief, probably due to Davis's judgment being warped by the pride he now had invested in keeping Holmes on the west bank and not appearing to adopt the policy for which he had rebuked Randolph. In any case, the course of action recommended by Johnston was not taken.

Holmes continued to insist that he could not reinforce Pemberton. For the time being at least, Davis continued to argue that he do so. Johnston continued to argue that it made far more sense to send troops from Holmes than from Bragg. Meanwhile, Grant's army continued to advance, and no troops were started on their way to Pemberton from either Holmes or Bragg. Each dispatch from Holmes painted a gloomier picture of the military situation in Arkansas than the last. The aged

Trans-Mississippi commander's estimate of the time it would take to reach Vicksburg rose successively from two weeks to twenty-five days to thirty days. Finally, Holmes stated that should "the President insist on the order of the 29th ultimo [for the reinforcement of Pemberton] . . . solemnly, under the circumstances, I regard the movement ordered as equivalent to abandoning Arkansas."[42]

Now Davis started backing up. In a letter to Robert E. Lee he mentioned that he had "called on Genl. Holmes to ask him, if it can be safely done, to send reinforcements to Genl. Pemberton." This was a far cry from a peremptory order. Davis went on to state, "I propose to go out there immediately," perhaps to view the situation for himself. Several days later Cooper as well, no doubt on the president's orders, was backing away from the previous relatively strong stand he had taken with Holmes. "You must exercise your judgment in the matter," he telegraphed Holmes. "It is impossible at this distance to judge of your necessities, but if you could give aid it was hoped you would do so."[43] The Richmond authorities had backed down. Davis simply did not have the self-assurance to force cooperation between the Trans-Mississippi forces and the rest of the Confederacy.

Davis did, as he had told Lee he would, travel to the Mississippi Valley. There Johnston apparently took the opportunity to press personally his argument that Holmes should be required to reinforce Pemberton. Davis was swayed enough by such arguments to write a long letter to Holmes, not ordering but urging the Trans-Mississippi commander to send the troops in question. "In my former communications to you I pressed the necessity for co-intelligence and co-operation of our armies on the opposite sides of the river . . . to prevent the enemy getting control of the Mississippi and dismembering the Confederacy," the president wrote.

> It seems to me then unquestionably best that you should reinforce Genl. Johnston, so as to enable him successfully to meet the enemy, and by his defeat to destroy his power for such future operations against you as would be irresistible by your isolated force. . . . Nothing will so certainly conduce to peace as the conclusive exhibition of our power to hold the Mississippi River, and nothing so diminish our capacity to defend the Trans-Missi. States as the loss of communication between the States on the Eastern and Western sides of the river. I have thus presented to you my views, and trusting alike in your patriotism and discretion, leave you to make the application of them which circumstances will permit.[44]

He might as well have saved himself the effort. Holmes had consistently resisted efforts to diminish the size of his command, even when such efforts took the form of almost peremptory orders. He was hardly likely to accede to the president's request now. In reply he sent another woeful report of how weak were his forces and how seriously threatened by the enemy. Predictably, he could spare no troops. "If you had given me an order I should have believed it best but you leave the matter at my discretion, and what I have said makes me feel that if I send the troops Ark. will fall."[45]

Grant's late 1862 offensive against Vicksburg was finally stopped, almost anticlimactically, by cavalry raids under the leadership of Nathan Bedford Forrest and Earl Van Dorn that cut the Union army's vulnerable supply lines. Yet before the success of these raids was known, Davis saw fit to detach ten thousand men from Bragg's army and send them to Pemberton. As a result, Bragg was seriously weakened in his battle with Rosecrans at Murfreesboro (Stones River), possibly changing the outcome of that battle.

Though Vicksburg was saved—or rather reprieved—temporarily, no substantial force of Confederate troops ever again crossed the Mississippi, nor did any significant cooperation occur between the Confederate forces on either bank. The Confederacy had been dismembered, not by enemy action so much as by the failure of Jefferson Davis to create a departmental arrangement that would be conducive to cooperation by Confederate forces in the Mississippi Valley or to compel such cooperation by his own orders.

Six

SOLDIER WITH A BLUNTED SWORD

*Braxton Bragg and His Lieutenants
in the Chickamauga Campaign*

W ELL BEFORE Nathan Bedford Forrest's gray-clad troopers clashed with elements of George H. Thomas's Union army corps in the woods around Jay's Mill, at the northeastern end of the Chickamauga battlefield, much of the course and even the outcome of the struggle that was to rage over this ground during the next thirty-six hours had already been set up by developments within the Confederate Army of Tennessee's high command. Though the soldiers of both sides would have to fight and die in order to make reality of the situations their generals had developed, the fact remains that the Confederate soldiers, though they did not know it, were condemned to fight against the long odds of a frontal assault, contending for what at best could be little more than an indecisive victory. They were neither the first nor the last Civil War soldiers asked to face such odds in hope of such scant gains, but their lot appears the more dramatic in the light of history because, up until just a few days before, it could have been entirely different. That it was not was the fault of the Army of Tennessee's generals, and for once, their failure had been not so much the result of incompetence as of contentiousness. Even more ironic, their commander, General Braxton Bragg, was almost as much the victim of this situation as were the common soldiers themselves, about to be fed into the meat-grinder of battle. The fact was that the fires of contention and bickering within the top ranks of the Army of Tennessee, originally kindled by just a few

70

discontented individuals, had by the time of the Chickamauga campaign spread so far and grown so hot that the entire command structure was warped and almost useless. Despite the strategic insights of Bragg and the courage of his troops, the army had become no longer a sharp weapon that could strike fatal blows to the opposing army, but rather a blunt instrument fit only for the crudest sort of bludgeoning.

To understand the situation in the Army of Tennessee's high command at the time of the Chickamauga campaign, it is necessary to step back some twelve months, to the Confederate invasion of Kentucky. In the late summer of 1862 the Confederacy had seemed about to reap a rich harvest of victories that might well bring Southern independence. Lee was advancing into Maryland for the first time in the war, and in Kentucky separate Confederate forces under Bragg and Edmund Kirby Smith controlled the bluegrass region and seemed to threaten both Cincinnati and Louisville. After the summer of 1862, however, Confederate fortunes had steadily declined.

That this was the case in Kentucky was largely the fault of Confederate President Jefferson Davis. Davis, at the outset of the invasion, had failed to place Smith under Bragg's orders. Consequently, at crucial moments during the campaign, Smith had refused to cooperate with his senior general, making it impossible for Bragg to win the victory over Buell that his superior strategy and hard marching should have gained him. Another error of Davis's was his refusal, before Bragg's army had left its former base in Mississippi, to take the commander's advice and remove incompetent generals—Bragg called them "dead weight"—from leadership of its corps and divisions. At the brigade-command level were a number of young, energetic, and talented officers such as Patrick R. Cleburne and Alexander P. Stewart, and Bragg wanted to see men like these promoted to fill the higher spots. The president's reason for refusing to act on Bragg's recommendation was the presence among the high-ranking incompetents of his old friend and West Point crony, Leonidas Polk.[1]

Polk had been a year ahead of Davis at the academy back in the 1820s. He was highly persuasive and had a winning personality. After graduation Polk had resigned immediately and become an Episcopal clergyman—eventually a bishop—and in the thirty-four years between that time and the outbreak of the Civil War, he apparently never read a single book on military matters. In fact, Polk did little reading of any sort. His strong suit was influencing people, and that he did very well indeed.

When war came, Davis had made Polk a major general. Only Davis's inordinate dependence on old friends could explain his giving that kind of rank to a man with Polk's almost complete lack of qualifications, and the new general's performance early in the war proved to be every bit as questionable—even disastrous—as his poor credentials gave cause to expect.[2]

Bragg, who was a good judge of military competence, though he tended to be rather naive about other men's personalities, had not taken long to realize that the bishop-general was a liability to the Confederate war effort. Thus when he had written to the president before the Kentucky campaign, he had suggested that of his top officers, only William J. Hardee was worth keeping. The implication was, of course, that Polk was not. That was the truth, but Davis would hear none of it. He refused Bragg's request, and that was that. The senior generals would stay, competent or not. During the Kentucky campaign Polk gave his commander plenty of cause to be dissatisfied. He provided Bragg confused reports of the situation in his front, delayed carrying out orders and thus endangered the army, and on one occasion simply refused to obey an order from his commanding general. Several months later, Bragg summed up a large part of the problem with Polk when he wrote in a letter to the president, "Genl. Polk by education and habit is unfitted for executing the plans of others. He will convince himself his own are better and follow them without reflecting on the consequences." The bishop-general was proud and willful and would make trouble if he did not get his way.[3]

And make trouble he did. After the army's return from Kentucky, Polk began a regular campaign to have Bragg removed from command. The reasons for this were plain: first, Polk resented anyone who gave him orders. Then, as second-ranking man in the army, Polk would— theoretically at least—succeed to army command should Bragg be removed. To accomplish his goal, Polk launched a stream of misleading letters to his old West Point friend Davis, begging for Bragg's removal. He fed false information to congressmen. He boasted in letters to friends that things would have been different if he "had been in chief command." In that case, he crowed, defeating Buell and taking Kentucky "could have been easily done." Even worse, he began to stir up discontent among the army's other officers.[4]

Being an influential man, he soon won over to his opinion his fellow corps commander William J. Hardee. Hardee was inclined to be critical of superiors in any case, though reluctant to assume responsibility himself.

He had far more practical influence within the army's officer corps than Polk could ever hope to have because of his reputation as an expert on tactics. Prior to the war he had produced the army's standard manual of infantry tactics, and although the work was largely cribbed from previous French publications and was not particularly brilliant for all that, it gave Hardee a formidable reputation. Within his corps of the Army of Tennessee he held regular classes for his officers, instructing them in the basics of troop handling and command, and, as he came increasingly under the influence of Polk, also insinuating to them that Bragg was incompetent and could do nothing right. Most of the junior officers, from division commanders on down, often had no way of seeing the larger strategic and tactical picture, and so they drank in Hardee's distortions about Bragg.[5]

Another group within the army's officer corps that had a special grudge against Bragg consisted of officers from Kentucky. Such influential men as former Vice President John C. Breckinridge and Simon B. Buckner, along with several other Kentucky generals, hated Bragg because it was the most obvious alternative to facing the fact that their home state by and large had not chosen to side with the Confederacy. Bragg had pointed this out after the Kentucky campaign, citing the obvious fact that if the people of Kentucky did not support them, Confederate troops could not possibly remain in the state for long. It was no more than the truth, but the Kentucky Confederates could not accept that and instead chose to believe, falsely, that Bragg had lost the campaign through incompetence and thus betrayed their beloved state.[6]

The discontent within the Army of Tennessee's officers increased after the battle of Murfreesboro. At that battle Bragg had handled the Union army about as roughly as Lee and Jackson were to do with Joseph Hooker's troops at Chancellorsville four months later. But Rosecrans was not Hooker, and the Army of the Cumberland was not the Army of the Potomac. The Federals did not retreat, and as they continued to bring up reinforcements, Bragg found that it was he who would have to retreat. Though the move was taken only at the intense urging of a number of his generals, including Polk, Bragg immediately came under intense criticism throughout the Confederacy and in the press for supposedly having thrown away another victory. The denunciations were almost certainly fed at least in part by Polk and possibly others within the army. Bragg, naively believing that his generals would support him since he had acted on their advice, sent each of them a note asking if they had advised retreat and stating as sort of a closing flourish that if he found that he had indeed acted without the support of his generals in this, he would resign at once. Polk, Hardee and his minions, and the Kentucky clique saw their chance. Admitting that they had counseled withdrawal after Murfreesboro, most of them went on to state bluntly that they thought the army would be better off without Bragg.

When President Davis learned of this bizarre situation, he ordered the western theater commander, Joseph E. Johnston, to go to the army's new base at Tullahoma, Tennessee, and investigate the matter. Johnston went and found the army in good shape and well led, the only problem being the attitudes of many of its top generals. He reported this to the president, but by this time, the constant bombardment of negative distortions about Bragg from Polk and whomever else Polk could recruit for the task as well as Kentucky generals, congressmen, and the like had finally persuaded Davis that the Army of Tennessee's commander must go. The president thought it would be easy enough to supersede Bragg. Since Johnston was Bragg's superior and theater commander, whenever he was present in person with the army, he would, of course, command. All that was necessary was that Johnston stay with the Army of Tennessee and actually exercise that command. But the president had not reckoned on the stubborn and contrary Joe Johnston. That Davis wanted a thing was almost reason enough for Johnston to oppose it, and besides that, the Virginian coveted glory but feared responsibility more, and though he would complain at not being given a field army to command, he would not take one when it was given. Consequently, and despite the president's wishes, Bragg remained in command of the Army of Tennessee.[7]

Eventually, Davis acquiesced, but the hostile generals within the army never did. Polk continued his campaign of trying to undermine Bragg, concentrating on those outside the army, especially President Davis, while Hardee continued to spread the poison of distrust within the army's high command. Relations between Bragg and many of his generals, particularly his two corps commanders, grew so bad that communication between them virtually stopped. Thus Bragg's subordinates had little knowledge and less understanding of their commander's operational plans and ideas and had become convinced that any movement Bragg ordered simply had to be ill-conceived and potentially disastrous— merely because Bragg had ordered it. This situation, far more than any strategic mistake Bragg could possibly have made, was to have disastrous results of its own.[8]

On June 24, 1863, the series of events leading directly to the battle-field of Chickamauga began, miles to the northwest of the meandering Georgia stream of that name. Rosecrans, moving south from his base at Murfreesboro, Tennessee, advanced toward Tullahoma, in front of which Bragg had positioned the two corps of the Army of Tennessee, blocking the road to Chattanooga. Bragg hoped to be able to deal Rosecrans a severe defeat, and for that purpose he knew he would have to do more than stand passively on the defensive. Rosecrans was a resourceful officer, and given time he could be counted on to find a way to put the Confederates at a disadvantage. Bragg did not plan to give him that opportunity. As he envisioned it, Hardee's corps, stationed nearer to the road and railroad lines of supply to which Rosecrans was tethered, was to serve as a blocking force, compelling the Federals to deploy in line against it and delaying them just long enough to allow Bragg to land the haymaker of this one-two combination. Polk's corps was positioned just to the west, and Bragg envisioned it swinging to the right, striking the flank of the Federal forces deployed to face Hardee, and winning a crushing victory, much like Lee's at Second Bull Run.

By the time Rosecrans began his advance, Bragg must have suspected that the plan probably was not going to work. Relations between himself and his two top generals had been so bad that they were hardly on speaking terms with each other. Consequently, it had been difficult to make sure that Hardee and Polk each understood what was expected of them. Bragg apparently thought they did. They apparently did not, and in any case they were not much inclined to cooperate in any plan of Bragg's. Hardee had almost inexplicably failed to entrench the position from which he was to stall the oncoming Union army, and Polk seemed to have no idea of cooperation. Rosecrans opened his campaign with a clever feint that seemed to fool Hardee completely and easily got past the Confederate positions. Bragg fell back on his prepared positions around Tullahoma, hoping to make a stand there. But by this time Hardee and Polk were convinced that Rosecrans could not be stopped. More to the point, they probably had convinced themselves by this time that any plan of Bragg's would fail. Their belief became, in effect, a self-fulfilling prophecy.

The two corps commanders pressed Bragg to agree to retreat farther, but Bragg resisted at first. At this point, the malcontents actually appear to have considered the possibility of mutiny—forcibly removing Bragg and seizing control of the army. That would seem to be the only reasonable interpretation of a letter Hardee sent to Polk about that time. He labeled it "confidential," and from the nature of the contents, one can easily see why. Hardee said that he "had been thinking seriously of the condition of affairs with this army." He believed that Bragg was not fit to command it. That being the case, he proceeded to ask, "What shall we do?" "What is best to be done to save this army and its honor?" Apparently, the thought of obeying orders and cooperating with the commanding general did not occur to him, for he continued, "I think we ought to counsel together." Concerned that they have the complicity of other top-ranking generals, particularly the influential and embittered Kentucky clique, Hardee went on to ask, "Where is Buckner? I would like Buckner to be present."[9] Whether Hardee and Polk would have had the nerve to go through with such a plan had it come to that, we can never know. Before matters had progressed much further, Bragg, weakened by physical illness and bombarded by his subordinates' demands for retreat, finally gave in and ordered the army to fall back.

In the next few days, Rosecrans followed one flanking movement with another, and the Army of Tennessee, with its almost dysfunctional high command, seemed less and less able to respond adequately and rapidly. The constant agitation of Bragg's generals had produced a situation in which the army's command apparatus had become virtually paralyzed and an easy prey for a resourceful enemy. The series of retreats that began in Middle Tennessee ended with Bragg sadly abandoning Chattanooga and falling back into Georgia.[10]

In Richmond, Jefferson Davis was not unmindful of the plight of Bragg's army and the Confederacy's fortunes in Tennessee. To the enormous disgust of his old friend Polk—and by now of many others as well—he did not see Bragg's removal as the solution to the problem. With Joseph E. Johnston on duty in Mississippi and unavailable for command of the Army of Tennessee, Davis knew of no one else whom he preferred to Bragg. While Bragg had never been a personal friend of the president, Davis did respect Bragg's ability and his loyalty to the Confederacy. To Polk, this was nothing but willful stubbornness. In a remarkable letter written about this time, the bishop-general told a friend, "The truth is, I am somewhat afraid of Davis. He has so much at stake on this issue [Bragg] that I do not find myself willing to risk his judgment. . . . He is proud, self-reliant, and I fear stubborn." As far as Polk was concerned, Davis should "lean a little less on his own understanding" and realize that "there were some minds in the land from whom he might obtain counsel worth having." Davis's friendship toward Polk was the only thing that had raised the pompous and self-important bishop as high as he was in the Confederate army and also the only thing that had kept him there. Now Polk was becoming bitter and contemptuous of Davis because presidential favoritism was not forthcoming to raise him the rest of the way to an independent army command. The letter reveals a great deal about Polk's personality.[11]

Rather than remove Bragg, Davis's solution to the plight of the Army of Tennessee was to reinforce it from Lee's army in Virginia. The decision to take this step was made before Bragg was forced out of Chattanooga, and was motivated primarily by the desire to prevent the cutting of the railroad line that ran through Chattanooga, Knoxville, and southwestern Virginia to Richmond. Davis ordered Lieutenant General James Longstreet and two divisions, about ten thousand men from Lee's army, to be detached and sent to Bragg. Substantial reinforcements were also ordered to Bragg from Mississippi. Once all these forces arrived in northwestern Georgia, Bragg would enjoy a luxury rare for Confederate commanders—he would actually outnumber Rosecrans by a small margin.

While the forces were on the way, however, opportunity presented itself to Bragg in a form that was rare for any commander on any side in any war. Rosecrans, elated at the bloodless success he had achieved simply through maneuvering, now seemed to forget that the Army of Tennessee was not a disorganized foe fleeing from a crushing defeat, but was still intact, a dangerous army spoiling for a fight, if its generals could ever give it a fair chance. Bragg encouraged Rosecrans in the delusion of Confederate disintegration by sending fake deserters into Federal lines with made-up stories of demoralization, desertion, and headlong flight among the Rebels. Under this false impression, the Federal commander divided the three corps of his army and sent them on widely divergent paths through the mountain passes in hopes of catching Bragg or at least keeping him on the run. The result was Rosecrans's presenting Bragg with an unbelievable opportunity to destroy the Federal army piece by piece, before the widely separated Union columns could come within supporting distance of each other.[12]

Bragg was not slow in responding to this invitation. On the afternoon of September 9, 1863, he set troops in motion to crush a substantial segment of Rosecrans's center column, the army corps of Major General George H. Thomas. By early morning of the tenth, all was to be in readiness. Confederate forces with more than a twofold superiority in numbers would strike both flanks of the foremost Union division. Calling on the troops closest to hand, lest the opportunity slip away while others were coming up, Bragg ordered the division of Thomas Hindman to strike one side and that of Patrick Cleburne, a part of D. H. Hill's corps, to hit the other. Then things began to go wrong. A good bit of what went wrong at this point had to do with Daniel Harvey Hill himself.[13]

Hill had served with the Army of Northern Virginia earlier in the war and had earned a well-deserved reputation as a ferocious fighter. Yet although he was one of that hard-fighting army's best combat leaders, he had proved to be a detriment to it nevertheless. His problem was his personality. He was bitter, sour, critical, and contentious, ever ready to pick nits and find fault. Lee also believed that Hill's organizational abilities were not all that might be desired. At any rate, probably both for that reason and because of his habit of carping criticism, Lee had suggested to Davis that Hill be transferred to other service. As with most of Lee's suggestions to the president, this one had met with swift compliance, and Hill had spent the year of the war leading up to Chickamauga in relative backwater commands. Sent to the Army of Tennessee to replace Hardee, who was needed at the time in Mississippi, Hill filled his predecessor's place in more ways than one, and proved to be almost the worst possible addition to the Army of Tennessee. The sour, critical Hill quickly picked up the bad attitude that infected its high command, and he was soon parroting Polk's denunciations of its commander.[14]

Thus he, like many of the other officers of the army, was conditioned to believe that an order from Bragg could not possibly be wise. When, on the night of September 9, he received Bragg's order to send Cleburne's division against the exposed portion of Thomas's corps, he began thinking of obstacles to action and excuses for inaction. He claimed the roads were obstructed but took no steps to clear them, and he complained that Cleburne was ill but made no move to substitute another commander or another division. Indeed, evidence suggests that Cleburne may not have been sick at all. The plain fact was that Hill did not trust Bragg and therefore feared to make the movement. Hindman, for his part, was little better. An officer of uncertain capability, Hindman had a service record that could, at best, be described as uneven. Now, as senior officer of the attack Bragg had ordered to beat the Army of the Cumberland in detail, Hindman lost his nerve and ordered the movement halted.[15]

Still, an opportunity remained for September 11. The Union officers did not yet realize their predicament and the exposed force remained in position. Since Hill seemed certain that Cleburne's division would not be available, Bragg selected the next nearest troops, Buckner's, to make the attack, sending an order for the Kentuckian to send two divisions to reinforce Hindman. Buckner, too, was little inclined to trust Bragg. As soon as he could meet with Hindman, the two of them discussed Bragg's order and decided it had better not be carried out. They so informed their commander. Bragg was not to be deterred from such a golden opportunity and insisted that they go ahead. At that, Buckner and Hindman simply refused to obey Bragg's order and pulled their troops back into defensive positions.[16]

No third chance to destroy Thomas's force presented itself, as the Union general became aware of his danger and pulled back out of reach, but again on September 13 an opportunity almost as inviting beckoned to the Confederates when Rosecrans's left wing was found to be isolated from the rest of the Federal army. Again Bragg set up his forces to crush the exposed Union corps. This time the task of making the attack fell to the troops of Leonidas Polk. The bishop-general, however, believed he was facing an overwhelming Union force, when in fact matters were quite the other way around. He informed Bragg that he would not attack but instead would take up a defensive position. Again, Bragg insisted that the chance be seized and the attack made. "We must force him to fight," he wrote, "at the earliest moment and before his combinations can be carried out." He assured Polk that his information about Federal vulnerability was solid and promised to increase the already decisive superiority Polk enjoyed by even further weakening other parts of the army to reinforce him, and he stressed that the attack must be made soon, lest "another golden opportunity . . . be lost by the withdrawal of our game." Of course, Polk disobeyed his orders and remained on the defensive, and the Union force escaped.[17]

Six days later Bragg launched the battle of Chickamauga. His tactics were simple, a frontal attack en echelon intended to hammer the enemy back and to one side, push him into a mountain cul-de-sac called McLemmore's Cove, and destroy him. Over the years Bragg has been criticized for the use of such a straightforward and unimaginative plan. If he had been a competent general, his critics argue, he would have attempted some sort of turning or flanking maneuver or have endeavored to catch and defeat the enemy in detail. They overlook the fact that Bragg had tried and succeeded in doing just that, not once but three times, during the fortnight prior to the battle. That no such relatively crushing and inexpensive victory was won was not the fault of Bragg so much as of the endemic dissension within the army's high command and of the officers—particularly Polk—who had fostered that dissension. Perhaps, if Bragg had been among the handful of truly great commanders in the history of warfare, if he had been another Lee or another Jackson, he might have succeeded in winning a decisive victory anyway. Yet even such an extraordinary commander might well have failed under these circumstances. As it was, Bragg had done all that should have been necessary to secure success, but he fought with a disadvantage he could not overcome. He was like a warrior with a dull and heavy sword. The instrument in his hands was simply not suited for quick, skillful, and dexterous work. Thus if he fell to hacking and bludgeoning his foe in a rather unsophisticated manner, we must look for the reason not merely by analyzing his own skills as a tactician, but also by considering the nature of the army—and particularly the generals—he commanded.

Seven

THE PRESIDENT'S CHOICES

*Confederate Command Options on
the Eve of the Atlanta Campaign*

MANY OF THE decisions made by Jefferson Davis in assigning commanders for the South's unsuccessful 1864 western campaign have been explained, and in some cases were justified by Davis himself, on the basis that no other options were available. When removal of the unpopular General Braxton Bragg from command of the Army of Tennessee finally became unavoidable late in 1863, there was supposedly no viable alternative to assigning that post to two-time failure General Joseph E. Johnston. When Johnston, true to form, backpedaled instead of standing his ground against the advancing Union army of General William T. Sherman, Davis met the clamor for Johnston's removal with the challenge to the general's detractors to come up with a better choice. They did not. When, with the Southern army backed up against the outskirts of Atlanta, Davis finally exercised the "nonexistent" option of sacking Johnston, no alternative remained to him, or so it seemed, but to give the command to the badly crippled John Bell Hood.

Thus Davis had no choice. His actions were inevitable. No other course lay open to him. Or did it? In fact, a number of options were available to Davis in late 1863 and early 1864, and some of them were quite attractive and had the potential to alter the course of events. Additional—and more attractive—options would have been available by the latter stages of the Atlanta campaign if Davis had made different choices at the outset.

The purpose of this essay is not to engage in a profitless chain of counterfactual speculations, but rather to suggest what possibilities lay open to the Confederate president as he pondered the always thorny problem of arranging the high command of the South's western army. Recognizing and understanding these possibilities is vital to realizing the significance of the command choices that were in fact made.

On November 25, 1863, the Army of Tennessee had broken and run from Federal troops storming its seemingly impregnable position on Missionary Ridge, southeast of Chattanooga. The debacle cost the Confederacy its last foothold in that state and Braxton Bragg the command of the army that bore the state's name. Long the target of carping and intrigue, Bragg had become thoroughly discredited, and for weeks had been retained in his position by Davis against the advice of a number of the army's high-ranking officers, including Bragg himself. Now, of course, Bragg would have to go, but who should replace him? For the moment, the command went to senior corps commander Lieutenant General William J. Hardee, who was also among the choices Davis considered for commanding the Army of Tennessee.[1]

First consideration, of course, would go to the Confederacy's top-ranking generals. Five men held the rank of full general in the Confederate army at that time. Bragg, of course, was out of the question, as was the aged and desk-bound Samuel Cooper. That left Robert E. Lee, Joseph E. Johnston, and Pierre G. T. Beauregard. For various reasons, none of them proved to be a very attractive choice to Davis.

Lee was obviously—and by far—the best of the lot. A clever strategist and tactician who was daring almost to a fault, Lee was also tactful and gracious in his dealings with fellow Confederates, which allowed him to get along well with Davis and most others. Accordingly, he was the president's first choice to serve as a replacement for Bragg to lead a desperate attempt to recoup the Confederacy's sagging western fortunes. Lee, however, simply did not want to go west. This was probably because of his sentimental attachment to Virginia, but in responding to a note from Davis inquiring as to his willingness to go, he raised two very practical objections. First, he believed he was needed with the Army of Northern Virginia. Second, he expressed his doubt that he would "receive cordial cooperation" from the Army of Tennessee's officer corps. Lee's second objection was a reference to the constant murmurings and machinations of men such as Leonidas Polk and William J. Hardee, who had helped to ruin the effectiveness of Braxton Bragg.[2]

Lee was right on both counts. The second was important but irremediable by that time. No commander ever received "cordial cooperation" from the band of chronic malcontents that officered the Army of Tennessee. It was the first point, however, that was decisive. Lee might or might not accomplish anything in Georgia, but he was definitely accomplishing a great deal in Virginia, and while the Confederacy might or might not survive the fall of Atlanta, it was very unlikely to survive, for very long, the fall of Richmond. In late 1863, the South simply needed Lee in Virginia more than in any other threatened area. Davis may have been slow to grasp this, since he responded to the general's note by summoning him to Richmond for what Lee himself believed would be immediate assignment to the West. If that was indeed the president's intent, Lee was able to dissuade him, and Davis's attention turned to the other candidates.[3]

In a week of discussions in Richmond, Lee urged on Davis his own choice for the job, the Confederacy's fourth-ranking full general, Pierre Gustave Toutant Beauregard. "Hero" of the 1861 victories of Fort Sumter and Manassas, both of which had been won primarily by luck, the colorful Louisiana Creole had subsequently fallen afoul of Davis. Beauregard was a man of colossal ego, and not above crass publicity seeking. Davis had been patient with him, but not patient enough to maintain good relations—that might well have been an impossibility. Hostility had resulted. Beauregard's questionable performance at Shiloh (April 6–7, 1862) and in the subsequent Corinth campaign had confirmed Davis in his negative opinion, and when Beauregard had—with amazing nerve—simply taken a sick leave from the army he was supposed to be commanding, the president had quite properly relieved him. Thereafter, Beauregard seethed with hatred for the commander-in-chief, referring to him as "that living specimen of gall and hatred," who must be "either demented or a traitor to his high trust." The president's assessment of his unhappy general was at once more sober, more just, and much more accurate. In a letter to his wife, Davis wrote, "There are those who can only walk a log when it is near to the ground, and I fear he [Beauregard] has been placed too high for his mental strength."[4]

Davis had good reasons, then, for not wanting to give Beauregard the crucial Army of Tennessee command. Beauregard had lost his nerve on the eve of Shiloh and again, with possibly serious results, on the evening of that battle's first day. Both there and at First Manassas, he had organized his troops poorly and given muddled orders. In the Corinth campaign he had again demonstrated little ingenuity in what appeared to be halfhearted attempts to stop a larger enemy army. President Davis need not have relied solely on his disgust for the Creole's repulsive personality in making his decision. However, Beauregard's record had not been all bad. Assigned to Charleston in 1863, he had done a credible job in the defense of that vital seaport. Had Beauregard grown as a commander if not as a person? Some would assert, then and later, that he had. In the summer of 1864 he would enjoy his finest hour, brilliantly directing the defense of Petersburg until Lee's forces came up and saved the railroad center from capture, a feat that prolonged the fighting in the East for some nine months. Yet just a few weeks before that, during the late spring of 1864, Beauregard turned in one of his vintage performances in the Bermuda Hundred campaign, indulging in unrealistic planning and loss of nerve on the battlefield. As a result, he merely drove back an extremely inept enemy when much more was possible and needed. He was, after all, the same old Beauregard—almost, but not quite, a good general. Though the events of the spring 1864 campaign in Virginia were still in the future when Davis made his choices, their nature was such as to bear out the president's assessment of Beauregard and justify his decision to pass over the Creole for important assignment in the West.[5]

That left Joseph E. Johnston, the man who finally took over command of the Confederacy's second-largest army. Johnston was Lee's second choice, after Beauregard, and was also supported by Secretary of State James A. Seddon and General (and personal friend of Davis) Leonidas Polk, as well as a sizable contingent within the Confederate Congress, many of whom merely used Johnston as a sort of political blunt object with which to belabor the president. Personally, Johnston was almost as repugnant to Davis as was Beauregard, but the president continued to think of him as a highly skilled general. In that much, at least, he was probably correct. Johnston seemed to be skillful, but he lacked nerve. Obsessed with his reputation, Johnston would not risk it on the outcome of a battle unless the conditions were perfect and success seemed certain. Since such situations rarely occur in warfare, the reputedly brilliant Johnston made a specialty of retreating. In Virginia in 1862 he had retreated to the outskirts of Richmond before directing the bungled battle of Seven Pines, in which he was wounded. After returning to duty later that year he had been sent west, and in 1863 he had hesitated outside Vicksburg while the last slim hopes of raising the Union siege vanished. The president had good reason to expect that Johnston would behave in a similar manner in 1864 but, imagining himself to be out of options, he gave Johnston the crucial Army of Tennessee command.[6]

So much, then, for the three full generals who were considered by Davis. Lee was simply not available; he was needed in Virginia. Beauregard was a possibility, though a questionable one. He might have performed acceptably, possibly better than Johnston and probably no worse, but to the president he was simply out of the question. Certainly neither man was an inspiring option.

Davis did seriously consider one other possibility before settling on Johnston, and that was the Army of Tennessee's interim commander, Lieutenant General William J. Hardee. Nicknamed "Old Reliable," Hardee was the author of a prewar infantry tactics manual and had served with the western army from Shiloh to Missionary Ridge. He had never accomplished anything striking, but at least he had committed no disastrous blunders. He had a bad habit of finding fault with his superiors, but in the Army of Tennessee that shortcoming seemed to be endemic. Davis had not only considered the lackluster Hardee but actually offered the command to him before looking elsewhere. Hardee refused. Ever ready to pick at what he saw as the failures of others, Hardee was hesitant to risk failure himself. Besides that, the forty-eight-year-old Hardee, a widower, was engaged to be married to a twenty-five-year-old Mobile, Alabama, woman, and he required a few days' leave to travel there and marry her—an unlikely scenario as long as he remained in command of the army.[7]

Whatever Hardee's motivation in turning down the command, Davis chose to accept his demur as final. Apparently, he need not have. Six months later when Davis passed over Hardee to position John B. Hood as commander of the Army of Tennessee, Hardee was outraged. Clearly, he was not as unambitious as he sometimes liked to appear, and a little extra urging by Davis might have persuaded him to take the job at the outset of 1864. He would probably not have been a spectacular success—he was not spectacular at anything—but throughout the Atlanta campaign he was more eager to fight than was his commander. Admittedly, that might very well have changed abruptly if the whole responsibility had been placed on him, for Hardee did not like responsibility and shied from it habitually. Still, like Beauregard, he probably would have done no worse than Johnston and possibly somewhat better. On the whole, he was probably the best realistic option available to Davis for command of the Army of Tennessee in early 1864, and the president should have insisted that he take the job, if necessary after returning from his furlough in Mobile.[8]

Far from having no alternatives, Davis actually had in Hardee at least one fairly acceptable option available to him for a commander of the luckless Army of Tennessee, and in Beauregard he had another, albeit highly questionable, possibility. The latter would have been the most daring choice, with even the long-odds chance for spectacular success—or for failure as dismal as Johnston's. Hardee would have been the cautious choice, providing skill and experience nearly comparable to Johnston's without the demonstrated record of failures of nerve and habitual retreats.

Even had Davis held his nose and appointed Beauregard—or been a little more persistent and given the job to Hardee—the possibility remains that he would have eventually found himself in the situation in which he finally did find himself with Johnston, i.e., a failed commander who needed to be replaced if Atlanta were to be saved. When that situation did arise, Davis found himself in a position of limited and unattractive options. However, this need not have been the case. Wise decisions by Davis at the outset of the campaign could have ensured that if things went wrong—and the weakness Davis perceived in his options for the top spot should have forewarned him that they well might—other alternatives would be available. In other words, Davis made what he knew was a weak choice, without providing for a backup plan.

In the first place, Davis's limited high command selections at the time Johnston was removed as head of the western army later that summer stemmed from a problem of organization. When Johnston took command of the Army of Tennessee late in 1863, it was an organizational mess. Its corps and divisions had been rearranged several times over the preceding few months, and a fair number of its higher-ranking officers had been transferred or demoted for failing to carry out their duties. When Johnston arrived on the scene, the army consisted of two infantry corps, but it had only one officer (Hardee) of the proper rank (lieutenant general) to command such a formation. By early January 1864, Johnston believed the army would be handier and more maneuverable if it were organized into three corps. That would require two new lieutenant generals and, of course, the president's approval.[9]

And that is precisely where the plan got stuck, for Davis would have none of it. Perhaps the problem was partially that he had appointed an army commander in whom he had little confidence. Any idea of

Johnston's was almost sure to be rejected by the president. In any case, Davis maintained that two corps were plenty for an army the size of Johnston's. The decision was Davis's first mistake. While the relatively small numbers in Johnston's army meant that the two corps would not be awkwardly large, it did not change the fact that an army of three, four, or even five corps would be more flexible, more nimble, and better able to meet the enemy's superior masses with its own superior maneuverability. Napoléon, who had all but pioneered the use of the *corps d'armée* and partially by means of it had conquered most of the continent of Europe, had favored a formation of four army corps supporting each other. Sometimes he had used five or more corps. Clearly, two corps was at least two too few.[10]

Beyond that, and of more direct importance in supplying himself with future options, Davis should have realized that if it became necessary to replace the commanding general in the presence of the enemy, the only viable replacements would be the corps commanders. By limiting these to two at first and later three (after the arrival of Leonidas Polk with a corps-sized contingent of troops from Mississippi), the president effectively reduced his own options to just that many men when and if the time should come to replace Johnston during the summer's campaign.[11]

Davis's second mistake—or category of mistakes—involved personnel. Hardee would command one of the corps of the Army of Tennessee. By mid-May Leonidas Polk, an earlier unfortunate choice of the president's, would be leading another of the Army of Tennessee's corps. Both incompetent and insubordinate, Polk was steadfastly sustained by Davis as a result of their prewar friendship. It would now be necessary for the president to select another corps commander, and Davis was not an especially good judge of officers.

Johnston was ready with recommendations. Besides Hardee's corps, the army's other corps was being led temporarily by Major General Thomas C. Hindman. Early on Johnston suggested to Davis the propriety of promoting Major General W. H. C. Whiting to the rank of lieutenant general and appointing him to take command of the corps. That he would suggest such a thing is characteristic of Johnston's tendency to antagonize Davis. Indeed, in this case it almost appears deliberate. Whiting was an odd character, perhaps not entirely stable mentally. He had graduated first in his West Point class of 1845, and in doing so had set an academic record that was not equaled until Douglas MacArthur excelled it more than half a century later. Early in the war he had been quite a favorite of

Johnston's, serving with him as a division commander and right-hand man when the latter had commanded the Confederate forces defending Richmond against George McClellan in the 1861 Peninsula campaign. Yet for all his brilliance, Whiting had a strange morose streak in him, and he fed Johnston's morbid fears with a double portion of his own.[12]

His chief sin in Davis's eyes, however, had occurred early in 1862. Whiting was commanding a brigade composed of regiments from various states. It was Davis's ambition so to organize the army that only regiments from the same state would be brigaded together, beginning with those from his own native Mississippi. Whiting was from Mississippi, and Davis offered him command of the first all-Mississippi brigade. Johnston and his coterie despised the president's plan, and Whiting responded to Davis's offer with an abusive letter denouncing the president and his plan and refusing the proffered command. Davis was livid, and it was all Johnston could do to prevent Whiting's being drummed right out of the army. The strange Mississippian's career was damaged but not destroyed.[13]

That Johnston would now recommend yet another promotion for Whiting, along with a high-priority assignment such as command of a corps in the Army of Tennessee, was a virtual slap in the face to Davis, and it is hard to imagine that Johnston did not know it. Davis ignored the request and no doubt at least mentally recorded another black mark against Johnston.

His first choice, such as it was, having been rejected, Johnston made two more selections almost equally bizarre. Hindman should be promoted to appropriate rank for the de facto corps command he now exercised, and Major General Mansfield Lovell should be promoted to three-star rank to lead the new corps that Johnston wanted to create in the army. These were interesting choices, to be sure. Hindman was a Tennessee-born lawyer and Mexican War veteran who hailed most recently from Helena, Arkansas. Not only had he once gone over a convent wall to get himself a wife, but on another occasion he engaged in a shootout with political opponents on Helena's main street at high noon. Given an important assignment in Arkansas in 1862, Hindman had acted with a ruthless efficiency that had impressed his commanding officer. Unfortunately, he then disobeyed orders, which resulted in the unsuccessful battle of Prairie Grove, Arkansas, on December 7, 1862. After joining the Army of Tennessee in the fall of 1863, Hindman and other officers failed to carry out one of Bragg's orders, which, if executed on time, almost certainly would have resulted in a resounding

Confederate victory. During the battle of Chickamauga, Hindman had redeemed himself—insofar as that may have been possible—by his reckless courage. Brave in battle though he might be, Hindman was nevertheless extremely unprofessional and unpredictable, and Davis did well to pass him by.[14]

Johnston's other recommendation, Mansfield Lovell, was far less colorful and had a curious past in Confederate uniform. Lovell was a West Point trained Northerner who had sided with the South. He was also a friend and protégé of his former boss in the New York street department, Kentucky-born Confederate General Gustavus W. Smith. Smith, for reasons that now seem obscure, had a towering reputation in the South for a few months in late 1861 and early 1862. On his recommendation, Lovell was made a major general and given command of the defenses of New Orleans.[15]

The promotion ultimately proved unfortunate for Lovell. Neither he nor anyone else could have done much to stop the determined David G. Farragut from running the forts below the city and capturing New Orleans. Many Southerners, however, viewed the loss of New Orleans as evidence that the Northern-born Lovell had betrayed the Southern cause. Shortly after the loss of the Crescent City, Jefferson Davis's brother Joseph, a Mississippi planter, had written a letter to the president complaining that Lovell "had become so obnoxious that he could do no good." Davis's confidence in him was shaken, but not destroyed. Subsequently, Lovell had served as a corps commander in northern Mississippi under the dashing Major General Earl Van Dorn. But giving Van Dorn command of infantry was asking for trouble— trouble that became a reality at Corinth, Mississippi, on October 3– 4, 1862. Although Lovell was not the one chiefly at fault in that affair either, it made him even more unpopular, and in December of that year he was relieved of the last significant command he was to hold during the war. It was his unpopularity that made Lovell an unattractive choice to fill the vacant corps command in the Army of Tennessee at the beginning of 1864. Confederate Secretary of War James A. Seddon warned the president that "it would be injudicious to place a corps under the command of Gen. Lovell" because "it would not give confidence to the army."[16]

This was probably true, but if anyone could have persuaded the troops to accept Lovell it would undoubtedly have been the extremely popular "Uncle Joe" Johnston. As for Lovell himself, he may well have been a serviceable corps commander, though he had not particularly distinguished himself in the few opportunities he had gotten thus far. At any rate, he was not the choice of Jefferson Davis.

The Confederate president had other choices available to him. One was Army of Tennessee division commander Major General Patrick Ronayne Cleburne. A native of Ireland and a veteran of the enlisted ranks of the British army, Cleburne had come to America and settled in Helena, Arkansas, where he later joined the state bar in 1856. A prewar friend of Thomas C. Hindman, he had been with him—and been wounded—in Hindman's high-noon shootout in the streets of Helena. Though without the formal education of an army officer, Cleburne proved to be one of the most gifted amateur officers of the war. By the winter of 1863–1864, Cleburne had been a major general for a year, had led his divisions with conspicuous success in three of the Army of Tennessee's toughest fights, and had, in covering the retreat from Chattanooga, exercised virtual corps command—also with great success under trying circumstances. That Davis passed over him seems almost incomprehensible. Perhaps it was because Cleburne had unwisely allowed himself to be drawn into the ugly politics of the Army of Tennessee's high command the previous year. It may also have stemmed from Cleburne's involvement that winter in advocating a scheme for freeing and arming Southern slaves for use against the Federals. Less likely, it may have had something to do with Davis's normally healthy predilection for West Point trained officers. Whatever may have prompted it, the failure to promote Cleburne to higher rank was a costly mistake for the Confederacy.[17]

Yet if it was West Pointers the president was seeking, these too were available. Most attractive among them was Major General Alexander P. Stewart. A member of the remarkable West Point Class of 1842, many of whose members went on to become generals during the Civil War, Stewart had ranked twelfth out of fifty-six, sixteen places ahead of Daniel Harvey Hill, forty places ahead of Earl Van Dorn, and forty-two places ahead of James Longstreet. His prewar career had been primarily that of an educator, first at West Point and then, after his resignation from the U.S. Army in 1845, at various colleges in Tennessee. Among his students had been Union General George B. McClellan and Confederate Thomas J. Jackson, one day to be "Stonewall," with whom Stewart shared a devout Presbyterianism. Stewart's wartime record with the Army of Tennessee had been good. He rose to division command and gave promise of aptitude at higher levels. He was seven months Cleburne's junior in rank, but when a vacancy opened late in the Atlanta campaign, it was Stewart who received the promotion to the coveted rank of lieutenant general. Either man was worthy of it, but the president would have done well to have promoted one or both of them at the outset of the campaign.[18]

Yet another West Point graduate and good available choice was Major General Stephen Dill Lee. Lee had performed good service in the East in the Army of Northern Virginia before going west, where he ultimately became one of the best of the brigadiers fighting for Vicksburg's defense in Lieutenant General John C. Pemberton's ill-fated army. Exchanged shortly after the fall of Vicksburg, Lee had promptly been promoted to major general and given command of the cavalry of the Department of Mississippi and East Louisiana. When Polk was called east to reinforce Johnston at the outset of the Atlanta campaign in May 1864, Lee succeeded to command of the department. When John B. Hood moved from corps to army command later that summer, Lee was assigned to take over Hood's old corps. As a corps commander in the Army of Tennessee, Lee gave a tolerable account of himself over the remainder of that army's service. He, too, would have been a viable alternative to command a corps in the Army of Tennessee at the beginning of 1864; not as good an option as Patrick Cleburne or A. P. Stewart, but a solid choice nonetheless.[19]

President Davis selected none of these men. Rather, his choice fell on Major General John Bell Hood. At thirty-three years of age, Hood was a year older than Stephen D. Lee, three years younger than Cleburne, and a decade younger than Stewart. Hood was a fierce fighter and had won a well-deserved reputation as a successful, hard-hitting brigade commander in Robert E. Lee's Army of Northern Virginia. His experience at higher levels of command, however, was scant. Hood had commanded a division at Gettysburg but was wounded almost as soon as his troops made contact with the enemy. Two months later at Chickamauga, he had in effect been responsible for a corps, but there too he was wounded. Hood's record as a corps commander with the Army of Tennessee in the summer of 1864 would demonstrate that he was struggling with the transition from brigade to division to corps command. During the army's long retreat from Dalton to the outskirts of Atlanta, he proved sometimes inattentive to details and sloppy in organization, shortcomings that greatly diminished his value as a corps commander despite his undeniable strengths as a combat leader.[20]

Young officers often had to learn the hard way when promoted to higher levels of responsibility. Stewart had stumbled at Shiloh, his first battle as a brigade commander, and also at Hoover's Gap, his first action in division command. Cleburne too had had a tough first experience at Shiloh, and in July 1864, Stephen Lee would demonstrate at Ezra Church that he too was susceptible to serious blundering when newly thrust into corps command. In many ways Hood was not a bad general at all, and especially after taking over command of the army on the doorstep, as it were, of Atlanta that July, he would do a number of things right.

The real problem with Hood was that by the time he was assigned to corps command in the Army of Tennessee in February 1864, he was a badly maimed man. He had lost the use of an arm as a result of his Gettysburg wound, and his Chickamauga wound had resulted in the amputation of a leg. Hood's physical handicaps meant that often during the coming campaign, he would suffer from excessive fatigue and chronic pain, factors that could possibly cloud judgment and warp the personality. Some scholars also suggest that Hood may at times have resorted to alcohol, opium, or a derivative of laudanum to dull the pain caused by his multiple wounds, with obvious consequences for his generalship. Even if he did not, he would always find it difficult to move about constantly viewing his troops and their positions and keeping up the frenetic pace of activity that was necessary for a man who would give orders to twenty thousand (later sixty thousand) other men and see to it that those orders were carried out.[21]

Thus the crucial 1864 campaign in the West began with Joseph E. Johnston, the least desirable of several less-than-perfect options, leading the Army of Tennessee without the confidence of his commander-in-chief. With the arrival of Polk and his troops from Mississippi, the army had three—rather than four or five—corps commanders. These consisted of the president's incompetent crony, Leonidas Polk; the badly crippled Hood; and the steady but lackluster Hardee. Polk was killed by artillery fire in mid-June and was eventually replaced by A. P. Stewart. When in July Davis finally felt the situation was desperate enough to warrant removal of Johnston on the eve of the struggle for the city of Atlanta itself (a struggle which, in all fairness to Davis, probably would not have taken place at all had he not had the courage to sack Johnston), Stewart had barely one month's experience at the corps level and so could hardly be considered for the top responsibility. The president's choices had indeed narrowed to two men, Hardee and Hood. Robert E. Lee's advice and the president's inclinations were in favor of Hardee, but Hood, true to his not-quite-stable self, had produced a stream of more-or-less honest letters that finally succeeded in convincing the Richmond authorities that Hardee had favored and abetted Johnston's policy of endless retreat. In addition, Hardee had already turned down command of the army on one occasion. That left just one option.[22]

Under the circumstances, the choice Davis made was probably the best available. With the army backed up into the Atlanta defenses, and with so much military and political importance riding on the successful defense of that city, it was no time for a plodder like Hardee. If the president had better, more viable choices available to him, he might have made his move before things became so desperate. Now they were almost hopeless, Hardee was probably not equal to the extremity of the situation, and the only other choice was the desperate gamble on John Bell Hood.

Yet the circumstances need not have been what they were. Other options were available and were successively rejected by the president, perhaps in part unwittingly, over the course of the winter of 1863–1864. He could have had Hardee or Beauregard as the Army of Tennessee's commander for the 1864 campaign. He could have had a more flexible army, subdivided into four or five corps; he could have had in place corps commanders who would not only have been more capable subordinates to their commanding general, but who would have provided a pool of excellent potential replacements if the removal of the army's leader became necessary. And it might well never have become necessary. One can only wonder how events might have played out had 1864 opened with Beauregard in command of an Army of Tennessee composed of three corps led by William J. Hardee, Patrick R. Cleburne, and Alexander P. Stewart, and joined by a fourth corps coming up from Mississippi led, not by Polk, but by the much more competent and reliable Stephen D. Lee. That scenario, however, is in the realm of speculation, and it is not the purpose of this article to explore such themes.

To claim, as Davis and some of his defenders have done, that no viable alternatives were open to him in 1864 other than the ones he chose, is to narrow one's understanding and appreciation of the events of that year. The circumstances were what they were because of the choices made by Jefferson Davis. This is not to say that he had no talent as commander-in-chief or that he lacked dedication to the cause of Southern independence. He had considerable talent and he was supremely dedicated, if only because his own career and place in history were inextricably entangled with the Confederacy. But, like any human leader, he made his share of mistakes, and it is instructive to consider what they were. That consideration requires an awareness of the options that were available to him during the winter of 1863–1864.

Eight

Beauregard at Bermuda Hundred

O F A L L T H E events in the colorful Civil War service of Confederate General Pierre Gustave Toutant Beauregard, none appears so much to his credit as his defense of the vulnerable "back door" of Richmond south of the James River in May and June 1864. Without question, his defense of Petersburg with a shoestring force against Grant's masterful turning maneuver in June of that year was a notable feat of arms, even if it was unwittingly aided by the blundering and lack of enterprise of the officers Grant had trusted to carry out the Union attack. Beauregard's energetic and successful efforts to hold what its residents called "the Cockade City" constitute very likely the most useful two or three days in his Confederate career.

Yet the great bulk of Beauregard's operations in southside Virginia during the spring of 1864 came not during the June defense of Petersburg against Grant but rather in the defense of both Petersburg and Richmond against Benjamin F. Butler's Bermuda Hundred campaign in May. This too has been celebrated as a great success for the Louisiana general, who is credited with a series of actions that shoved Butler and his substantial army into a pocket formed by a bend of the James River, where it languished, in Grant's words, "as completely shut off from further operations directly against Richmond as if it had been in a bottle strongly corked." Here at last, claim the Louisiana general's defenders, is a demonstration of the battlefield genius obscured by various circumstances—or worse, by Confederate President Jefferson Davis's malignity—in Virginia in 1861 and Mississippi the following year. The success of the Bermuda Hundred campaign is presented as proof that Beauregard was a capable and practical field commander who might have accomplished far greater things for the Confederacy had Davis not conceived an irrational dislike for him.[1]

Beauregard's long journey to the May 1864 battlefield on the south bank of the James River began in Charleston, South Carolina. The Palmetto State was the scene of his initial taste of Civil War glory, when Fort Sumter surrendered under the weight of his bombardment during the first April of the war. The crucial port city had more recently been the scene of his most effective wartime service prior to 1864; Beauregard had directed the successful Confederate resistance to a months-long Union effort to capture Charleston. Though his military reputation was in a measure refurbished by his solid defensive performance, Beauregard grew tired of static service in what he considered a backwater of the war. As was often the case when he was unhappy, he began to complain increasingly of his chronic throat ailment. He was on the point of prescribing for himself another of his therapeutic vacations at his favorite spa at Bladon Springs, Alabama, when a dispatch arrived from Richmond that changed his mind.[2]

General Braxton Bragg, President Davis's chief military adviser, telegraphed to ask if Beauregard felt up to assuming a command in southern Virginia. The Old Dominion State was the place of action, glory, and widespread recognition, and the Creole had an ear keenly tuned for public acclaim. Throat ailment forgotten, Beauregard quickly replied that he was ready to travel north. The following day, April 15, 1864, the wire from Richmond carried a terse message from Adjutant and Inspector General Samuel Cooper: "Repair with the least delay practicable to Weldon, N.C., where instructions will be sent to you."[3]

Several reasons lay behind the summons. Command arrangements in North Carolina and southside Virginia were diverse and confusing. Command of the sector immediately south of the Richmond district was entrusted to the weak-minded Major General George Pickett, an adequate brigade commander whose promotion to major general was owing mostly to the favoritism of his mentor, Lieutenant General James Longstreet. Without Longstreet's overbearing personal presence, and faced with a task more complicated than leading a division on a battlefield, Pickett was even more inadequate than usual. Bragg—who with Davis's approval was giving considerable attention to the southern Virginia and North Carolina region—had felt that someone with more ability was needed. Also, Robert E. Lee had written the president to suggest that Beauregard and some of his troops around Charleston be moved northward to cover the southern approaches to Richmond.[4]

So it was that Beauregard moved a good deal closer to the scene of his earlier glory, Manassas, where in the summer of 1861 he had enjoyed the acclaim of the victor. Now he officially assumed command of the Department of North Carolina and Cape Fear, as well as that part of Virginia lying south of the James and Appomattox Rivers, on April 23, 1864. Promptly thereafter, he renamed his enlarged sphere of command the Department of North Carolina and Southern Virginia. The situation he found upon his arrival was little to his liking. For Beauregard, concentration of forces, always and for every purpose, was the ultimate distillation of military wisdom. Confederate units in his new department, however, were sprawled across the countryside from the Carolina coast to the Virginia piedmont. Their various errands included not only the securing of Richmond's inland approaches, but also the gathering of supplies and (as the authorities in Richmond devoutly hoped) the dislodging of the Federals who had early in the war established enclaves on the Tarheel State's long and intricate shoreline. A success had recently been scored at Plymouth, North Carolina, and Richmond hoped for similar results at New Bern. The policy made good sense during the winter's lull on the major fighting fronts, but now spring was coming on apace and Beauregard had no use for such a strategy. "It occasioned an untimely division of some of the most available troops in my new command," he later complained, "rendering their immediate concentration at any threatened point very difficult, if not impossible." Despite his perennial penchant for complaint, Beauregard was correct. Ulysses S. Grant was within a fortnight of launching the largest and best-coordinated set of offensive thrusts yet aimed at the Confederacy. As Northern preparations became increasingly obvious, Southern enthusiasm waned for sideshows like New Bern.[5]

Already doubtful about the enterprise but under orders to supervise its execution, Beauregard remained as aloof as possible from the New Bern expedition. The troops marched off toward their objective on May 2, but the operation was still in its preliminary stages two days later when a wire arrived from Davis: "Unless New Berne can be captured by coup-de-main," the president instructed, "the attempt must be abandoned, and the troops returned with all possible dispatch to unit in operations in N[orthern] Virginia. There is not an hour to lose. Had the expedition not started, I would say it should not go."[6]

Grant's grand coordinated offensive, which had opened that very day, lay behind this sudden change in Richmond's policy. While Major General George G. Meade's Army of the Potomac advanced across the Rapidan River against Lee's Army of Northern Virginia, Union forces led by cockeyed Massachusetts politician-turned-general Benjamin F. Butler were preparing to move up the James River toward the Confederate capital. Though Lee's army had not yet collided with Meade's, the Army of Northern Virginia's commander was convinced that the enemy's main thrust was aimed at him, and he was demonstrating in his dispatches to the president that he could, at times, be as much of an advocate of concentration of force as Beauregard. "I regret that there is to be any further delay in concentrating our . . . troops," Lee wrote. "I fully appreciate the advantages of capturing New Berne, but they will not compensate us for a disaster in [Virginia]."[7]

Sensitive as always to Lee's urgings, Davis immediately besought Beauregard for troops. The Creole, responding promptly and decisively, ordered the forces of Major General Robert Hoke's division to disengage and move north for Richmond with "utmost dispatch." Other units were soon on their way to Lee's front, both from North Carolina and southern Virginia as well as from Charleston, where the Federal threat was correctly judged to have diminished as Union troops departed for Virginia. Among the Confederate units moving north were two brigades from George Pickett's division, with Pickett himself accompanying them. Service south of the Appomattox River had been a distasteful exile for the Virginian, and he was eager to rejoin Lee, Longstreet, and a war he at least believed he understood.[8]

Amidst all the tension of an impending collision of the major armies in northern Virginia, no one seems to have remembered the threat posed by the Federals debarking down on the James River. Though Davis had mentioned in a dispatch to Lee on May 4 that "the enemy's forces from S[outh] C[arolina] and Florida are no doubt on the Peninsula," Confederate units moving up from the southern coastline were slated for transport through the Richmond area and on to Lee's army.[9]

That same day, the day before the combined Federal offensive, Beauregard wrote a friend that he saw "no prospect now, of active operations in this Dept." This amazing lapse in Confederate planning was not the result of poor intelligence information but rather of hesitance at the highest level of command. At the moment Davis had better information than Beauregard, but characteristically he was simply passing the raw data on to Lee and naively trusting that general somehow to know what was best to be done in the situation. Even as Butler's troops were landing and establishing their beachhead at Bermuda Hundred, the neck of land at the confluence of the James and the Appomattox Rivers, Davis was reporting the Union concentration to Lee on May 5, concluding, "With these facts and your previous knowledge, you can estimate the condition of things here and decide how far your own movements should be influenced thereby." Lee could do nothing of the sort. That morning he had hurled his division against Meade's army in the tangled thickets of the Wilderness, and it was 11 P.M. before he could so much as pause to scribble a few lines to the War Department, briefly describing the day's carnage. Lee's attention was fully occupied on his front. On the subject of other units he remained silent, no doubt hoping the Richmond authorities would send him whatever troops they could spare. For the moment, no military response was made to Butler's landing.[10]

This was a potentially fatal oversight. A Federal army at Bermuda Hundred would possess several strategic alternatives, all of them disastrous for the South. Most significant, a body of troops could either march up the James and take Richmond from the rear, or move up the Appomattox, seize the vital rail junction at Petersburg, and cut off Richmond's—and Lee's—supply conduit from the Deep South. A third possibility involved a lunge for the Richmond and Petersburg Railroad, a vulnerable single line of track connecting the Confederate capital and Petersburg. Federal success in any of these movements or a combination of them would amount to the same thing: an end to Confederate hopes of independence.

The first high-ranking Confederate officer to begin to grasp what the Federals were about was the hapless Pickett. Not yet having left Petersburg to join his brigades in northern Virginia, Pickett could hardly have helped but notice the oncoming Union juggernaut, for he stood almost directly in its path and less than a dozen miles away. Beauregard had already given him permission to communicate directly with Richmond if the need arose, and Pickett frantically began to bombard Richmond and Beauregard both with pleas for troops and instructions.[11]

Beauregard in turn sent a string of messages to Braxton Bragg in Richmond, requesting that Pickett be allowed to keep the small force he had already at Petersburg and to stop other units passing through the town on their way from the southern coast to join Lee on the Rapidan. Davis took a direct interest in these matters, and while allowing that Pickett could keep the token forces then in Petersburg, insisted that the reinforcements bound for Lee must not be diverted. Beauregard's protests got the order at least partially rescinded, allowing one brigade to be halted at Petersburg for the defense of that point. He urged Pickett to do the best he could and ordered him to remain in command in the threatened city until the situation stabilized. At the same time, while assuring Bragg that "all possible will be done," Beauregard declined to go personally to the scene of action, pleading lamely that he was "too unwell to go to Petersburg tonight," but promising to "do so tomorrow evening, or next day." Richmond authorities—and Pickett—would have to content themselves with that assurance. For the moment the Creole remained in his secure headquarters in Weldon, North Carolina, well away from the arena in which crucial decisions had to be made.[12]

This was vintage Beauregard. Simply put, he did not handle stress well. Often when the military situation looked particularly bad, his mysterious throat ailment would flare up, allowing him a convenient excuse to decline to take command or responsibility. This occurred in West Tennessee in February and March 1862, and again in Mississippi that summer. It was an ironic quirk of Beauregard's personality that although he longed for military glory and pined for assignment to the chief seat of the war, where laurels were most likely to be won, he also had a dread of responsibility and tended to choke under pressure. The glories of command drew him like the Lorelei from afar, but its lonely decisions appalled him when their prospect arose immediately before his face. That, of course, was precisely the reason why for the last year and more he had been stationed in a backwater of the war. As Butler's Federals appeared to be about to advance through the almost nonexistent Confederate defenses south of Richmond, Beauregard found the heights of command and decision altogether too giddy, and his health, at least, failed him.[13]

There can be no denying that Beauregard had good reason to be nervous, and that by this time he had a far more realistic appreciation of the military situation south of the James than did anyone in Richmond, Davis not excepted. On May 6, the Confederate president wired Beauregard to express the hope that the general would "be able at Petersburg to direct operations both before and behind you, so as to meet necessities." That would have been fine if Beauregard had been on his way to the threatened city and if any substantial body of troops had been available for him to direct either before or behind. As it was, Beauregard replied that he was "still confined to [his] tent by sickness" but that he hoped to be able to set out for Petersburg in another day or so. Meanwhile, he was "concentrating as rapidly as possible all available troops." The troops were indeed on the way from all over Beauregard's department and South Carolina. As his dispatches and Pickett's almost frantic, well-nigh hourly telegraphic pleadings made their impact, Davis and Bragg began to grasp the gravity of the Bermuda Hundred situation. Authorization finally came to retain troops at Petersburg, and by May 6, it was Adjutant and Inspector General Samuel Cooper, on behalf of Davis, who was urging Beauregard to hasten "forward by rail the troops ordered from the south to Petersburg, which is much threatened."[14]

Fortunately for the South, the Confederate high command had recognized the danger to Petersburg in time to shore up its defense. The first brigade to halt there in its northward movement was able to baffle a pair of halfhearted probes by Butler toward the vital railroad between Richmond and Petersburg on May 6 and 7. Still, the Federal threat remained, and in Richmond anxieties continued to grow. On May 6, Beauregard, still in Weldon, sent duplicate messages to Cooper, Bragg, and Secretary of War James A. Seddon, asking if he were authorized "to control to best advantage I may think proper all troops now in this department or arriving?" It was natural for a commander to want to be sure of the extent of his authority, but from Richmond it may have appeared that the temperamental Creole was refusing to move to Petersburg and carry out his duty unless he were promised a free hand. However this may have appeared to Davis, the Southern president was quickly losing patience with Beauregard. He wanted troops brought up from the south more quickly, and he wanted "a prompt and earnest attack" against Butler's Federals.[15]

Davis now saw clearly that the Union movement represented a serious threat to Richmond. By this time he had also learned that the Federals were commanded by Benjamin "Beast" Butler, whose administration of occupied New Orleans earlier in the war had drawn from Davis a proclamation that he was to be hanged, without further ado, immediately upon capture. For Davis, the prospect of carrying out his decree, coupled with his desire to safeguard Richmond and Petersburg, provided strong incentive for a quick and decisive attack. He wrote in a note to Bragg on May 8 that "if General Beauregard's health disqualifies him for field operations, it would be well to order [Major General Robert F.] Hoke to proceed in advance of his troops and take command of the forces in front of Petersburg." In an offhand command that told much about what the Richmond authorities thought of George Pickett, Davis concluded, "For the defensive operations of that point General Pickett will be enough."[16]

Bragg communicated Davis's advice to Beauregard, along with the president's suggestion that the railroad through Danville, Virginia, might be used to move troops more quickly into Petersburg. The Creole responded with a stream of dispatches in which he promised that troops would "be pushed through as fast as possible," although he considered the president's suggested alternate route impractical. As for going to Petersburg himself, this was something he seemed always on the verge of doing. First he wrote, "I hope to leave today for Petersburg, where prompt and energetic measure will be adopted." Then he would "leave here tonight by the first train." This was postponed to "will leave here at 11 P.M. for Petersburg," which in turn finally gave way to an admission that he "should have started today for Petersburg," but a nuisance raid by some Northern cavalry had prompted him to postpone his going until morning. At that time, he insisted, "I shall run through and assume command as desired." In case the president might still be in a mood to take the general's poor health as an occasion to relieve him of command, Beauregard hastened to add the assurance, "The water has improved my health."[17]

All this proved to be sufficient to save Beauregard from removal, but he was not quick to forgive Davis for coming so close thus to committing, for a second time in the war, such an unpardonable sin. Long after the war he wrote of this period, "Rapid as were the movements of our troops . . . their celerity failed to satisfy or reassure the War Department, whose trepidation grew hourly more intense, and whose orders, telegrams, and suggestions became as harassing as they were numerous." Harassing or not, they did finally have the effect of budging Beauregard from his secure seat on the sidelines. On May 9 he reached Raleigh and telegraphed Richmond that he would proceed from there by way of Danville to Petersburg, where he finally arrived the next day.[18]

By that time, the flow of the campaign had shifted, and Petersburg was no longer the focal point of Butler's Federals. Acting on his understanding of Grant's grand plan of campaign, and in response to information he was receiving from north of the James, Butler shifted his attention from

Petersburg to the southern approaches of Richmond itself. Skirmishing with troops of the Richmond garrison slowed Butler's advance to a timid creep, but Richmond's garrison commander, Major General Robert Ransom, realized he did not have enough troops on hand to stop a resolute Federal advance. The Richmond authorities knew it too. At 10 P.M. on May 9, Bragg telegraphed Hoke, then assumed by the War Department to be at Petersburg, to advance with his "whole force" to join Ransom in the defense of Richmond. In fact, Hoke, along with his division moving up from North Carolina, did not arrive in Petersburg until 1:30 P.M. the following day, five and a half hours after Beauregard. At this point, some confusion arose as to whether the order to Hoke was still in effect, and if so, what was meant by his "whole force." Did Bragg mean just his division, or all the troops at Petersburg? Beauregard sent an inquiry to Richmond for clarification, proceeding with his own plans in the meantime.[19]

As it turned out, the issue was moot. On May 10, Ransom met elements of Butler's command just east of Chester Station, a small village south of Richmond. After inconclusive fighting, Ransom withdrew north into the fortifications around Drewry's Bluff, a Confederate strong point on the south bank of the James just below the city. The defensive bulwark at Drewry's Bluff had saved the Confederate capital in early 1862 by turning back a determined Union naval assault up the James River. Now, however, the position was threatened by Butler's ground troops, and defending it were Ransom's few, thin brigades. Davis and his advisers waited anxiously throughout May 10 for news of Ransom's action with Butler.[20]

As the day passed, they became aware of an additional danger. Union Major General Philip Sheridan, with two divisions of Union cavalry, had detached himself from Meade's army and was moving to destroy a key bridge on the Virginia Central Railroad at Beaver Dam Station. The loss of the bridge would seriously threaten the supply lines to Lee's hard-pressed army. With Ransom's Richmond garrison occupied south of the James with Butler, Sheridan's troops also posed a serious threat to the capital itself. At 3:30 P.M. Bragg wired Petersburg urging Beauregard to attack. "Let us know when you will be ready, that Ransom may cooperate. Every hour is now very important." Bragg spelled out the danger more fully in a later communication: "We are seriously threatened here from above," he explained. "You should make a heavy demonstration and change to attack, if practicable, at an early hour in the morning." In response, Beauregard telegraphed that night to promise that he would be ready for offensive operations the following evening.[21]

That was not good enough. Twenty minutes after midnight on the morning of May 11, Bragg fired off an order for Beauregard to send Hoke, along with all available field forces at Petersburg, directly north up the turnpike for Drewry's Bluff to join Ransom—even if they had to cut their way through Butler's command to do so. Beauregard responded, pleading for more time to get things organized before going over to the offensive.[22]

Receiving no reply, Beauregard had enough sense of the frustration in Richmond to realize this was an order that had best be carried out. He accordingly obeyed the order, and the troops prepared to move out. As daylight crept up the broad tidal rivers of eastern Virginia, Beauregard sent Bragg an upbeat message. "My forces are being united . . . You may then rely on my hearty co-operation in defense of Richmond." He then added cryptically, however, "Appearances here this morning are that the enemy is about withdrawing from this point to reenforce elsewhere. I will try to strike him a severe blow before he leaves." This, in fact, was a mistake. What Beauregard was perceiving was merely Butler's shift toward Richmond. In that city, Bragg and the rest of the circle around the president could hardly have known what to make of the statement, but it must have been good at last to hear Beauregard speaking of striking "a severe blow" to the enemy.[23]

At 7 A.M. further encouraging word came from the Creole. "Offensive movement against enemy has commenced," he grandly proclaimed. "General Hoke's division in the advance supported by Pickett's division." He concluded the short telegram by stating, "Give necessary orders to General Ransom," meaning that Ransom should be ordered to cooperate with him from Drewry's Bluff. This information from Beauregard was not exactly true either. The previous evening, Pickett, having fretted himself into a state of nervous prostration during his few days of responsibility for Petersburg, relinquished his duties and took to his bed.[24]

From Richmond's perspective, at any rate, Beauregard appeared to be proceeding as ordered. In a dispatch to Ransom through Bragg, however, Beauregard began to speak of "a forced reconnaissance" by Hoke and Pickett. His men would attack Butler "should [the] opportunity be favorable." He was proposing an attack—not toward Richmond and the threatened lines at Drewry's Bluff—but instead toward Bermuda Hundred. He even planned to send some of his men through Petersburg and around the south side of the Appomattox to attack City Point, across the wide confluence of the James and Appomattox Rivers from Bermuda Hundred. Beauregard was moving his troops sixty degrees in the wrong direction, and he was planning to straddle them across a broad tidal river controlled by enemy warships.[25]

Consternation reigned in the War Department at this shocking proposal. "Division of your forces is earnestly objected to," Seddon hurriedly replied. "It is decidedly preferred that you carry out the instructions given last night, and endeavor to unite all forces." At 12:45 P.M. Beauregard's reply was equivocal: "My division of force is only temporary to meet present emergency." He asked the secretary to "state [his] objections," and insisted, "I am carrying into effect to best of ability instructions received." The Creole concluded his message with a vague assurance—which was not very reassuring under the circumstances—that "the movement is now in progress."[26]

Shortly thereafter, Beauregard received a dispatch from Seddon that had crossed his in transit. "This city is in hot danger," the secretary raged. "It should be defended with all our resources to the sacrifice of minor considerations. You are relied on to use every effort to unite all your forces at the earliest practicable time with the troops in our defenses, and then together either fight the enemy in the field or defend the intrenchments."[27]

When Seddon received the general's reply, he fired back a message of stinging rebuke:

> Your two telegrams of this date are received. They pain and surprise. I do not feel this to be an appropriate time to reply fully to them. I may do that hereafter. At present I have only to say, that while your past service, patriotism, and reputation are fully appreciated, you are on those accounts only the more relied on and expected to use every effort in your power with all your forces to carry out the instruction of the Department and accomplish the junction of all our forces to fight the enemy or defend the capital.[28]

Beauregard took offense at Seddon's reprimand and replied with a longer dispatch, defending his actions and motives and pointing out that he had passed up a sick leave to take this assignment. "I am ready and willing to serve the cause to the utter sacrifice of health, but if my course be not approved by the War Department I wish to be relieved at once."[29]

To Davis, who was monitoring the correspondence, this exchange must have looked very familiar. Beauregard was in his usual form, spinning complex and unrealistic plans, indulging in melodramatic self-promotion, and taking offense at any suggestion of an authority above himself. Indeed, that Beauregard was worked up to a higher-than-usual pitch of strategic pipe-dreaming was evidenced by the fact that this plan abandoned even his cherished principle of concentration of force. Another aspect of the general's behavior might have put Davis in mind, unpleasantly, of the Creole's behavior at Shiloh: Beauregard had not gone forward with his troops. This became apparent for the first time to those in Richmond when Davis intervened in the process at 2:15 P.M. The distressed president dashed off a quick dispatch addressed simply to the "Commanding Officer, Petersburg." He inquired, "What forces have you today to unite with General Ransom? . . . When did General Beauregard leave?"[30]

The answer of course was that Beauregard had not left at all, and the general himself replied to the queries. "I have not yet left here," he wrote, "my presence being still absolutely necessary." He would go, he promised, "immediately after arrival of two last brigades—hourly expected from Weldon." He further informed Davis that he had canceled the movement on Bermuda Hundred in response to Seddon's rebuke, but that shortly thereafter, "the order to make forced reconnaissance was approved by General Bragg, and is now being executed." What, Beauregard wanted to know, did Davis think of all this?[31]

Without waiting for an answer, which apparently never came, Beauregard telegraphed Bragg a few minutes later, complaining of Seddon's interference and concluding, "I must insist on receiving order only from one source, and that from the general commanding."[32]

By this time, however, Beauregard's fitful gestures toward Bermuda Hundred had come to nothing after all. Hoke and his two divisions had proceeded directly up the turnpike without incident, and by 5 P.M. had easily made contact with Ransom. Beauregard seemed to reconcile himself to this turn of events, and the temporary storm between him and the secretary of war apparently blew over.[33]

It was fortunate for the Confederacy that Hoke arrived when he did. That day Major General Jeb Stuart's Confederate cavalry had clashed with Sheridan's troopers north of Richmond at Yellow Tavern. Stuart fell mortally wounded in the action, and the Federal horsemen were just a few miles outside the city. Davis and his advisers felt compelled to pull most of Ransom's division off the southern front to hold back Sheridan, a move made possible by Hoke's timely arrival. For the moment, Richmond was again secure. After briefly threatening the city, Sheridan retired to Butler's base on the James River. The authorities in Richmond, however, had worries enough, as the news from all fronts was disheartening. On May 12, Lee's army was nearly broken in two at the Bloody Angle at Spotsylvania, where hours of desperate fighting were needed to repair the rupture in the line. Twenty cannon and thousands of men were lost in the fighting. Lee, who had been asking for reinforcements to replace his heavy losses, also needed men to protect his flow of supplies from raiding Union cavalry. The only reasonable source for these reinforcements were the troops concentrated in the Richmond-Petersburg area. Butler, however, had yet to be decisively dealt with, and he still posed a considerable threat to both Richmond and the vital rail junction at Petersburg. On May 11 and 12, Beauregard had promised Ransom, Seddon, and Davis that he would leave for Drewry's Bluff on the twelfth, probably by noon. When he finally left Petersburg, it was twenty-four hours later on May 13. In Petersburg he left two brigades of troops along with Major General William Henry Chase Whiting, who had left his post at Wilmington, North Carolina, to travel to Petersburg merely to consult with Beauregard. Instead, Beauregard asked him to stay and command the city in his absence. By the time the Creole left for Drewry's Bluff with a small escort, pushing through to Richmond's southern defenses was a daring enough undertaking by any standard. The Federals controlled the turnpike, and Beauregard had to take a roundabout route that finally brought him into Confederate lines south of the James at 3 A.M. on May 14. Upon his arrival, he learned that Hoke, with a small force left him after troops were shifted north to counter Sheridan, had spent the day stubbornly skirmishing with Butler's men. Though he still held Drewry's Bluff, he had been forced back from the outer fortifications into the intermediate defensive lines.[34]

Beauregard discussed the situation with staff officers on the scene for about an hour before turning to his favorite military occupation: the manufacture of grandiose and far-fetched strategic plans. His new scheme called for Lee to fall back more than forty miles to the outer, or even intermediate, defensive works around Richmond, at the same time detaching ten thousand men to reinforce Beauregard. This addition to his force, plus the five thousand troops of Ransom's Richmond garrison, would bring Beauregard's numbers to twenty-five or thirty thousand men, perhaps more. With these he would assail Butler's right flank, aiming to pry the Union army away from the James River and its base at Bermuda Hundred. Simultaneously, proposed the Creole, Whiting would move up from Petersburg with four thousand men and strike the rear of the Union position. Beauregard believed that his plan would "insure his [Butler's] unconditional surrender." That accomplished, Beauregard would turn north with twenty-five thousand men, attack the left flank of Grant's army while Lee assaulted it in front, and thus win the war.[35]

Beauregard later admitted having formed this scheme "hurriedly," and he was no more inclined to lose time in getting it approved. He dispatched a galloping staff officer for Richmond to see Davis and gain his blessing for the plan—a program that had yet to be set down in writing. When the aide arrived in Richmond, it was still exceedingly early in the morning. Davis had not been well, and his aides were reluctant to disturb him with such a hasty plan. Instead, the officer gave his message to Bragg, who decided to ride down to Drewry's Bluff and talk to Beauregard about the matter. There, Beauregard presented his case in impassioned terms and urged Bragg to order its immediate execution on his own responsibility. Bragg was not about to do anything of the sort. He was polite but noncommittal, and he harbored a number of serious reservations about the plan, though he did not share these with Beauregard. Indeed, so anxious was Bragg to be pleasant, that Beauregard later claimed Bragg had fully agreed with the plan. The best the Creole could get from Bragg in concrete terms was a promise to put the matter to the president as soon as possible.[36]

Beauregard decided to follow up his discussion with Bragg with a written proposal of his plan, and its details were set down on paper for the first time in a dispatch that morning. To his written version he added a flourish or two—the undoing of Butler should be the work of, at most, two days, once Beauregard received the reinforcements he sought. The destruction of Butler would provide such a windfall of supplies that for "a few days" the Confederates could proceed in blissful unconcern to all considerations of logistics. The hours passed, however, with no instructions from Richmond as to whether his plan would be adopted. Finally, about midafternoon, Beauregard's suspense was ended, not by the arrival of an answer from Davis, but by the arrival of Davis himself.[37]

Beauregard endeavored to convince the president of the merits of his operation, but it was no use. Davis was too much of a realist to be drawn into approval of such a bizarre and unrealistic scheme. The president pointed out the obvious problems involved in having Lee make such a precipitate retreat on Richmond. He also objected to Beauregard's plan to have Whiting move from the opposite side of the enemy and yet coordinate his movements with those of Beauregard. With the state of communications as they were in the nineteenth century, such coordination was all but impossible and Davis knew it. Instead, he suggested that Whiting and his men make a night march, skirting Butler's positions by way of the Chesterfield Road, and joining Beauregard "by or soon after daylight' on Sunday, May 15. After a day of rest they would be ready to join in an assault at dawn on the morning of Monday, May 16.[38]

The general, of course, was not happy with this at all. Whiting's movement was, as Beauregard later put it, "a salient feature of my plan." Hoping to block the president's objections, he lamely complained that it would be terribly difficult to get "a courier who knew the route and could certainly deliver the order to General Whiting." Unfortunately for Beauregard, he had made a very ill choice of an excuse, for just at that moment a courier rode up, having come from Whiting by way of the Chesterfield Road. Thus checkmated, Beauregard, as he put it in a postwar account that dripped with bitterness, "reluctantly yielded to" the president's objection. He still had a trick or two up his sleeve, though. In agreeing to the president's plan, Beauregard "said the order [to Whiting] would have to be drawn with a great deal of care, and that he would prepare it as soon as he could." That seemed to satisfy Davis, who then returned to Richmond, no doubt to Beauregard's immense gratification.[39]

With the president gone, Beauregard sat down to prepare "with a great deal of care" his instructions to Whiting. Flagrantly ignoring Davis's orders, he directed Whiting to depart from Petersburg not at nightfall on Saturday, May 14, but at dawn on Monday, May 16. This directive, of course, would result in a two-day delay in opening the battle—unless Whiting were to revert to his original role of leading an independent force to fall against the rear of Butler's army while Beauregard was engaged in front. Clearly, Beauregard never for a moment intended to comply with Davis's orders regarding Whiting.[40]

Beauregard's true intent gradually began to dawn on Davis and Bragg the next day. On Sunday morning, May 15, Davis had Bragg send dispatches to both Whiting and Beauregard. He urged the former to "join [Beauregard] at the earliest moment with his whole force," while informing the latter officer, "It is hoped you may receive [Whiting]

in time to attack tomorrow. . . . time is all important to us, as the
enemy gains more by delay than we possibly can. Sheridan's cavalry,
with re-enforcements, will again threaten the city very soon, which
is almost stripped of troops to aid you." That this last statement was
true, Beauregard had good reason to know, for even then the troops
of Ransom's division—the only force available to protect the capital
from Sheridan—were filing into reserve positions just to the rear of
his lines at Bermuda Hundred. It was 4 P.M. before Beauregard replied,
"I have already sent General Whiting his instructions to cooperate with
me." The Creole haughtily informed Bragg, "Please telegraph him to
follow them. Yours may conflict with mine." By this point in the war
it is doubtful that any manner of insubordination could have shocked
Braxton Bragg, but this gross demonstration probably came close. One
can almost hear the sputter in his reply: "My dispatches of this morning
to you and General Whiting were by direction of the President and after
his conference with you."[41]

Since May 15 was a Sunday, Davis and Bragg were probably not in
close contact for much of the day. At any rate, it seems likely that after
ordering Bragg to send the dispatches to Whiting and Beauregard that
morning, Davis did not talk with him again until at least evening. The
president was learning of Beauregard's perfidy by other means. Sometime
before noon, a staff officer stopped by Davis's residence with another
oral message from Beauregard. The general had now decided, the officer
related, "to order Whiting to move by the direct road from Petersburg,
instead of by the Chesterfield route." This, of course, was a return to
Beauregard's original plan of launching Whiting against the Federal rear,
and Davis objected as he had before. In reply, the officer "said General
Beauregard had directed him to explain to [Davis] that upon a further
examination he found his force sufficient; that his operations, therefore,
did not depend upon making a junction with Whiting." Twenty-four
hours before, Beauregard had claimed that Whiting must approach the
enemy rear because the plan could not go on without him. Now the
Creole was claiming that Whiting was free to approach the enemy rear
precisely because his force was not essential to the plan. The contrary
claims, one coming close on the heels of the other, made little sense, and
as events would prove, the latter contention was untrue.[42]

That Sunday evening, Beauregard took time out from his preparations
for battle to complete the job of deception he had begun on his superiors.
In response to Bragg's indignant protest, he wired blandly that a "change

of plan of operations since President was here necessitated a corresponding change in Whiting's instructions, which I have ordered accordingly." The president would require more verbal camouflage than Bragg, and consequently Beauregard prepared one of his lengthier dispatches of the campaign. He now claimed that "it was found he [Whiting] would require two days to reach here." Since the battle could obviously not be delayed that long with any degree of safety, Beauregard had "ordered Major-General Whiting to co-operate with all his forces by attacking the enemy in rear" while the forces at Bermuda Hundred attacked head-on the next morning. That, after all, had been Beauregard's original plan.[43]

Robert Ransom's four-brigade division, holding the Confederate left flank near the James River, was to lead off the attack. They went in "at the first glimpse of daylight," as Ransom recalled it, hindered by trees the Federals had felled in their front as well as by wire entanglements "interwoven among the trees" in front of the Union lines. The half-light of dawn and a dense fog aided them in their approach to the enemy position. Butler had planned to threaten the opposite end of the Confederate line along the axis of the Richmond Turnpike. As a consequence, he expected little trouble on his own right flank. Between the flank and the James River, Butler mistakenly left a substantial gap covered by nothing but cavalry—which promptly de-camped for the rear when Ransom's infantrymen emerged from the mist. Just to the left of the skedaddling troopers was the rightmost Federal brigade under Brigadier General Charles A. Heckman, a tough, battle-seasoned outfit composed of one New Jersey and three Massachusetts regiments. Caught by surprise while boiling their morning coffee, the Jerseymen and Bay Staters nonetheless stood their ground, hurling back the frontal assaults of Archibald Gracie's and Seth Barton's Rebel brigades.

Meanwhile, William R. Terry, another of Ransom's brigadiers, was guiding his Virginia brigade—which was but a shadow of what it had been when James L. Kemper had led it up the slope of Cemetery Ridge ten months before—around the exposed right flank of Heckman's hard-fighting Federals. The fog masked Terry's movement, allowing his men to fall on the exposed flank and rear of the Union battle line. No troops could stand up to the terrifying crossfire that resulted, and the collapse that followed triggered a chain reaction that soon had the entire Federal right rolling backward while Ransom's brigades surged forward in pursuit. The Federal commanders actually had more men on the ground than did Ransom, but in the dense mist they could not effectively concentrate them against the hard-charging Confederates, who were sweeping down their line from the right, rolling it up like a blanket. Before they could stabilize their position they had lost three-quarters of a mile of ground and an impressive collection of guns, flags, and prisoners—including Brigadier General Heckman.[44]

By this time, however, Ransom's attack was beginning to unravel. Fog, wire, and abatis had snagged and torn the fabric of the division's organization, and the shock and casualties of combat had shredded it still more. On top of that, Ransom's soldiers were reaching for the last few rounds in their now alarmingly light cartridge boxes. The assaulting brigades desperately needed a pause to catch their breath, restore their alignment, and refill their cartridge boxes. Hoping to retain the initiative and preserve the momentum of the assault, Ransom asked Beauregard for the use of a large brigade from the general reserve. Beauregard, who was concerned about the state of affairs on the army's right flank, where things were not going nearly as well, refused Ransom's request. As a result, Ransom's attack stalled. Delays were also encountered in attempting to resupply ammunition to the men at the front. Ransom once again renewed his request for additional troops, but Beauregard deemed he could spare him only a couple of weak regiments, which Ransom was forced to commit almost immediately to blunt a Federal counterstroke that nearly caved in the junction between his division and Robert Hoke's troops on his right. When ammunition finally arrived and the division moved forward again, it advanced only a short distance to, or just beyond, the line of the old breastworks from which Hoke had been driven several days before. There, further delay occurred as it became necessary to correct the alignment of two of Ransom's brigades. Riding off to report the delay to Beauregard before continuing the advance, Ransom found his superior only a few hundred yards away. To his surprise, Beauregard seemed almost relieved. "It is as well," he responded. "I am hard pressed on the right, and we may have to withdraw to the breastworks, and most of our force come to the right." Beauregard went on to explain to the stunned officer, "I fear my flank may be turned."[45]

Things were not as bad as that, but the right wing of Beauregard's army had not been very successful. Hoke's division had attacked the left front of Butler's army from their entrenchments, and the direct assault exacted a correspondingly high price. The proverbial "fog of war" had been compounded by the literal fog that morning, to say nothing of woods, abatis, and wire entanglements. Attempting to wheel to the right too soon, before Ransom's brigades had rolled the enemy's line back that far, Hoke exposed his left flank to the Union counterattack that had forced the commitment of Ransom's scant reserves. Another Union counterattack had torn at the division's (and the army's) right flank. Though the Confederates had held on this part of the field, it was this event that prompted the concern Beauregard expressed to Ransom regarding his right flank.[46]

The army had not been fought to a standstill, but it was clear that further advance, if any, would come at the cost of substantial losses. This was all the more true because of the equally obvious fact that Butler's army simply was not going to be pried loose from the James River and cut off from its base of operations—at least, not by Confederate troops advancing from Drewry's Bluff. But what of Whiting, and the column he was supposed to be leading from Petersburg against the Federal rear? As his frontal attack against Butler sputtered out, Beauregard pinned his hopes increasingly on the aspect of his battle plan that he had for the previous two days been assuring the president was inconsequential. All would now hinge on Whiting's timely and forceful arrival.[47]

In Richmond the president and his advisers anxiously awaited news of the battle. At 8:30 A.M. Beauregard had sent word to say that all was proceeding well. Ransom had turned the enemy right and was driving them. "I think," Beauregard stated reassuringly, "I can rely on Whiting's support. Distant firing now heard in direction of Petersburg." A 9:45 A.M. dispatch told of Ransom's delay to replenish ammunition. "When he comes up," expounded a confident Beauregard, "I will push the enemy. . . . I hope soon to make a junction with Whiting." The situation, as far as Davis could see, was still encouraging.[48]

Later that morning, a dispatch announced that Hoke had driven the enemy back, "capturing several siege field pieces and many prisoners." It was, Beauregard assured his superiors, "a brilliant success." Conspicuous in its absence was the issue of Whiting, of whom Beauregard said nothing at all. At 1:15 P.M., he wrote that there was "no material change since last dispatch." Beauregard's troops were stationary with the enemy still before them. For the first time the general related something of the damaged condition of his army—"some of the brigades are much cut up"—but he stated hopefully that he was "preparing for a combined attack." That could only mean an assault in concert with the forces moving up from Petersburg, but of them Beauregard only related ominously, "I hear nothing yet of Whiting's movements." That was about as much as the patience of Jefferson Davis could endure. Always eager to take to the battlefield whenever possible, he had his horse saddled and set off for Drewry's Bluff. About midafternoon he rode up and joined Beauregard near the point where the turnpike for Petersburg crossed the Confederate front lines. His presence would probably have been acutely embarrassing to Beauregard in any case. It was made infinitely more so, however, by the fact that the Creole's entire plan of battle was about to founder on precisely the rocks Davis had foreseen and ordered him to steer clear of. Together, silent for the most part, they waited for the sound of firing to the south that would tell them that Whiting had finally moved up and engaged the enemy. The afternoon wore on. Then, from the direction of Petersburg, came the boom of a cannon. "Ah!" said Davis with a smile, "at last!" But after the solitary shot, silence stole down again, and with the passing minutes it became clear that no push was yet being made from the south.[49]

At 5:45 P.M. Beauregard sent word to Bragg back in Richmond that he was still hoping for that "combined attack," but that he had "nothing positive as to position of Whiting save the knowledge that he was at Port Walthall Station [between Petersburg and Drewry's Bluff] this morning at 10 o'clock." As Beauregard's troops waited in formation, prepared to renew the assault, hope of a complete victory on this day faded with the waning light of evening. By 9:30 P.M. Beauregard finally gave up on Whiting. "The approach of darkness," he wired Bragg, "made it imprudent to execute this evening the plan set forth in my dispatch of 5:45 P.M." He still hoped to carry out the design at daylight next morning, in conjunction with Whiting, to whom he had been sending dispatches all day urging haste and aggressiveness in joining the concentration against Butler. But all was for naught. At four o'clock that afternoon, the Federals had begun withdrawing to their base on Bermuda Hundred, and the following morning found Butler and his army well along toward barricading themselves into the peninsula. There, his communications would be secure and no amount of Confederate troops Beauregard was remotely likely to gather would possibly be able to dislodge them.[50]

Why had Whiting failed? What went thorough the mind of William Henry Chase Whiting on May 16, 1864, is one of the Civil War's enduring command and leadership mysteries. Whiting the general was a puzzle; he was alternately brilliant, temperamental, and unstable. Despite his record-setting academic achievements at West Point, his wartime career is marked by more failure than success. No failure, however, seemed as inexplicable as his simple refusal to make more than the most halfhearted of efforts at moving toward Drewry's Bluff to assist Beauregard in his desperate attempt to crush Butler. A brief and belated advance had stopped at Port Walthall Junction before hurrying back to Petersburg without any discernible reason. Whiting's contemporaries were at a loss to explain his behavior. Some believed it was the result of drunkenness, for Whiting had given himself increasingly to drink during his sojourn at Wilmington. On May 16, one of his brigade commanders observed him mounting a horse with great difficulty and concluded that strong drink was the source of his distress. Still others believed Whiting to have been under the influence of narcotics. Confederate Postmaster General John H. Reagan, who, like Davis, had ridden out to the lines that afternoon to see the action, claimed Whiting later wrote a letter to Davis admitting to intoxication at the time of the battle. If Reagan's improbable claim is to be believed, the letter has since disappeared. Publicly at least, Whiting denied having taken anything stronger than coffee during the entire episode. Instead, he claimed his failure was the result of extreme exhaustion and prolonged lack of sleep. Modern historians have tended to accept Whiting's own explanation and suggest that his anxiety may have compounded the problem.[51]

The specific cause of Whiting's failure, however, is largely beside the point. Beauregard's decision to base his plan of battle on the convergence of two separate columns of troops—divided from each other by the enemy's force—created so many possibilities for problems that the chances of one or another of them actually occurring were high to the point of near certainty. For a general preparing his battle plans, what would go wrong was not as significant as the failure to realize that *something* almost undoubtedly would go awry with such a complex plan. In Beauregard's case, when the unexpected occurred, it was serious enough to destroy the effectiveness of the entire operation. Davis had recognized this and had ordered Beauregard to eliminate from his plan the ill-conceived idea of having Whiting's force approach the battlefield separately. Beauregard disobeyed this order, and the result was as Davis had foreseen. A malfunction in the plan had ruined the effectiveness of the attack. The specific malfunction was probably a failure of nerve on the part of Whiting, but Beauregard's plan was preprogrammed for failure.

The most striking thing about all of Beauregard's behavior during the campaign is the remarkable continuity with his performances throughout the war: Beauregard at Bermuda Hundred was virtually indistinguishable from the Beauregard of 1861–1862. He did not transcend himself or reveal talents previously obscured by Davis's enmity or unfavorable circumstances. His talents and his failings were as they had been since his arrival on the Manassas line some three years before. In the early days of the crisis he had shown a remarkable slowness about going in person to the threatened points; he did not arrive in Petersburg until May 10, by which time the focus of the Union advance had shifted from that point to Drewry's Bluff. Again, he did not depart for the new scene of action until May 13, when it was almost too late to affect the outcome. This reluctance to be in the thick of the campaign did not spring from any lack of physical courage. Beauregard had displayed much of that on the field of First Manassas. Even at Drewry's Bluff, he had stood under enemy artillery fire almost to the point of recklessness. Rather, the delays seem to point to Beauregard's reluctance to take responsibility and make vital decisions. As had been the case in the western theater in 1862, the Creole had plenty of courage but not quite enough nerve. In that, he was anything but alone among Civil War officers.

On the other hand, Beauregard had displayed considerable strategic insight in recognizing—well before the Richmond authorities had done so—that the Federals were making a major effort on the south side of the James. Along with Pickett, who from his fortuitous position at Petersburg could hardly have thought otherwise, he may indeed have helped to save Petersburg—and thus Richmond—by his insistent messages calling for the diversion of troops to that sector. Yet, the Creole's worst enemies had never accused him of a lack of strategic ability or mental acuteness. Davis himself had merely suggested, two years earlier, that Beauregard was unable to use his great mental gifts to advantage when placed in a position of extreme responsibility. In this way also, Beauregard in the Bermuda Hundred campaign had proved true to his earlier form.

His various plans for dealing with Benjamin Butler had shown a characteristic mixture of brilliance with almost absurd flights of fancy. Just as before First Manassas, he had prepared to open his campaign by suggesting to his superiors in Richmond a grandiose and unrealistic scheme for shuffling armies about the country—heedless of issues of transportation and supply—while his enemies presumably stood inertly by to be defeated in detail. Beauregard simply could not resist the temptation to let his overactive imagination run away with him. His plans were elaborate to the point of being unwieldy and unrealistic. This was equally true of his final plan for the battle of Drewry's Bluff. The failure of his unrealistic scheme to unite his and Whiting's forces on the field of battle, from opposite sides of the enemy, had extinguished the last hopes of a decisive Confederate victory south of Richmond. Here, too, as in his battle plans for Manassas and Shiloh, Beauregard displayed a characteristic trait that accompanied him throughout the war.

Of course, Butler's army did end up "tight corked" in the "bottle" formed by the curving loops of the James and Appomattox Rivers at Bermuda Hundred, and Grant was understandably disgusted with Butler's equally inept performance. Still, the Union Army of the James remained intact, dangerous and uncomfortably close to Richmond. Though Beauregard might eventually establish the shortest and most fortified lines he could across the neck of the peninsula, keeping Butler's troops corked would require several thousand Southern soldiers that the Confederacy could well have used elsewhere.

Also, Beauregard had let an important opportunity slip through his fingers. The total defeat and subsequent capture of even a moderate-sized Union army such as Butler's would have had an important impact on Northern morale at the beginning of a campaign season when the chief Southern goal would be to bring Union war-weariness to the point of Northern collapse. How often could the Confederacy hope to find such an army in hands as incompetent as Butler's? His assignment to such responsible duty was an important Union mistake, and Beauregard's shortcomings allowed the North to escape without paying the price for it.

When Grant finally stole a march on Lee in mid-June 1864 and crossed the James River for Petersburg, the logistical bases at Bermuda Hundred and City Point, just across the river, were of some considerable value to him, a residual effect of the failure to defeat Butler decisively. On the whole, Beauregard's failure to win the kind of victory Butler's incompetence offered him cost the Confederacy significantly. Such success as Beauregard did achieve in bottling Butler up at Bermuda Hundred was more the result of Yankee miscues than Rebel tactical or strategic genius.

Thus Beauregard was not, after all, the flawless hero of Petersburg and savior of Richmond—not exactly, anyway. He was, as he had always been, complicated, frustrating, and paradoxical, a general of many excellent parts but unsatisfactory as a whole. As Jefferson Davis rode back to the Confederate White House through the gathering darkness of the evening of May 16, 1864, he might have had much to contemplate in disappointment, but likely very little in surprise. The Louisiana general of Napoleonic pretensions had performed throughout the Bermuda Hundred campaign precisely as his previous record had given cause to expect.

Nine

HOOD, DAVIS, AND THE ARMY OF TENNESSEE

Elements of a Confederate Debacle

T HE SHOCKING carnage at Franklin and the subsequent devastating Confederate defeat at Nashville have marked John B. Hood as one of the Civil War's most spectacular failures in army command. Hood's attack order at Franklin stands out as perhaps the war's foremost tactical blunder; as for Nashville, it is unlikely that any other Civil War army was ever as thoroughly routed on the battlefield. How could this happen? How could a general follow a course of action so drastically contrary to his own and his army's best interests? Various solutions have been suggested by scholars of the campaign, ranging from narcotics to physical exhaustion to serious mental and emotional instability. Perhaps at least some of these factors did play a part in Hood's behavior. Yet they can hardly provide a full explanation. One of the most important questions that remains unanswered by such factors is how a man of that description could ever have been appointed to command the army in the first place. If Hood was indeed a sort of military disaster looking for a place to happen, how did he continue to rise through the ranks of the Confederate officer corps? How did he gain a respected position in the Confederacy's most successful army, the Army of Northern Virginia? And how was it that Jefferson Davis, himself a man of military training and experience, could make such an incredible mistake as to assign Hood to command one of the Confederacy's most important armies? Almost as incredible as Hood's horrendous failure is the inescapable fact that he came to army command as a trained, experienced, and successful commander who possessed the confidence of his commander-in-chief. Hood did not gain the high opinion of many of those with whom he served or a reputation as a fine officer by displaying the sort of behavior that all but destroyed the Army of Tennessee at Franklin and Nashville. How could a soldier of such high reputation come to such a disastrous defeat? To find answers to questions like this one, we must take a careful look at the road that had brought John B. Hood to command of the Confederacy's second-largest army and the disastrous campaign in Middle Tennessee.[1]

The Kentucky-born Hood gained an appointment to West Point from his uncle, who was a member of Congress. At the academy he compiled a mediocre record, ranking forty-fifth of the fifty-two graduates in the class of 1853. After two years' service in the infantry, he apparently used political connections to gain assignment to the prestigious new Second Cavalry Regiment. In his leadership of the troopers on the Texas frontier, Hood was most notable for his audacity.[2]

Though he had gotten both his West Point berth and his commission in the Second Cavalry through political influence and though his record at the academy had not been good, the fact remains that the young lieutenant must have had some ability. He had, after all, graduated— never mind what rank—from a fairly demanding school, and if his tactics against the Comanche seemed a bit reckless, he at least avoided the sort of disaster that could befall careless cavalry commanders who chased Plains Indians a ridge too far.[3]

When the Civil War came, Hood chose the Confederacy, and when Kentucky failed to secede, he made Texas his adopted state. The Confederacy (the Union too, for that matter) was sorely in need of trained officers, and such men could expect a rapid rise through the ranks. Hood was no exception to that rule, and by early 1862 he commanded the Texas Brigade of the Army of Northern Virginia, ever afterward known as Hood's Texas Brigade. His finest moments in battle came at the head of this unit. In June 1862 he led his Texans in breaking the Union line at the battle of Gaines Mill. Near the end of a day in which Robert E. Lee's battle plans had gone almost completely awry, Hood and his brigade were part of a full-scale frontal assault on an entrenched Federal position. Hood's men were among the first, if not the very first, to breach that position and thus change the entire course of the battle.[4]

In September of that year, Hood led his own brigade and another in a sort of improvised division at the desperate battle of Sharpsburg (Antietam). His men defended the hard-pressed Confederate left flank in the West Wood and the Cornfield and around the Dunker Church with frenzied tenacity. His casualties were appalling—Hood himself was appalled by them, reportedly almost in tears by the end of the day—but then so were those of the whole Confederate army at Antietam, and somehow, against very long odds, Hood had managed to keep the Federals from taking his key position. In an army that was constantly in need of capable replacements for the higher-level generals who seemed to fall in every battle, as well as for those whom Lee found inadequate for his purposes, Hood's performance was good enough to gain promotion to major general and regular command of a division.[5]

The year that followed was one of frustration for Hood. At Fredericksburg in December 1862, his division was not seriously engaged. When the Army of Northern Virginia fought the battle of Chancellorsville the following spring, Hood and his division were on detached duty in North Carolina. At Gettysburg, he received a key assignment, attacking the Union left flank, but he was wounded by a shell fragment almost at the very outset of the battle. Thereafter, his left arm remained all but useless. Returning to duty early, he accompanied his troops to Georgia to take part in the battle of Chickamauga. In this engagement he exercised a sort of de facto corps command, but during the second day's fighting he suffered a bullet wound in the right thigh, necessitating the amputation of his leg. Early reports in Richmond had it that Hood was dead; he was not, and within a few weeks he was in the Confederate capital himself, for a long convalescence.[6]

In Richmond, Hood came into contact with Jefferson Davis, and a friendship developed between them. Perhaps Hood genuinely admired Davis; perhaps he was merely ambitious. At any rate, he was soon much in evidence around the Confederate White House and in the reserved Davis pew at St. Paul's Episcopal Church. He socialized with Mrs. Davis and, as his strength returned, made long rides with the president around the outskirts of Richmond, wearing a cork leg and strapped securely into the saddle. They discussed the strategic situation and Hood's place in the further prosecution of the war. By late winter they had decided that the place for Hood was the Army of Tennessee, then encamped at Dalton, Georgia, and under the command of General Joseph E. Johnston. Hood would be promoted to lieutenant general and given command of a corps.[7]

In many ways it was an obvious choice. Hood was one of the Confederacy's war heroes, a successful general from the South's most successful army, and a key participant in the only Confederate victory west of the

Appalachians. He had never been involved in any serious battlefield failure. It would have been difficult for anyone in the spring of 1864 to criticize his promotion to a more responsible position. Yet at the same time, Davis's choice of Hood for a corps command in the Army of Tennessee was a key element in the conjunction of circumstances that produced disaster in Tennessee that fall. The tell-tale signs of Hood's unsuitability were present even then, though they are much more visible in hindsight than they possibly could have been to the Confederate president in the fourth springtime of the war.

All of Hood's actual battlefield success had come leading either a brigade (at Gaines Mill) or a very small division (at Antietam). Since his promotion to regular division command, he had been engaged in only two battles, Gettysburg and Chickamauga, in both of which he was wounded. At Gettysburg, he had fallen before he had really had any chance of exercising his command. In the woods and thickets of Chickamauga there had been little enough chance for anyone above the level of brigade commander to exercise command. When at noon on the battle's second day a Union mistake allowed Hood's provisional corps to break through into a fluid situation in which skillful corps command would make all the difference, Hood was again promptly wounded.

On close examination, these circumstances reveal two facts about Hood's generalship. First, Hood had not been very thoroughly tested at any level much above that of brigade command. In combat situations of extreme crisis, he had no experience—and the president had no capability of assessing his performance—at leading more than a couple of thousand men. In effect, Davis's assignment of Hood in the spring of 1864 was equivalent to jumping an excellent brigade commander all the way to corps command.

This is particularly significant because brigade and corps command in the Civil War were two very different matters requiring very different sets of skills and mental aptitudes. There are two essential roles that a commander can fulfill. One is a matter of motivation, the other, of planning. In the Civil War, the brigadier was called upon to exercise much more of the first than the second. He led troops into battle, he could usually see all of the men under his command at one time, and they could often see him. While such officers had important duties to fulfill in maneuvering their handfuls of regiments, what really distinguished the great brigade commanders such as Hood was their ability to infuse into their troops on the battlefield a fearless, driving will to victory.

The corps commander faced a much different task. His opportunities for battlefield heroics and for inspiring his men in the midst of the fight were much less than those of a brigadier. Occasionally, his appearance at a key point would fire up the troops to extraordinary efforts, but properly he had to give his first attention to other matters. His task in planning and organizing victory was infinitely more complex than that of the brigadier. On most Civil War battlefields, he could not see all of the troops fighting under his command; he nevertheless had to visualize—often from sketchy reports or the sound of their firing—just how they were situated and what might be accomplished by them. The really successful corps commanders infused their troops with what martial qualities they could long before they marched into battle, then carefully gathered and analyzed intelligence and painstakingly planned every detail in advance. They made success seem easy because they had taken care of all the little matters first. The composition of such a man's personality required a good deal more of cold calculation than of fiery ardor.

All of this is very pertinent to Hood's case, for the second thing revealed by his wartime experience prior to 1864 is that he possessed far more of the first type of leadership skills than of the second. It is interesting to note the fact of his wounding both at Gettysburg and Chickamauga. At Gettysburg he was one of five Confederate division commanders to be wounded. At Chickamauga, no other Confederate division or corps commander was wounded. Hood's propensity for drawing fire may indicate that he was still trying to exercise command much like the commander of a very, very large brigade. He was well to the front, visible to his men, trying to inspire them, but also visible to the enemy.

A third ominous item in Hood's résumé was not a factor of his personality, intellect, or style of command, but it was nevertheless an indirect result of his personal aggressiveness. By this time he was a physical wreck. His left arm was limp, and his right leg was missing. It is interesting to note that while several Civil War generals returned to duty and served effectively and successfully after the loss of an arm, none ever did after the loss of a leg (for example, Philip Kearny and Oliver O. Howard enjoyed considerable success as one-armed generals, but Richard Ewell was a consistent disappointment after he lost a leg at Groveton). Probably a leg was simply too large a part of the body to lose without very serious impairment to the entire system. One depends so constantly on one's legs in order to function on a daily basis (obviously much more so in the world of the 1860s than today), that the loss of one would probably entail stresses hard to imagine for those who have not experienced it. And while Hood might demonstrate to the president his newly regained strength by making those long horseback rides around Richmond, that was not at all the same thing as enduring day after day of hard rides with no soft beds in between them—little sleep, poor food, and bad conditions— and then remaining clear-headed under great mental stress. If Davis had possessed a better concept himself of the purely physical demands on a general, he might have thought twice about subjecting Hood's stamina to such a test.

Still, in all fairness, many factors could have obscured these insights from Davis's view in the spring of 1864. Circumstances are sometimes such that good corps and division commanders do come under enemy fire. Perhaps Hood's conduct at the 1863 battles had thus been appropriate. The most that could probably be said of Hood at the time of his promotion is that he had gotten very little opportunity to prove his aptitude for his new position. Promotion of relatively untried men is sometimes unavoidable in wartime, and some of them prove successful. Besides all that, an additional factor was at work on Davis, prodding him to appoint Hood to a position in the Army of Tennessee.

From late 1862 to late 1863, the Army of Tennessee had been commanded by Braxton Bragg. Though not a particular friend of Bragg's, Davis had appointed and sustained him because of his ability and his devotion to the Confederate cause. Unfortunately, the Confederate president had refused to give Bragg an officer corps he could work with. Instead, he had insisted on the retention of incompetent and insubordinate generals, particularly his own old crony of West Point days, Leonidas Polk. Polk had sown discord among the Army of Tennessee's generals, and when Bragg had failed to win spectacular successes, feeling against him, both inside and outside the army, had become extreme. After the army's defeat at the battle of Chattanooga in November 1863, Davis had finally felt compelled to remove Bragg from command.[8]

The general's effectiveness had been entirely destroyed by the wellnigh mutinous actions of his subordinates, but Davis's political enemies, who by this time were legion, exulted in Bragg's removal as an admission that they had been right all along in indicting the president for stubbornness for retaining Bragg. Worse still, they brought heavy pressure to bear on Davis to appoint Joseph E. Johnston to fill Bragg's place.[9]

A two-time proven failure in army command, Johnston nevertheless continued to possess a considerable reputation and a certain amount of military skill. What he apparently lacked was a deep devotion to the Confederate cause and, it seemed, the nerve to commit an army to battle. Davis's political enemies, including some generals, had seized on Johnston as a convenient blunt instrument with which to beat the president over the head. After Bragg's removal, Davis tried to dodge Johnston by appointing William J. Hardee, one of the Army of Tennessee's corps commanders, to take over the leadership the army, but Hardee had declined to take the position on anything more than a temporary basis. Perhaps Hardee hoped to force Davis to appoint Johnston, or perhaps he simply did not want the responsibility.[10]

At any rate, Johnston got the appointment, but not the confidence of the president. Johnston's perceived timidity and propensity to retreat in order to avoid contact with the enemy were sources of considerable uneasiness to Davis, as was the general's reluctance to communicate adequately with his superiors. All of these considerations led Davis to reflect that two things were needed in the high command of the Army of Tennessee: an aggressive corps commander who would push Johnston to fight the enemy, and a good friend of the president who could be counted on to communicate freely and reliably about the army's plans and situation. Hood seemed to answer both requirements.

In the Atlanta campaign that followed, Hood did not exactly fulfill Davis's expectations, though Davis remained largely ignorant of that fact. Interestingly, Hood seemed to realize that the proper place for a corps commander was not the front line. To be sure, a certain sensitivity to enemy fire may have been an understandable result of having received two life-threatening and maiming wounds within the past year. At any rate, Hood took to commanding from the rear, but he did not begin to display the talents desirable in a corps commander. It was a role that fit perhaps better than any other the epigram that "genius is an infinite capacity for taking pains," and Hood was never one to take pains about things. As a corps commander he simply did not prepare adequately or give sufficient attention to detail. As Lee summed it up a few months later when asked to assess Hood's aptitude for command based on his experience in Virginia, Hood was "very industrious on the battlefield, careless off."[11] In other words, Hood had what it took to be a good brigade commander and an atrocious corps commander.

The result, ironically, was the opposite of Hood's previous reputation and of Davis's expectations in sending him to the Army of Tennessee. Hood became in effect an advocate of retreat. On the one occasion during the entire campaign when Johnston had determined to strike the enemy a blow, he very reasonably assigned Hood's corps to lead the attack. Hood, having prepared inadequately, was unnerved when unforeseen difficulties arose. He pressed Johnston to call off the attack, and Johnston did. The retreat toward Atlanta was resumed, and Hood on several occasions gave his consent to Johnston's unaggressive policies.[12]

In one way Hood did fulfill Davis's expectations: he wrote frequently to the president, outside the chain of command, bypassing Johnston. Unfortunately, however, Hood let his ambition get the better of his honesty in these communications, leading him to shade the truth rather heavily in his own favor. At least, that is the most generous interpretation that can be put on his actions. An unsympathetic observer might say that he lied through his teeth—habitually. He consistently represented himself as the lone advocate of aggressive operations, which was false on several counts. Hood communicated the same story in even more virulent form to Braxton Bragg when Bragg visited the army on a fact-finding mission for Davis. This time Hood made sure to implicate Hardee, his fellow corps commander—and rival for promotion—in the habitual retreats. Hood seems to have been angling to take over command of the army when, as seemed inevitable if the retreat continued, Davis sacked Johnston after the latter abandoned Atlanta. In mid-July, however, just a few miles in front of Atlanta, Hood got a surprise. His propaganda campaign with the president proved more successful than he had reckoned. That, and the fact that Davis was determined not to yield Atlanta without a fight and finally summoned the nerve to remove Johnston, led to Hood's appointment to command the Army of Tennessee even as its back was up against the city it was supposed to defend. Hood telegraphed Davis to request that Johnston be left in command until the fate of Atlanta was decided. That, of course, was precisely what Davis was striving to avoid, and he insisted that Hood take over the army at once.[13]

It was not an enviable position for a commander. He was expected to save Atlanta, but his predecessor had already surrendered so much territory that he had no room to maneuver. If Sherman made a move, Hood would have to respond, and the result would be a battle. In fact, Hood fought three major battles within his first eight days in command. Intriguingly, these battles show him to have been a slightly better army commander than corps commander. The two job descriptions required many of the same aptitudes, but the weight of detailed preparation may have been a bit heavier on the corps commander. The army commander's role offered more opportunity for the exercise of strategic imagination. In a sense, it was the army commander's job to devise a good plan and the corps commanders' job to make it happen, and if Hood had possessed excellent corps commanders he might have enjoyed about as much success as anyone could have under the circumstances.

He did not have excellent corps commanders, however. Hardee was knowledgeable and skillful, but he was also mortally offended that Hood had been promoted over his head. He sulked and did not yield hearty and enthusiastic cooperation to Hood's plans. Alexander P. Stewart was a competent officer, but terribly new in his position. Then there was Benjamin Franklin Cheatham. He was enormously popular with his Tennessee troops, and he did seem to be able to inspire them in battle. When sober, he probably would have made an adequate brigadier. He had been an indifferent division commander, and as a corps commander he made Hood look like a model of efficiency. At the time of the fighting around Atlanta, he was as new to corps command as Hood was to the command of the army. He was promptly and wisely replaced by Stephen D. Lee. A bright, young officer, Lee had plenty of aptitude but a lot to learn. He added his share to the blunders that led the army to several costly defeats.[14]

Because of the inexperience, uncooperativeness, or inadequacy of its corps commanders, the Army of Tennessee's commander needed an even greater than usual—perhaps greater than human—ability to plan, organize, and take care of details. Hood was simply not the man for that job. As a result, the three battles fought around Atlanta, although launched according to very promising plans and enjoying some initial success, ultimately failed to do significant damage to Sherman's army and incurred an unpleasant number of casualties for the Army of Tennessee. Hood, a general who needed better than average corps commanders, had, in effect, worse than average men in their place, and so he simply could not translate his fairly good plans into reality.

And so Atlanta fell. Hood was able to extricate his army, and the next issue was what to do next. With Davis's approval, Hood tried a strategy of basing his own army in northern Alabama and threatening Sherman's supply lines in North Georgia. It was a fairly successful plan, and Sherman was soon sorely frustrated with chasing the elusive Hood around and around the North Georgia hill country, trying to keep the Rebels off his railroad. Ironically, each commanding general grew tired of the program at about the same time. Hood could not decisively cut Sherman's supplies in North Georgia and so decided to strike out for Middle Tennessee and see what mischief he could cause there. Sherman could not catch Hood and so decided to cast loose his supply line and strike out across Georgia for the sea. And so the two main armies marched away from each other. Sherman would face only Confederate cavalry and Georgia militia during his march to the sea. Hood would face a Union army larger than his own commanded by George H. Thomas.

The Tennessee campaign included all of the ingredients of the Atlanta campaign along with a couple of additional items. Hardee pouted about having to play second fiddle to Hood until he finally succeeded in gaining a transfer to other duties. In his place, Cheatham once again took over corps command, this time on a permanent basis. The resulting command structure was an uneven one—Hood, who could make some tolerably good plans but was incapable of translating them into action, along with one incompetent corps commander and two others who were bright and gifted, but inexperienced. The situation was aggravated by the fact that for all practical purposes the war's outcome had already been decided by the time Hood moved his army northward in November 1864.

When Hood could no longer hold Atlanta and the city had fallen to Sherman back in September, it had provided all the boost Northern public opinion had needed to ensure the reelection of Lincoln. Perhaps Lincoln would have been reelected anyway. At one point, it had appeared he would not. In any case, his resounding electoral victory was a clear mandate from the Northern people to continue prosecution of the war to ultimate victory, restoring the Union and ending slavery. If necessary, the North was prepared to carry on the war through the end of 1868. The South, by contrast, was nearing the end of its strength. To any impartial observer, it had to have been clear by this point that the Confederacy was not going to last until the end of 1868—or even the end of 1865. While neither Hood nor Davis could see as much at the time, they could see that the situation was exceedingly desperate. Thus when Hood marched northward into Tennessee in November 1864, it was with the knowledge that desperate measures were required and that only a truly resounding success would be good enough. That awareness made the Army of Tennessee's command arrangements that much more volatile.

Davis himself added another difficulty, although he intended it as a source of stability. That was the presence, in a sort of supervisory theater commander, of General P. G. T. Beauregard. Beauregard was one of the most intelligent commanders of the war, surpassed on the Confederate side only by Robert E. Lee. He was one of the few generals with a truly Napoleonic grasp of strategy and operations, but somewhere in his generalship there always seemed to be a fatal flaw. His plans were brilliant, elaborate, and usually not very closely tied to reality. Like Hood, he seemed to lack the ability to translate his ideas into real actions on the part of his troops. In that sense he was a strange man to send as an overseer for Hood's operations. However, Beauregard was older and far more experienced, and that would count for something.

Precisely what Davis expected Beauregard to do remains a mystery. It is not at all clear that Davis himself had precise ideas on the matter. Though Beauregard and some historians have concluded that the assignment was simply an elaborate way to make it politically possible to keep Hood and shelve Beauregard in a do-nothing job, it seems far more likely in view of Davis's personality and the way he approached matters such as this that his vague directives conceal nothing but vague thinking. Davis apparently intended the higher-ranking general to go out west and make himself useful some way or another.[15]

About the only thing that is clear in the matter of Beauregard's assignment to oversee the western theater, including Hood's army, is that Hood did not like it at all. During the weeks immediately preceding and following his Tennessee campaign he avoided communicating with his new superior and even avoided his presence, at one point going so far as to move his own headquarters across the Tennessee River just to be farther away from Beauregard. What effect this had on the campaign is difficult to say. Perhaps it had none. Or perhaps Hood might have been irritated enough to pursue a more rash and aggressive course of action. In any case, it is clear that for the 1864 Tennessee campaign, Davis's attempt to add Beauregard's experience and maturity to the command mixture had not been successful.[16]

The disastrous development of Hood's campaign in Tennessee displays in Hood the traits his previous performance had given cause to expect. On November 29 he successfully turned Schofield's Union army at Columbia, taking up a position near Spring Hill that should have made this operation one of the most successful turning movements of the Civil War. Instead, it has become one of the most famous fiascoes. Hood's lack of extremely detailed planning and provision hindered the operation. Then the final execution of the plan, actually seizing the road near Spring Hill, fell to Cheatham, who was far from equal to the task.

Hood, who had been riding strapped into the saddle since 3 A.M., was exhausted and possibly plagued by pain in the stump of his leg. He was incapable of personally supervising the carrying out of his orders. And so the orders were not carried out, and the enemy escaped. The next day, Hood's frustration and miscalculation combined to produce the disastrous slaughter at Franklin. The enormous casualties there, the loss of key generals, and the demoralization of the rank and file, virtually sealed the outcome of the campaign—if it had ever been in doubt in the first place.[17]

No one, least of all Hood and Davis, had planned or desired the sort of berserk generalship that destroyed the Army of Tennessee. Rather, it was the result of a series of errors, wrong choices, and miscalculations by which the wrong man was entrusted with a position in which he could do incalculable damage. For us as students of history more than a century and a quarter later, the hardest thing in understanding it all may be realizing that this unbelievable disaster was the outcome of a series of decisions, each one of which seemed logical and reasonable at the time it was made. If we imagine that it would have been easy to avoid a disaster such as that into which Hood and Davis blundered, we will have missed one of the most important lessons of this episode of history.

Ten

Homespun Generals

Nonprofessional Officers in the Confederate Army

A SINGLE RIFLE-SHOT cracks the predawn stillness of a Virginia morning, and out of the darkness and mist, crouching riflemen lope forward. The skirmishers come first, a scattering of vague shapes against the paler darkness around them, then, looming up behind them, the main battle line, really more an elongated swarm of soldiers spreading out into the darkness on either side. The lack of precise formation belies the battle-tested fighting prowess of these veteran soldiers as well as the thorough planning and preparation that has gone into the assault. Their commanding general has thought of everything right down to strips of white cloth to be worn on the front of uniforms of troops in the leading elements, to aid friend-or-foe identification in the dark. Preparations for the advance have been stealthy, and surprise is complete. The objectives are clear, and key personnel are thoroughly aware of what is expected of them and what they need to do to accomplish it. Within minutes the attackers overrun the powerful enemy strong point on this sector, taking hundreds of prisoners, then fan out to exploit the breakthrough. In short, it is a thoroughly professional job.[1]

It was March 25, 1865, and the Army of Northern Virginia was making its last great assault. Commanding the attack—and for the occasion about one-half the troops Robert E. Lee still numbered in his depleted ranks—was Major General John Brown Gordon. The assault was doomed to failure, and by midmorning superior Northern numbers had slammed the attackers back to their starting point with heavy losses despite all that they or Gordon could do. Yet none of that could obscure the valor of the Southern soldiers or the obvious skill, thoroughness, and flair of Gordon in planning and leading the attack. No career officer could have done a more professional job, but Gordon was no career officer and had received no formal military training before he marched off in 1861, leading a company of his equally inexperienced fellow citizens. The story of how he and more than two hundred other men of erstwhile peaceful pursuits became generals in the Provisional Army of the Confederate States is an epic of courage and resourcefulness. It is also a singularly instructive lesson in military leadership.

Four hundred twenty-five men would rise to the rank of Confederate general between secession and the collapse of the rebellion. Of those, 146 were graduates of West Point. About ten more had received one or more years of training there but had not yet graduated. Another seventeen were graduates of the Virginia Military Academy and four were of South Carolina's Citadel. At least a couple of others had come up through one of the South's many other military schools, and one even had the benefit of a diploma from France's famous École Militaire. Finally, nineteen had served as regular officers in the prewar U.S. Army without having received an academy education at all. The other 226 generals were presumably more or less rank amateurs.[2]

Of course the categories do not break down that neatly. Many of the amateurs had at least a smattering of exposure to things military. A number had served, either as volunteer officers or enlisted men, in the Mexican and Seminole Wars, and two had been enlisted men in the British army. A good many of the nonprofessionals had held rank in the state militia, although that was often little more than a combination drill team and social club. In short, these men were practically devoid of training as officers. In the past, when need had arisen they had gone and done what their country needed—or what their pride demanded—and then they had got back to the business of living their lives in the civilian world. Even those who were in the militia would not, as a general rule, have been much bothered with military affairs.

On the other hand, not all of the "professionals" were all that professional either. Leonidas Polk, for example, had graduated from West Point in 1827 and then immediately resigned, never having held a command, and became an Episcopal priest. Through the favoritism of his old West Point friend Jefferson Davis, Polk received an appointment as major general direct from civilian life. His performance in command, until he was killed in action in June 1864, was all that such lack of preparation might lead one to expect, made worse by his proud and contentious nature: he would neither learn his duty nor follow orders. Clearly a West Point education, by itself, was no guarantee of creditable performance by a general.[3]

The same could be said of service, even many years of service in the "Old Army." William Wing Loring had served briefly against the Seminoles during his youth. Then, in 1846, he parlayed a bit of political prominence (he was a member of the Florida legislature) into a direct commission as captain in the regular U.S. Army. He could at least say that he had not shirked danger in the Mexican War, for he lost an arm at Chapultepec and won two brevet promotions. In 1856 he became, at age thirty-eight, the youngest line colonel in the Old Army. He went with the South, being appointed first brigadier and later major general. Still, he remained not only a very bad officer but a very unprofessional one too. He never seemed to grasp the business of obeying orders, and his stubborn contrariness almost drove Stonewall Jackson out of the Confederate army. Later, it helped doom John C. Pemberton to disastrous defeat at Vicksburg—a superfluous act, to be sure, since Pemberton had needed no help in that process, but a culpable one nonetheless.[4]

Granted, then, that military professionalism and its attainments did not always "take" with those who were exposed to it in one form or another, as well as that the nonprofessionals were not wholly ignorant of military matters, the fact remains that well over half of the Confederate generals had nothing like a real preparation for the roles they were asked to play during the nation's greatest conflict. They were, in fact, civilians pressed into service as officers.

The reasons for this use of civilians as generals were twofold. First, it was a matter of philosophy, at least for some people. The idea of the citizen-soldier went back a long way in America. In the earliest days of the English colonies on these shores, citizen-soldiers had been the only kind available. They had staved off extermination in King Philip's War and captured the menacing French fortress at Louisbourg, Cape Breton Island, during colonial times. George Washington had served as a militia officer, had led his Virginians along behind Braddock's British regulars, and had performed well when Braddock suffered humiliating defeat. In the Revolution, Washington had been only the most prominent of citizen-generals. In that conflict, the trained officer was the exception, an ideal borne out when after the war the former officers, now returned to civilian pursuits, organized a sort of old-soldiers' club called "the Society of the Cincinnati." The name came from the Roman hero Cincinnatus, who left his plow to lead the republic's armies and then, the danger past, returned to his agrarian pursuits.

The War of 1812 was not exactly an advertisement for nonprofessional officers, but then the resounding victory of Andrew Jackson in the war's closing battle at New Orleans seemed to answer all doubts. The quintessential amateur general had led an army of plain frontiersmen in butchering the vaunted British professionals. During the years that followed, many Americans continued to feel that any man of ability could supply the military leadership that was needed in war. Politicians frequently questioned the need for the United States Military Academy and suggested that it was a veritable pesthole of aristocratic, antirepublican thinking.

They had a point, of course, despite all their windy foolishness. Professionals are people hired to do a job. People who plan to defend their freedom do well to think twice before hiring their fighting done for them. If they are not capable of doing their own fighting, perhaps hiring professionals is simply exchanging one master for another. Or so it seemed to many Americans from the founding era to the Civil War. That being the case, it was natural that both sides would readily look to nonprofessionals for at least a good deal of their military leadership when they went to war in 1861.

Yet even if the South had wanted to officer its armies entirely with professionally trained men, the inescapable fact was that there were simply not enough of them. The entire U.S. Army in 1860 boasted some 950 commissioned officers, exclusive of the Medical Department and military storekeepers. Of that total, 555 hailed from the free states and 395 from south of the Mason-Dixon line. Of those Southern officers, 213 resigned to go with the South when the Civil War broke out, and they were joined by another 26 Northern officers who also left the service to join the Confederacy. Of more significance to the number of professional officers available for early promotion to general officer rank is the number of field-grade officers in the Old Army. Of the 76 men who held such rank, 30 were from Southern states. Many of those, from Brevet Lieutenant General Winfield Scott to Major George H. Thomas of the Second Cavalry, chose to remain loyal to the Union. Others, such as Major Richard Gatlin of the Fifth Infantry, were too old to be of extensive use in a long and intense war. On the other hand, some Southern officers who had left the army in favor of civilian employment years earlier now came forward to serve the Confederacy. Among these were Thomas J. Jackson and Braxton Bragg, though their status as field officers was based only on brevet rank. Finally, there were Northern officers of field rank who chose, for whatever reasons, to fight for the South, though some of these, like U.S. Adjutant General Colonel Samuel Cooper, were of the superannuated type. The numbers, then, complicated as they are, do not express the full complexity of the situation. Still, the obvious fact remains: the Confederacy could have made generals of virtually every former field officer at its disposal, and a good many company-grade officers as well, and still had plenty of slots open for men whose qualification was status as a successful lawyer, businessman, or planter.[5]

The first broad class of nonprofessional Confederate generals to make an impact in the war was perhaps the most notorious—the political generals. A political general was an officer whose appointment, by itself, was supposed to increase the public's support of the war, apart from what results he might achieve on the battlefield. Sometimes such a general might be appointed by an optimistic president, eagerly anticipating the effect the move would have in a particular segment of the population. This seems to have been Davis's attitude in appointing Leonidas Polk. While Polk's military background would have made him well qualified for a commission as second lieutenant—had it not been for the thirty-four years since he had left the military—Davis made him a major general with responsibility for the defense of the Mississippi Valley in large part because he believed that Polk, as a result of his service as an Episcopal bishop over the region, knew its people well and was well-known and liked by them. Davis's objective may in part have been successful, since Polk enjoyed considerable popularity with his troops right up until his death.[6]

More often, however, the practical reality of the political general was that he was a politician who had ambitions for military glory and also had political power enough to make the president pay a prohibitive price for failing to gratify those ambitions. The president chose him not so much to gain political points as to avoid political damage. Both Lincoln and Davis were saddled with far more of this species than they would have liked. Indeed, Lincoln's miseries with political generals are better known, but Davis suffered with them as well and could afford it less.

Sometimes the political pressure that led to the appointment of such a general could take place with only a moderate amount of encouragement from the prospective general himself. This was the case with Nashville newspaper editor Felix Kirk Zollicoffer. Zollicoffer had enjoyed a successful career as a politician, serving in Congress for a time, in addition to editing for many years the influential *Nashville Banner*. He had also served as a lieutenant of Tennessee volunteers during the Seminole War. That, however, was not his chief qualification for the wreath-and-stars insignia of a Confederate general. That distinction instead came to him because he was a prominent Whig. Tennessee had not been quick to secede, and even when it did, along with other upper-South states such as Virginia, it contained a large and vocal Unionist minority, composed to a large degree of the state's prewar Whigs. Except in East Tennessee, most of these Whig-Unionists were now falling dutifully into line in support of their state's secession, but Tennessee governor Isham G. Harris was worried about divisions that might lead to a relapse into old allegiances. The state's political situation would definitely need very careful handling.

It was therefore, with alarm, that in July 1861 Harris observed that all of Davis's appointments of generals from civilian life from the state of Tennessee had gone to men who were both prewar Democrats and early advocates of secession. As far as Harris was concerned, that was dangerous, since it might convey to the state's large Whig minority precisely the wrong message, to wit, that this war was purely the business and the problem of the hotheads in the Democratic Party. To avoid that appearance, Harris sent Davis an urgent plea that one or more Whigs be made generals. He even sent along a list of worthy candidates. Felix Zollicoffer's name stood at the top. The Nashville newspaperman had done what he could, in a modest sort of way, to further his own cause, sending Davis a number of reports on the situation in Tennessee, along with his assessment of the strategic outlook. Also, when the president's old West Point crony Polk passed through on his way to his own new command in West Tennessee, Zollicoffer may well have talked to him about the need for a good general in the eastern part of the state and his own qualifications for that job. At any rate, Polk wrote to Davis recommending him for the job. Zollicoffer's first campaign proved a complete success, as Davis duly appointed him a brigadier general and gave him command of politically troubled East Tennessee.[7]

Davis had appointed Zollicoffer to a command that seemed highly unlikely to see serious combat. Since in July 1861 Kentucky still clung to its bizarre status of neutrality and banned entry to all warring armies, no enemy could threaten Zollicoffer's district. The only thing the new brigadier would thus have to deal with was internal unrest from the stubborn Unionists in that part of the state—a political problem for a political general. The trouble with appointing such politicians to special commands that might seem peculiarly suited for their talents was that once a man was a general, there was really no way to guarantee where the tides of war would—or would not—carry him.

In September 1861, a political miscue by—of all people—the politically appointed Polk at the other end of the state scotched Kentucky neutrality, and suddenly Zollicoffer commanded a district with a wide-open frontier on enemy territory. What he lacked in knowledge and experience, the Nashville newspaperman tried to make up in aggressiveness, and with the approval of his immediate superior, western theater commander Albert Sidney Johnston, he promptly moved his force forward to seize Cumberland Gap, Kentucky, the northwestern gateway to East Tennessee. That went well enough, but by the following January, Federal forces were advancing into eastern Kentucky in such a way as to threaten Zollicoffer's front. Taking the initiative again, he advanced his outnumbered force to the north bank of the Cumberland River, this time without checking with his superior, who was several hundred miles away. The position he took up seemed to make sense to the man whose only military experience came in the Seminole War. He put his troops inside a horseshoe bend, with the river at their backs and on both sides. That way, as he reckoned it, the foe could attack from only one direction. Of course, to a trained military man the position was readily apparent as a potential trap, where Zollicoffer's force could easily be cut off and captured. In fact, a trained military man arrived about that time, Davis having thought better of Zollicoffer's leading a field army. George B. Crittenden (West Point, 1832) was sent to take command of his force, retaining the Tennesseean as a subordinate. Crittenden was appalled at Zollicoffer's deployment and would have pulled him back across the river save that the advancing enemy was already within striking distance and he deemed the move too dangerous. Rather than wait and meet the enemy in the riverbank position, Crittenden ordered Zollicoffer forward in hopes of striking the enemy by surprise. The January 19, 1862, battle of Mill Springs did indeed surprise the Union force under Brigadier General George H. Thomas, but Zollicoffer's men were outnumbered and facing what would prove to be some of the North's most accomplished combat troops and one of its best defensive commanders. To seal the Confederate defeat, the inexperienced Zollicoffer, who was still enormously popular with his men, became confused in the thick battle smoke and already low visibility of a rainy day, and rode into Union lines. He was promptly shot dead.

The defeat at Mill Springs would have been even more disastrous for the Confederacy if it had not been almost immediately overshadowed by twin disasters of immense magnitude that illustrate even better the hazards of using political generals. When Jefferson Davis had made brigadier generals of Tennessee lawyer/politician Gideon J. Pillow and former Virginia Governor and U.S. Secretary of War John B. Floyd, he could hardly have intended that they end up in top command of one of the most vital positions in the Confederacy, but so it happened.

Floyd was a Virginian who had graduated from South Carolina College, failed as a cotton planter in Arkansas, and then had come back to his native state to launch a successful career as a lawyer and politician. The first stop in his rise to prominence was the Virginia House of Delegates, then the governor's mansion, and finally appointment as U.S. secretary of war by President James Buchanan in 1857. In the last role Floyd won a questionable reputation, amid allegations of fraud. He also incurred the wrath of the North by allegedly shifting heavy guns to Southern locations where they could readily be seized by the seceding states. He resigned when Buchanan refused to order Major Robert Anderson out of Fort Sumter. After the fort fell and Virginia seceded, Floyd offered his services to his state, and, as a Confederate brigadier general, he became an asset of the South's war effort along with more desirable personnel such as Robert E. Lee.[8]

Floyd and his brigade drew service as part of the Confederate effort to hold what would become West Virginia that fall, and there he encountered another former Virginia governor in uniform. Henry A. Wise had a career in Virginia twice as long as Floyd's, and Wise had been governor more recently. Some men were simply too influential for a president to pass over their military abilities, real or imagined; Wise and Floyd were two such. A month after Floyd, Wise got his own commission as Confederate brigadier, and the following autumn, he too got orders for western Virginia. There the two men had staged an incredible exhibition both of incompetence and pettiness, making foolish decisions and refusing to cooperate with each other so stubbornly as to convince observers that each actually hoped for the other's defeat. They probably did. As it turned out, there was enough Confederate defeat to go around that fall and winter in western Virginia. With the debacle there ended, authorities at Richmond did the wisest thing they could have done (short of having both brigadiers court-martialed and shot) by sending the two in opposite directions, Wise to the Atlantic coast, and Floyd to Tennessee. Unfortunately, it was that transfer to Tennessee that put Floyd in position to do his greatest damage to the Confederate cause.[9]

With Floyd came his brigade, some of the only reinforcements Richmond believed it could spare for Johnston's hard-pressed western Confederate armies. In early February the desperate need for troops on Johnston's front seemed most acute at Fort Donelson, guarding the Cumberland River against ascent by Union gunboats and river-borne forces that would put them in control of Middle Tennessee and squarely in rear of Johnston's main force. Another Confederate fort, Henry, on the Tennessee River, had fallen to Union gunboats a few days before, so Johnston was under no illusions about the long-term prospects at Donelson. Still, he needed the garrison there to buy him time to extricate his army from Middle Tennessee, and then he needed that garrison intact, not captured, so that it could join his none-too-numerous forces. To accomplish those two goals, he determined to reinforce the garrison strongly enough to allow it to brush aside the Union investing force and make its escape after a sufficient delay had been achieved. Floyd's brigade was to be a part of those reinforcements.[10]

At the fort, Floyd found himself senior Confederate officer. He also found that his second-in-command was another politician-in-arms, Brigadier General Gideon J. Pillow. A successful trial lawyer from Tennessee, Pillow actually had some military experience, for this was not his first war as a political general. He had been appointed a brigadier general in the Mexican War by his good friend and close political associate President James K. Polk. Pillow's combat record in Mexico had been, at best, uneven, and he was most remembered in the army for having a set of fortifications built backwards, something he still had not lived down, among professional officers, a decade and a half later. But Pillow had not spent the decade among professional officers. Even had he wanted a military career, it was not open to him, for Congress had refused to approve his nomination as a general. So it was back into law and politics in Tennessee for the decade of the 1850s, then back into uniform when his state seceded and made him, briefly, the commanding general of its independent forces. Absorption into the Confederacy had left Pillow an ordinary brigadier general, a perceived slight that brought him near to resigning. Instead, he remained in the service, and the Confederate crisis of February brought him and his brigade to Fort Donelson.[11]

The presence of Floyd and Pillow in the number one and two command spots at a crucial post such as Fort Donelson is a prime illustration of how generals have a way of turning up in unexpected assignments. A president who appointed officers of deficient abilities simply could never be sure these defective cogs in his war machine would not turn up in precisely the places where inefficiency would cost it the most severely. If Davis's experience with Floyd and Pillow is any indication, he would have been well advised to count on their turning up in such places— repeatedly.

Their performance was all that a West Point trained Confederate might have feared and a Yankee could have hoped. Floyd showed a shortcoming unusual among politically ambitious generals, a simple and glaring lack of courage. He all but panicked at the first attack by the Union gunboats, frantically telegraphing his superior, "The fort cannot hold out twenty minutes," when in fact it was not seriously threatened by the gunboats the Federals then had on the river. After the first day's success, Floyd called a council of war and urged that it was now time to break out and flee. When the attempt was made the following day, it succeeded admirably. They surprised the Federals, and the large force Johnston had sent now proved itself by driving back the Federals and opening an escape route to Nashville.

Floyd gave the order to march out, but then Pillow approached him and urged the necessity of letting the men rest up, gather their effects, and have a nice warm meal before starting their long march. To the horror and amazement of professionally trained Confederate officers in the garrison, Floyd changed his orders accordingly. Floyd and Pillow were both shocked when Union forces quickly recovered, reoccupying their former positions and then some, making the fort now truly untenable. When the officers of the garrison discussed surrender at a second nocturnal council-of-war, Floyd and Pillow nervously insisted they could never allow themselves to be taken prisoner. Northerners had been talking about hanging Floyd for his questionable dealings while secretary of war, and neither man wanted to be the first experiment to see what the national government would do with a captured Rebel general. In a preceding very likely unique in the history of warfare, Floyd relinquished command to Pillow, who passed it to their junior, Brigadier General Simon B. Buckner (West Point, 1844), so that he could surrender the command while his superiors made their personal escapes as best they could. Both succeeded. Floyd met a couple of steamboats full of reinforcements arriving at the landing next morning, ordered the fresh troops off, sent his own Virginia regiments aboard, and departed, leaving the others to their fate. Pillow also made good his escape by river, paddling off in an abandoned scow one of his staff officers had found tied up along the bank. Meanwhile, as Grant and Buckner sat down to discuss the surrender, Buckner mentioned Pillow's escape. Grant was unconcerned: "If I had captured him," he replied, "I would have turned him loose. I would rather have him in command of you fellows than a prisoner."[12]

It was not an inspiring performance, even for political generals, and neither Floyd nor Pillow was to hold an important combat command again except for when Pillow commanded a single brigade for a single day of fighting at Murfreesboro. That action led to a story being told by his immediate superior to the effect that Pillow had hid behind a tree in the rear while his troops had gone forward. Pillow would hotly deny the report, and later historians would question it, but his performance at Fort Donelson made it believable.[13]

The only consolation in this from the Confederate point of view was that the miscues of Floyd and Pillow were serious enough to end their careers. Other political generals of less spectacular incompetence simply could not be humored by further promotions, and their pride balked at continued taking of orders, as in the case of former Confederate Secretary of State Robert Toombs, who resigned his brigadier general's commission over lack of promotion. He went back to Georgia, inveighing all the while against the evils of the West Point clique that was keeping for itself the privilege of leading the Confederacy's armies and ruining its cause in the process. Still others, exercising the one element of combat leadership that political generals rarely lacked—courage—managed to get shot. Such was the case of Georgia politician—and member of the Confederate constitutional convention—Thomas R. R. Cobb, who became one of the relatively few Confederate casualties in the Sunken Road at Fredericksburg. One way or another, by the middle part of the war, relatively few truly political generals were still to be found at the head of Confederate combat formations.

An exception, and probably the best actual political general in the Confederacy, was John C. Breckinridge. A Kentucky lawyer, Breckinridge served in the state legislature, the U.S. Congress, and then, at age thirty-five, was elected vice president of the United States on the Buchanan ticket in 1856. Kentucky elected him to the U.S. Senate upon the expiration of his term, but when the state declared for the Union in September

1861, Breckinridge went the other way, joined the Confederacy, and by November was a brigadier general. The following April he rose to major general. His appointment was clearly aimed at influencing the people of Kentucky, where Breckinridge was still immensely popular, and at first it appeared the Confederacy would pay the usual military price for such a political ploy. The following autumn he led an unsuccessful expedition to take Baton Rouge, Louisiana, and that winter, at the battle of Murfreesboro, Breckinridge's performance was questionable at best. In the first day's fighting he badly misinterpreted raw intelligence, was halting and indecisive, and responded to Braxton Bragg's call for troops by forwarding his brigades in piecemeal fashion. In the final day's action Breckinridge balked at carrying out his orders, then gave in and provided bold and inspirational leadership for a dramatic charge. To complete the day's checkered performance, he then lost control of his troops, allowing them to over-pursue and suffer a severe repulse.[14]

Yet Breckinridge proved capable of learning, and he served without mishap through operations in Tennessee and Mississippi over the next nine months. At Chickamauga, in September 1863, his performance was quite creditable. In the second day's fight, his division flanked the Federal line and he led two of his brigades in an assault that came within a whisker of beginning to roll up the Union army in what would have been a truly decisive Confederate victory. After the battle, Breckinridge bitterly complained that his attack would have been successful if he had been properly supported, and he was probably right. Bragg recognized Breckinridge's performance with enlarged responsibilities, command of a corps in the crucial Missionary Ridge sector of the Army of Tennessee's lines around Chattanooga. Then, however, with an inconsistency that often characterized amateur generals, he blundered badly. The lines in his sector of the front were disastrously ill-sited, and when a Union attack finally came, Breckinridge's leadership was less than inspirational. Very shortly thereafter, Bragg informed Davis that the battle had come on the tail end of a three-day drunk by Breckinridge. The charge is difficult either to prove or disprove today, but there is no denying that the Kentuckian was deeply fond of bourbon. At any rate, his career survived the debacle at Missionary Ridge, perhaps because the disaster was so dismal and unrelieved that Confederates had little stomach and less patience for detailed postmortems.[15]

Landing on his feet, Breckinridge's next assignment gave him command of Confederates in southwestern Virginia, and in that capacity he enjoyed his finest hour as a general. When Federals under Major General Franz Sigel penetrated deep into the strategic Shenandoah Valley while Lee was locked in a death-grapple with Grant in eastern Virginia, Breckinridge moved to check Sigel at New Market and defeated him in a dramatic battle. He continued to serve in Virginia, and ended the war back in politics, as Confederate secretary of war.[16]

Like other political generals (and some who were not), Breckinridge sometimes was insubordinate to his superiors, undermining their authority. He also behaved in ways prejudicial to good discipline among his subordinates. At his imperious worst he could be disdainful of everyone's authority but his own. Yet he was greatly loved by his men, another trait that he shared in common with most political generals, and unlike most of them, he showed some real talent for the business of soldiering.

Political generals were not, however, the only type of nonprofessional general used by the Confederacy nor even the most numerous. Of a total of 425 men who eventually served as Confederate general officers, only 24 were politicians. The other 273 generals who were neither professional soldiers nor politicians before the war were drawn from the South's lawyers, businessmen, farmers, planters, educators, and others. Their number even included four physicians and three ministers. These men, as a group, presented striking contrasts to the political generals. One of the first of those differences was the rank at which they began their army careers. William Barksdale and Joseph B. Kershaw began their Civil War odysseys by being elected the colonels of their respective regiments. Richard Taylor, son of Mexican War General and U.S. President Zachary Taylor, was appointed colonel of a newly formed Louisiana regiment by that state's governor during the summer of 1861, but only after serving several months as a volunteer civilian aide on the staff of General Braxton Bragg. Patrick Ronayne Cleburne was first elected captain of his local company and only later chosen to be colonel of the regiment into which it was incorporated. Francis Marion Cockrell, who would later command the Army of Mississippi's crack Missouri Brigade, fought his first three actions of the war at the head of a company. Likewise, future corps commander John B. Gordon began as a captain, was a major by the time of his first battle, Manassas (at which his regiment was not engaged), and still only a colonel when he first saw significant combat at Seven Pines, more than a year after putting on the uniform. Firebrand Army of Tennessee division commander William B. Bate enlisted in the

Confederate service as a private, as did the redoubtable Nathan Bedford Forrest.[17]

Some of these men numbered among those who were politicians before becoming Confederate generals. Barksdale was a congressman from Mississippi from 1852 until his resignation upon his state's declaration of secession. Kershaw served two terms in the South Carolina legislature and was a delegate to the state's secession convention, and Taylor served in the state senate of Louisiana from 1856 until he went into uniform in 1861. Yet Kershaw and Barksdale were not political generals, and Taylor was at most a partially political colonel—general officer rank he earned on his own. If there were insufficient trained military men to serve as generals for the Confederate army, this was doubly—or trebly—true of colonels. The same factors that led the American populace to think of civilians as suitable candidates for the rank of general operated even more powerfully for colonels. The distrust of West Point–trained professionals was expressed by Taylor himself in describing that species of officer: "Take a boy of sixteen from his mother's apron-strings, shut him up under constant surveillance for four years at West Point, send him out to a two-company post upon the frontier where he does little but play seven-up and drink whiskey at the sutler's, and by the time he is forty-five years old he will furnish the most complete illustration of suppressed mental development of which human nature is capable." The active man of affairs looked more promising to many Americans at the outset of the war, and thus any prominent local man who inspired confidence in his fellow citizens might well be selected as colonel of the regiment the community was then forming, particularly if he had played a leading role in recruiting and organizing the regiment. In an age not yet grown entirely cynical about its politicians, they were prime candidates. The military positions they received upon their first enlistment were not bestowed on the basis of any hoped-for political bounce they might produce for the government, but rather each of them was simply selected as the most promising potential leader among a group of military innocents as green as themselves if not more so.[18]

And some of these men had previous military experience, even if they could not by any stretch of the imagination be considered trained or prepared for the ranks they occupied at the outset of the war. Cleburne had served several years in the peacetime British army, rising to the rank of corporal. Kershaw had been lieutenant for a year in South Carolina's

Palmetto Regiment during the Mexican War. Barksdale entered a volunteer regiment as an enlisted man in that conflict and rose to officer rank before the war was over, while Bate also had Mexican War experience as an enlisted man.[19]

In contrast to the political generals, who were, as a group, an almost unrelieved disaster, these more or less ordinary citizens in high military rank provided some first-rate generals who were among the most successful of any who wore the gray, and their careers are illustrative of the ways in which nonprofessional generals proved effective for the Confederacy.

After receiving his appointment as colonel of the new Ninth Louisiana, Richard Taylor got orders for the glamorous Virginia theater of war, arriving with his regiment only hours too late to take part in the Confederate victory at First Manassas. Incorporated in Joseph E. Johnston's army, Taylor's regiment became part of the all-Louisiana brigade of Brigadier General William H. T. Walker, a West Point graduate, twenty-four-year professional soldier, and many-times wounded veteran of both the Seminole and Mexican Wars. Walker was a thorough military instructor and a rigorous disciplinarian, and he drove his men hard to make the brigade the best-trained in the army. His tenure in command of the organization lasted only until October of that year, when Taylor's brother-in-law, Davis, transferred him to a Georgia brigade as part of a campaign to place troops from a given state together under officers from that same state. Walker, a Georgian, thus seemed an inappropriate commander for a Louisiana brigade. While there might be a certain logic in that, nothing but personal favoritism could have determined the president's choice of a successor, for, passing over the three senior colonels of the brigade, Davis elevated his kinsman Taylor to command and to the rank of brigadier general. Taylor was much embarrassed, and a disgusted Walker resigned from the service (for a time), but Davis stuck to his decision.[20]

This sort of personal favoritism of someone whose initial rank had not been earned in battle could well have been disastrous. For two key reasons it did not turn out to be so in Taylor's case. The first of these was the effect of Walker's training on the brigade that Taylor would lead through the dramatic campaigns of 1862. By forging this collection of northern Louisiana farm boys and New Orleans riffraff into an effective military formation, Walker had given Taylor a tool that could do much in the hands of a good general and that would bring its commander favorable recognition. As much or more of good generalship lay in the preparation of the troops as in leadership in actual campaigns and battles. By training Taylor's first brigade for him, Walker had launched the Louisianan on a successful trajectory in command.

A second reason that Taylor rose to the unusual demands and opportunity that Davis placed upon him was the effect of Walker's training on Taylor himself. The former president's son was an educated man and knew how to learn, having graduated from Yale in 1845. Walker proved both a high example and a rigorous teacher of what a brigade commander should be and do. It would be difficult to overestimate the importance of this, Taylor's first lesson and observation of command, for he had seen little of his father on duty. Even before coming under Walker's tutelage, Taylor had showed himself prepared to be a demanding, even imperious, superior. Having benefited from several months under the irascible Georgian, Taylor could channel his sometimes domineering nature into the effective training and discipline of his brigade. As he later put it, "Owing to the good traditions left by my predecessor, Walker, and the zeal of officers and men, the brigade made great progress."[21]

This was important, because much would be demanded of the Louisiana Brigade in the coming campaign. Spring of 1862 found Taylor's brigade a part of Ewell's division. With Richmond desperately threatened by Union General George B. McClellan's advance up the Virginia peninsula, that division was under the orders of Major General Thomas J. "Stonewall" Jackson, commanding Confederate forces in the Shenandoah Valley and contemplating offensive movements that few, as yet, understood. Unfortunately, Taylor and Ewell were among those who did not understand what their commander was doing. With the encouragement of the professional soldier Ewell, who should have known better, Taylor made the trip from the Blue Ridge to Richmond to complain to his brother-in-law the president that Jackson was crazy and should be removed or superseded. Davis had had his doubts about Jackson's sanity for some time, and readily agreed, assuring Taylor that James Longstreet would be sent to take command over Jackson and his force. This would have been an unqualified disaster in every way except perhaps shortening the war by about three years. That it did not in fact take place seems to have been the subtle work of Robert E. Lee, who at that time was posted to Richmond in a supervisory role over all Confederate armies.[22]

Jackson remained in independent command and carried out the brilliant Valley campaign, utterly baffling Union commanders in the region, winning several battles, and often using Taylor's Louisianans as his shock troops. Taylor and his men performed brilliantly, winning an excellent reputation and ensuring Taylor's further advancement as a general. Meanwhile, Taylor came to love and respect Jackson and learned from this master the practice of the operational art. Walker had shown Taylor how to run a brigade; now Jackson showed him how to lead an army. Yet the fact remains that at the outset of the campaign Taylor had displayed one of the besetting sins of nonprofessional generals, particularly those with political experience. Aided and abetted by a professional officer—for this class by no means always lived up to its training—he had gone outside the chain of command, appealing over the head of a superior whom he did not understand and injecting civilian politics into the governance of the army in a way that was never intended in the concept of civilian control of the military. Only Lee's wise and skillful intervention had saved him and the Confederacy from the consequences of his action. Sometimes, a nonprofessional general needed not only good training and example from his more experienced superiors but also a deft hand in rescuing him from the miscues he made in the process of learning his new business.[23]

Later in the war, Taylor was assigned to command in his home state of Louisiana. There his performance on the whole was admirable. In the spring of 1864 he experienced his finest hour in command when he led his small army against the invading force of Union Major General Nathaniel P. Banks at the battle of Mansfield. Taylor wisely planned and skillfully executed the discomfiture of the inept Banks and won a devastating victory. Clearly, given the proper talents and tutelage and the right sort of character, a nonprofessional could develop into an excellent general. By the end of the war Taylor would be a lieutenant general, commanding what was left of Confederate forces in the Southern heartland between the Appalachians and the Mississippi.[24]

Another strikingly successful Confederate nonprofessional general was John B. Gordon. Unlike Taylor, Gordon lacked the favoritism of a brother-in-law in the Confederate White House, and his upward climb through the ranks was marked by even harder work and harder fighting. He was a colonel by May 1862, when he led his regiment into its first serious combat at the battle of Seven Pines. There he performed with notable coolness under fire, making a few mistakes—that was inevitable—but correcting them by quick thinking and impressive courage. By the close of the first day's fighting, his brigade commander, Brigadier General Robert E. Rodes had been wounded and had selected

Gordon as his successor, despite the fact that the latter was the junior colonel in the brigade. Notified of this change just before nightfall, Gordon once again took the new challenge in stride and got the brigade ready for renewed action the next day. As it turned out, they were not called on to enter combat a second time at Seven Pines, being held in reserve throughout the battle's second day, but Gordon remained in command for several weeks afterward while Rodes recovered, gaining valuable experience and impressing his superiors.[25]

By the time Rodes's brigade faced combat again, at Gaines Mill during the Seven Days' fighting, Rodes was back at its head, and Gordon ably led his own Sixth Alabama, demonstrating again as he had at Seven Pines that he was the most competent of the brigade's colonels. A single day of action prostrated the still weak Rodes, and Gordon took over the brigade a second time. His first chance to lead it into battle came just a few days later, at Malvern Hill. It was not an auspicious action for a neophyte brigadier to win his spurs, but Gordon performed magnificently. Not the least important part, by far, of the duties of a Civil War officer was that of inspiring his men by oratory and most of all by his own example of fearless courage. This was particularly true of officers up to and including the rank of brigadier, who was usually the highest-ranking officer to lead from a position almost right up on the firing line. At this sort of leadership Gordon excelled mightily, and he gave another demonstration of it at Malvern Hill. In the doomed Confederate assault into the face of massed Federal artillery, Gordon led his brigade forward in good order and, as he would later boast, got closer to the Yankee lines than any other Confederate unit that day. At two hundred yards' range, with the incoming fire too hot for the men long to endure, Gordon could see none of the promised support coming up in his rear or on either flank and ordered the men to lie down in ranks. Then, with the kind of stunning courage that the best Civil War officers displayed in such situations, he walked along his lines, speaking calmly to his men to bolster their nerve, while bullets and shell fragments buzzed around him, tearing his coat, and breaking his canteen and the handle of his revolver. Remarkably, he remained unwounded, but his bravery and that of his men went for naught. The support troops never arrived, the Union line proved impregnable, and the brigade had to withdraw with severe casualties.[26]

Gordon's courage and charismatic leadership ability had served him well in his first battles, prompting one observer to remark, "The capacity of inspiring courage in action, & holding men long under fire is an endowment characteristic, unique, almost peerless in the young officer," referring to Gordon. This gift in turn helped Gordon in the acquisition of all of the other skills necessary to make a good officer. His men's steadiness under fire brought him both reputation and confidence. "Nothing so increases an officer's confidence in our strength," he wrote, "as to lead such troops into battle." As usual, success had bred more success. Gordon's ability to inspire his men gave him the early successes needed to convince both him and his superiors that he had the capability of becoming a first-rate officer. Another advantage Gordon enjoyed early in his military career was service under an excellent commanding officer. Rodes would prove himself to be among the best of the Confederacy's brigade and division commanders. Professionally trained at VMI and for several years an instructor there, Rodes was ideal both as teacher and example.[27]

After Malvern Hill it was back to regimental command for Gordon, and he led his Sixth Alabama with much credit through the Second Manassas and Maryland campaigns. At South Mountain his regiment held a key position and fought stubbornly against superior numbers, finally retiring as the last unit in the brigade to maintain its cohesion, a nucleus on which Rodes was able to rally the fragments of the rest of his command. At Sharpsburg Gordon held the Sunken Road in the Confederate center, and he promised Lee that his men would stay there all day. They tried, and Gordon used well-thought-out tactics and his usual courageous leadership in the attempt. It proved to be in vain, however, and Gordon this time paid the price for conspicuous courage on a Civil War battlefield by being hit no less than five times. He was unconscious when his command retired from the position he had promised Lee to hold.[28]

His performance at the two battles in Maryland won him high praise. Rodes, in his report on South Mountain, referred to "Gordon's excellent regiment (which he had kept constantly in hand, and had handled in a manner I have never heard or seen equaled during this war)," and even the habitually critical D. H. Hill referred to Gordon as "the Chevalier Bayard of the army." Lee recommended him for promotion to brigadier general, but that had to await his recovery from serious wounds. He reported for duty on March 30, 1863, and twelve days later was assigned to command of a brigade in Major General Jubal Early's division. At Chancellorsville he mistook his orders, wrongly supposing that they called for an immediate attack. He did so without support but was successful. Early told him afterward, perhaps not entirely seriously, that if it had not succeeded, he would have had Gordon court-martialed. Still, Early was obviously pleased with his new brigade commander and even more so after Gordon played a skillful role in the Confederate victory at Winchester, June 13–15, 1863. That battle was part of the march that took the army north into Pennsylvania that summer and ultimately to Gettysburg. On July 1, it was Gordon's brigade that overran Barlow Knoll, north of the town, and first broke the Union flank. The collapse of the entire Federal position north and west of Gettysburg followed quickly thereafter. Gordon was among those officers who thought they should have pushed on beyond the town to attack Union remnants and reserves massed on Cemetery Hill, but the army halted, pressing neither its advantage nor its luck. Gordon's men saw little action during the climactic final two days of fighting at Gettysburg and then helped cover the long retreat back to Virginia.[29]

Gordon had done outstanding service in his second campaigning season as an army officer, and his merits did not escape the notice of General Lee himself, who twice the following winter mentioned Gordon in his dispatches to Jefferson Davis, praising the young brigadier as one of his best brigade commanders and someone well qualified to step up to division command. The outset of the 1864 campaign quickly demonstrated that this assessment was an understatement. Gordon was better qualified for high command than either his division commander, Early, or his corps commander, Ewell. When the opposing armies clashed in the tangled thickets of the Wilderness, Gordon correctly perceived that the Union right, opposite his position, was "in the air," unsupported and liable to be turned. In vain he pleaded with Early and Ewell to authorize him to attack or at least to come and view the situation themselves, but taking counsel of their fears, his two superiors refused. Not until late in the day did they finally give their approval. Gordon's attack scored a significant success during the closing hours of daylight, but darkness, the thick foliage of the Wilderness, and an alert Union response prevented it from producing decisive results. Still, Lee was impressed enough with Gordon's performance to promote him to division command, once again over the heads of senior officers.[30]

Gordon got his test as division commander almost immediately, and it was a rigorous one. A number of Civil War officers who performed well as brigadiers failed as division commanders. The jump from brigade to division command represented an important change in the nature of an officer's duties. Inspiring the troops with personal courage was much less important for the division commander, but wise planning, careful preparation, and clear thinking under pressure were vastly more so. Thrust into this new role in the midst of the war's bloodiest campaign, Gordon never missed a beat. At Spotsylvania, just days after taking over his division, he was alert and quick to react to the Union breakthrough at the Muleshoe Salient. He skillfully marshaled his division and led the initial Confederate counterattack after dissuading Lee from doing so in the second of the campaign's famous "Lee to the rear" incidents. Through the rest of the campaign all the way down to Cold Harbor he continued to perform well, and then was detached along with the rest of Early's II Corps, to which his division belonged, to operate in the Shenandoah Valley and threaten Washington. Gordon led his division in breaking the Union line at Monocacy, and was in the thick of the action at almost every encounter in the Valley, salvaging the army's retreat at Winchester, planning and leading the successful attack at Cedar Creek, and then pining in frustration when Early refused to order the follow-up assault that would have completed Confederate victory in a battle begun with such promise. Southern hopes for a strategic turn-around in the Valley that fall were bitterly disappointed, and for Gordon there was the added bitterness of Early's attempt to shift blame onto him. Yet in a decision that few professionals would have made, Gordon decided that no useful purpose would be served by contesting Early's unfounded claims and demanding a court of inquiry. Gordon had no career to protect; he had a war to fight. In the end, it appeared that neither Lee nor many others were taken in by Early's blame-shifting. Gordon was transferred along with his troops back to the main army in eastern Virginia, while Early was left in the Valley with a token force.[31]

With Gordon back in the Petersburg lines, Lee showed his confidence in him by assigning him to command of the II Corps in place of the otherwise occupied Early. Lee also assigned the junior corps commander to the vital and seriously threatened Confederate right, southwest of Petersburg, where Grant was constantly striving to cut the Southside Railroad and with it the flow of supplies to beleaguered Petersburg and Richmond. During the bleak winter months of 1865, Gordon became Lee's most trusted commander and military confidant, and the two discussed what to do in the current difficult situation. Get terms if possible, they agreed; fight their way out if necessary. Since Jefferson Davis would listen to no terms but total Confederate victory, the latter option was all that remained.

To lead the Army of Northern Virginia's last offensive, Lee chose Gordon, placing half the army's available force at his disposal. In his meticulous planning of the attack, Gordon reflected the foremost tactical thinking of the time in seeking to assure that his assaulting troops would proceed directly into the enemy position without pausing to exchange fire with the defenders—on hopeless terms—from no-man's-land. In some ways, he was half a century ahead of his time in providing for special details to infiltrate deep into the Federal defenses, a tactic used with devastating effectiveness by the Germans in 1918. But Gordon had nothing like the numbers available to him that Ludendorff would command during the last year of the First World War, and nothing like the numbers he would have needed to make a dent in the Union lines. The war had passed beyond the point where such things were possible, and barring a massive and catastrophic Union blunder, Gordon's attack never had a chance. That blunder did not occur.[32]

One week later, Grant finally took the Southside Railroad and the next day broke Lee's lines around Petersburg, precipitating the Army of Northern Virginia's final retreat. For the first few days of the march, Gordon's battered command served as rear guard, almost constantly in action with the hard-pursuing Federals. When the end finally came at Appomattox and Lee contemplated one more blow to try to break out of the trap, it was Gordon whom he ordered to lead it, and Gordon who finally gave the word that further attack was hopeless.[33]

Gordon's career was exemplary of the use that the Confederacy needed to make of nonprofessional generals. He was a man of enormous natural endowments for military command. His ability had been cultivated, recognized, and rewarded, and in four years he had gone from leading a company to leading a corps. He had shown that for a man of some natural aptitude, a couple of years of active wartime service would suffice to make him every bit the equal of a professionally trained officer. His military accomplishments would then be limited only by his character and his intelligence—or by the prejudices controlling promotion policies in his army's high command.

The idea that Davis was perniciously prejudiced against nonprofessional officers and would not promote them to high rank arose during the war itself and has had considerable life since then. During the war, the issue was as often as not raised by disappointed nonprofessionals such as political general Robert A. Toombs, who complained that the Confederacy's epitaph should be: "Died of West Point." Like Toombs, many who raised the complaint then were men whose talents and services were far from qualifying them for the ranks they held, much less the higher ones they coveted, and their whining has cast well-deserved doubt on their claims. There was, after all, a grain of truth in their lament, but the problem was sorting out the deserving from the undeserving among nonprofessionals (or professionals for that matter) and determining just how far up the chain of command an officer was qualified to serve.[34]

This difficulty is illustrated in the careers of two nonprofessional generals who served in the western theater, both of whom have long been viewed as victims of Davis's West Point bias. In one case this perception is perhaps partially correct; in the other it probably is not.

Nathan Bedford Forrest's life was "a battle from the start." Born in West Tennessee, he grew up in the rough frontierlike society of that area and northern Mississippi, where violence was common and life often cheap. Forrest had been involved in a shoot-out before he was twenty. He received little formal education, but he was a man of extraordinary natural strength, fierce determination, and, in a very unpolished form, probably considerable intellect too, though he was always more of a doer than a thinker. By the time the Civil War came he had made himself a success as a planter and a slave trader.[35]

At nearly forty years of age, he enlisted as a private in the Seventh Tennessee Cavalry in 1861. That fall he was discharged for the purpose of raising and equipping a battalion of cavalry, which he did, being elected its lieutenant colonel. He was present for Floyd's and Pillow's joint debacle at Donelson, but got permission to take his command out before the surrender, leading them by a back way not guarded by the Federals and crossing a swamp saddle-skirt deep in ice-cold water. At Shiloh he disobeyed orders that had him guarding the army's flank while the battle went on elsewhere. "War means fighting, and fighting means killing," he would later say, and that was what he and his men enlisted for. Leaving his post of duty, he led his troops into the fray. Fortuitously, no mischief followed. Covering the Confederate retreat two days later, Forrest had one of his trademark episodes. Leading a charge in his habitual furious style, he outran his men and suddenly found himself alone amid a crowd of Union soldiers. One of them placed the muzzle of his rifle against Forrest's side and fired. The impact of the slug lifted him in the saddle, but retaining his seat, he grabbed a Federal soldier and by force hauled him up onto the horse's rump behind him. Then, turning, he rode back out of range of the Union lines with the soldier as a shield before dumping the startled Yankee and riding off after his men.[36]

This incident was typical of a man who would kill more than two dozen of the enemy (and one of his own men) before the war was over. Forrest unquestionably excelled in personal fighting prowess any other general, or any commander for that matter, in any army, since warriors had stopped wearing chain-mail and started using firearms. He was big. He was fiery. He was intimidating, and he was an incredible warrior. Half a dozen centuries before his day, a man like him would have conquered an empire, for with all his other attributes he was also cunning. He had never studied the principles of war—he figured them out on his own. His men might not love him, but they respected him and, if necessary, feared him more than they did the enemy. As for his enemies—William T. Sherman called him "that devil Forrest."

During 1862 and 1863 he made a name for himself by leading highly successful raids behind Union lines in Tennessee, recruiting men and horses along the way and reequipping his troops by captures from the foe. On September 19, 1863, he did excellent service at the battle of Chickamauga, and the following spring, at the battle of Brice's Crossroads in northern Mississippi, he was brilliant. Using principles of war that later generations of officers would laboriously memorize, he trounced a superior Union army. Not until the spring of 1865 did the Union come up with the force to checkmate Forrest's independent cavalry command. Federal Major General James H. Wilson led ten thousand cavalry equipped with repeating rifles on a drive into Forrest's territory and soundly defeated him at Selma, but by that time, every Confederate force was suffering defeat. Forrest's career was nothing short of remarkable, and he has a fair claim to being the greatest true natural military genius of the war.[37]

Yet Forrest had his problems. He never took well to any authority above himself unless that authority was almost purely nominal. A superior who attempted to integrate Forrest into his operational plans, and thus give him orders, was likely to get into his bad graces. Forrest announced that he would never again take orders from Major General Joseph Wheeler. He made more or less the same statement regarding Earl Van Dorn and almost came to swords' points with him—literally. He screamed in Braxton Bragg's face the same sort of blanket refusal to obey future orders, adding, "If you were any part of a man, I would slap your jowls and force you to resent it [i.e., to fight a duel]. . . . If you ever again try to interfere with me or cross my path it will be at peril of your life."

That might have been the way a good frontier Mississippian handled a man who tried to tell him what to do and make him do it, but it was not an attitude suited to military life. Only those superiors who chose to allow Forrest more or less free rein enjoyed good relationships with him. Forrest's seeming inability to submit to a superior sharply limited his value as an officer.[38]

Forrest also displayed one of the typical shortcomings of the un-taught—or self-taught—amateur: his performance could be uneven. Though he had many an impressive success to his credit, there were other outings as well. In a raid against Fort Donelson in February 1863 and at Tupelo, Mississippi, the following year, Forrest blundered badly through impetuosity. The day before his fine performance at Chickamauga in September 1863, when his cavalry was supposed to cover the approach march of an important Confederate column, Forrest's brigades were not on hand, and the redoubtable general, instead of going to hurry them along, pitched into the battle with his escort troops alone. He might have been a veritable host in himself, but he could not do the screening job of a whole division of cavalry. The march was delayed, with important consequences for the course of the battle.[39]

Was Forrest then a victim of West Point prejudice, denied promotion he merited and not used by the Confederacy to the degree that he might have been? Davis later all but admitted as much, stating at Forrest's funeral years later that the Confederacy's top western generals had presented Forrest in their reports as nothing more than "a bold and enterprising raider and rider," and that the president had not known the true greatness of Forrest until too late to advance him more rapidly in rank.

Yet Davis was mistaken. True, Forrest was never a failure at any level of command. He was promoted to brigadier general in July 1862 and major general in December of the following year. Lieutenant general's rank did not come to him until the end of February 1865, and he performed with credit in each rank that he held. Yet he had done his best service as "a bold and enterprising raider and rider." He was at his best at a level of command that allowed him a great deal of personal supervision and leadership, and that meant brigade or at most division command. While he was able to function efficiently at higher levels, it was often without the dash he exhibited in his true element. It is also clear from his record of mistakes and "growing pains," mixed in with his sterling successes, that he was probably advanced in rank about as rapidly as he was capable of learning and taking on the higher levels of responsibility. In short, the Confederate command system functioned well in Forrest's case, allowing him to rise commensurate with his merit and employing him mainly at that at which he was best. No West Point prejudice appears to have been at work here.[40]

The case of Pat Cleburne may have been different. Born in Ireland, Cleburne had served several years as an enlisted man in the British army before coming to America and settling in Helena, Arkansas. He worked first as a druggist, then as a lawyer, and when war came he raised a company and went off to fight for the Confederacy. He was promptly elected colonel of the regiment into which his company was incorporated and saw his first action at Shiloh. He was not an instant success. In the woods and morasses there, he found it hard to keep his brigade together. In fact, he entirely lost control of about half of it. Still, everyone was having a hard time that day, and Cleburne's first outing, if not flawless, was undeniably plucky and diligent.

Like Taylor and Gordon, Cleburne had a good teacher. His was Major General (later Lieutenant General) William J. Hardee, sometime commandant of cadets at West Point and author of the Old Army's prewar tactics handbook. Hardee held regular classes of instruction for the officers in his corps of the Army of Tennessee, and Cleburne turned out to be his star pupil. Over the course of the war in the West he performed brilliantly again and again at brigade and division level. His defense of the Tunnel Hill sector of Missionary Ridge during the November 1863 battle of Chattanooga and his defense of Ringgold Gap while covering the Confederate retreat afterward compare well with any operations by any general in the war.[41]

Yet he remained a major general in division command while his juniors, with less impressive records, were promoted over his head. Why? No clear reason emerges as certain, but several are possible. The first, of course, is West Point bias. Yet there is no clue as to why it should have operated in Cleburne's case and not in those of Forrest, Gordon, and Taylor. A more likely explanation is that a paper Cleburne presented to his fellow generals in the Army of Tennessee at the beginning of 1864, advocating the freeing of slaves and their recruitment into Confederate armies, turned the administration against him. Still more probable is the possibility that Cleburne's involvement in the anti-Bragg cabal within the army's high command soured Davis's opinion of him. Hardee was a good teacher of tactics, but a bad one of military subordination. He infected virtually all of his officers with subversive attitudes toward Bragg, and Cleburne was no exception. At any rate, Cleburne, who was perhaps the most qualified of any of the nonprofessional Confederate generals for the exercise of high command, remained a division commander until his death in battle at Franklin in November 1864.[42]

What lessons then can be drawn from the experience of the Confederacy with its nonprofessional generals? The first is that every Civil War general had to learn his trade. While an old saying might have it that good sergeants are made but good generals born, that is true only in the sense that generalship requires an extremely high degree of mental aptitude which, if not present naturally, can never be trained in. Yet, given that level of intelligence, a man still had to go through a laborious process of learning before he could be a good general.

For this to happen, several things needed to be true. First, he needed time to learn. A too rapid rise in rank—the hallmark of the political generals—was almost sure to produce a failure. Officers who spent some time at each level of command, at least beginning at the level of colonel, did much better. The general also needed the ability to learn the art of war. Some men simply lacked the aptitude. No amount of training or experience would ever make good generals out of them—a limitation apparent among West Pointers as well as nonprofessionals. Also, if a general was to master his trade, he would need to have a willingness to do so. For a man to learn a new line of work in the middle of life, it helped if he was not already stuffed full of himself. That may have been a further disqualification of most politicians, particularly those who coveted—and thought themselves likely candidates for—military glory. Finally, it was especially helpful if the new officer had a good instructor and example early in his military career. Zollicoffer, stationed by himself out in East Tennessee, never had the benefit of a well-trained immediate superior present with him until it was too late to make any difference. On the other hand, Taylor, Gordon, and Cleburne all profited from instruction by such superiors.

The final lesson of the Confederacy's use of nonprofessional generals is that it worked. Men totally or largely devoid of any military training or experience became, under the stern necessity of war, truly excellent generals. The graduates of West Point, VMI, and the other military schools had a head start in learning the art of war and had been, to some degree, winnowed of the most obvious failures. Yet performance in lower ranks during time of war provided an even more rigorous winnowing, and given a couple of years to learn the business, those erstwhile civilians who possessed the basic aptitudes for command could perform just as well as their professional comrades in arms. The Confederate experience thus demonstrates that wise promotion policies at each successive level of command could select out of the ranks of ordinary citizens the men who were capable of leading a republic's armies.

Notes

Chapter One. Davis, Beauregard, and Washington, D.C., 1861

1. William C. Davis, *Jefferson Davis: The Man and His Hour* (New York: Harper Collins, 1991), 328.

2. Ibid., 337.

3. Steven E. Woodworth, *Jefferson Davis and His Generals: The Failure of Confederate Command in the West* (Lawrence: University Press of Kansas, 1990), 75–76; Douglas Southall Freeman, *Lee's Lieutenants: A Study in Command*, 3 vols. (New York: Charles Scribner's Sons, 1942–1944), 1:4, 7; Alfred Roman, *The Military Operations of General Beauregard*, 2 vols. (New York: Harper and Brothers, 1884), 1:66–67.

4. Roman, *Military Operations*, 1:78.

5. Freeman, *Lee's Lieutenants*, 1:38.

6. Roman, *Military Operations*, 1:77.

7. Ibid., 1:77–78; William C. Davis, *Battle at Bull Run: A History of the First Major Campaign of the Civil War* (Garden City, N.Y.: Doubleday, 1977), 64; T. Harry Williams, *P. G. T. Beauregard: Napoleon in Gray* (Baton Rouge: Louisiana State University Press, 1954), 71; Freeman, *Lee's Lieutenants*, 1:39–40; Davis, *Jefferson Davis*, 345.

8. Freeman, *Lee's Lieutenants*, 1:41–42; Davis, *Battle at Bull Run*, 65; Roman, *Military Operations*, 1:81–82, 82–83.

9. Ibid., 1:84.

10. Davis, *Battle at Bull Run*, 66–67.

11. Roman, *Military Operations*, 1:84, 87; Williams, *P. G. T. Beauregard*, 75; U.S. War Department, *War of the Rebellion: A Compilation of the Official Records of the Union and Confederate Armies*, 128 vols. (Washington, D.C.: Government Printing Office, 1881–1901), 2:506–7 (hereafter *O.R.*: all volumes cited are from Series 1).

12. Roman, *Military Operations*, 1:88.

13. Davis, *Jefferson Davis*, 348; *O.R.*, 2:980; Roman, *Military Operations*, 1:91, 90.

14. Freeman, *Lee's Lieutenants*, 1:50–72; Davis, *Jefferson Davis*, 347.

15. E. Porter Alexander, *Military Memoirs of a Confederate: A Critical Narrative* (New York: Charles Scribner's Sons, 1912), 43.

16. Ibid., 44, 43; Roman, *Military Operations*, 1:109–10.

17. Alexander, *Military Memoirs*, 45.

18. Ibid., 42.

19. Freeman, *Lee's Lieutenants*, 1:76, 77; Roman, *Military Operations*, 1:110–14; Davis, *Battle at Bull Run*, 243–44.

20. Gilbert E. Govan and James W. Livingood, *A Different Valor: The Story of General Joseph B. Johnston, C.S.A.* (Indianapolis: Bobbs-Merrill, 1956), 59–60.

21. Davis, *Battle at Bull Run*, 244; Roman, *Military Operations*, 1:114; Alexander, *Military Memoirs*, 49–50; Govan and Livingood, *A Different Valor*, 49–50, 59–60.

22. Davis, *Battle at Bull Run*, 244; Roman, *Military Operations*, 1:115–16, 121–22, 137–39, 142–45; Freeman, *Lee's Lieutenants*, 1:102–4; Govan and Livingood, *A Different Valor*, 74–75; James M. McPherson, *Battle Cry of Freedom: The Civil War Era* (New York: Oxford University Press, 1988), 345.

CHAPTER TWO. DAVIS, POLK, AND
THE END OF KENTUCKY NEUTRALITY

1. McPherson, *Battle Cry of Freedom*, 356–57.

2. Haskell M. Monroe and James T. McIntosh, eds., *The Papers of Jefferson Davis* (Baton Rouge: Louisiana State University Press, 1971), 1:liii-lxv, lxxxiv; Clement Eaton, *The Mind of the Old South* (Baton Rouge: Louisiana State University Press, 1967), 209–12; Joseph H. Parks, *General Leonidas Polk, C.S.A: The Fighting Bishop* (Baton Rouge: Louisiana State University Press, 1960), 33; Herman Hattaway and Archer Jones, *How*

the North Won: A Military History of the Civil War (Urbana: University of Illinois Press, 1983), 164; Jefferson Davis to Leonidas Polk, February 7, 1862, National Archives.

3. Isham G. Harris to Jefferson Davis, July 2, 1861, Dearborn Collection, Houghton Library, Harvard University, photocopy.

4. Stanley Horn, *The Army of Tennessee: A Military History* (Indianapolis: Bobbs-Merrill, 1941), 48; James T. McIntosh, Lynda L. Crist, and Mary S. Dix, eds., *The Papers of Jefferson Davis* (Baton Rouge: Louisiana State University Press, 1981), 3:91n; Milo Milton Quaife, ed., *The Diary of James K. Polk* (Chicago: McClung, 1910), 4:5–9, 22; Thomas Lawrence Connelly, *Army of the Heartland: The Army of Tennessee, 1861–1862* (Baton Rouge: Louisiana State University Press, 1967), 47.

5. Gideon J. Pillow to Jefferson Davis, May 16, 1861, *O.R.,* 52.2:100–101.

6. Ben Anderson to Jefferson Davis, June 2, 1861, The Samuel Richey Collection of the Southern Confederacy, Miami University Libraries, Oxford, Ohio; *O.R.,* 4:179.

7. John B. Jones, *A Rebel War Clerk's Diary,* ed. Earl Schenck Miers (New York: Sagamore Press, 1958), 28, 21, 41; Parks, *General Leonidas Polk,* 166–67; Mary Boykin Chesnut, *A Diary from Dixie,* ed. Ben Ames Williams (Boston: Houghton Mifflin, 1905), 84; Jefferson Davis to Leonidas Polk, September 2, 1861, Leonidas Polk Papers, Southern Historical Collection, University of North Carolina at Chapel Hill Library.

8. *O.R.,* 4:181, 188–89; Bruce Catton, *Terrible Swift Sword* (Garden City, N.Y.: Doubleday, 1963), 37; William C. Harris, *Leroy Pope Walker: Confederate Secretary of War* (Tuscaloosa, Ala.: Confederate Publishing Co., 1962), 110–11.

9. Connelly, *Army of the Heartland,* 25–45; *O.R.,* 4:180, 188–89, 190.

10. Endorsement by Jefferson Davis, September 5, 1861, on telegram from Isham G. Harris to Jefferson Davis, September 4, 1861, National Archives, RG109, "Documents in the *Official Records,*" microfilm; *O.R.,* 4:189, 181.

11. *O.R.,* 4:180.

12. Ibid.

13. Ibid., 4:181.

14. Ibid.; Jefferson Davis to Leonidas Polk, September 5, 1861, Polk Papers, Library of Congress.

15. *O.R.,* 4:396–97; Jones, *A Rebel War Clerk's Diary,* 46.

16. *O.R.,* 4:179–84.

Chapter Three. Confederate Command in Microcosm: The Case of Williamsburg

1. Gustavus Woodson Smith, *Confederate War Papers* (New York, 1884), 46; *O.R.*, 11.1:602; Stephen W. Sears, *To the Gates of Richmond: The Peninsula Campaign* (New York: Ticknor and Fields, 1992), 61.

2. Sears, *To the Gates of Richmond*, 47, 68–69; Smith, *Confederate War Papers*, 41–42; Joseph E. Johnston, *Narrative of Military Operations* (New York: Appleton, 1874), 114–15; Jefferson Davis, *Rise and Fall of the Confederate Government*, 2 vols. (New York: 1881), 2:86–87; Joseph E. Johnston, "Manassas to Seven Pines," in Robert U. Johnston and Clarence C. Buel, eds., *Battles and Leaders of the Civil War*, 4 vols. (New York: Century Magazine, 1884–89), 2:203; Steven Harvey Newton, "Joseph E. Johnston and the Defense of Richmond" (Ph.D diss., College of William and Mary, 1989. Ann Arbor: UMI, 1991. 9102176), 242–43, 246–47, 253, 255–56, 261, 263, 273–74; James Longstreet, *From Manassas to Appomattox* (Bloomington: University of Indiana Press, 1960), 66; William C. Davis, *Jefferson Davis*, 414; Douglas Southall Freeman, *R. E. Lee: A Biography*, 4 vols. (New York: 1934), 2:21–22.

3. Johnston, *Narrative*, 116, 118 127; Johnston, "Manassas," 204; *O.R.*, 11.1:455–56, 458, 469.

4. Douglas Southall Freeman, *Lee's Lieutenants: A Study in Command*, 3 vols. (New York: Scribners, 1942–1944), 1:175–76.

5. Johnston, *Narrative*, 120.

6. Mary Boykin Chesnut, *Mary Chesnut's Civil War*, ed. C. Vann Woodward (New Haven: Yale University Press, 1981), 268.

7. *O.R.*, 11.1:564.

8. Ibid., 580.

9. Sears, *To the Gates of Richmond*, 70–71.

10. *O.R.*, 11.1:564, 590, 564, 575, 584.

11. Ibid., 564, 580, 590–91.

12. Newton, "Johnston," 345; *O.R.*, 11.1:580, 582.

13. *O.R.*, 11.1:571, 580, 582, 584, 587–88, 591.

14. Ibid., 576, 580, 590–91.

15. Ibid., 582, 588, 591, 595, 594–96, 598.

16. Ibid., 576, 591, 598.

17. Ibid., 587–88, 591.

18. Ibid., 585, 591–92, 596–98.

19. Ibid., 584–85, 591–92, 598–99.

20. Longstreet, *From Manassas to Appomattox,* 74; Newton, "Johnston," 352–53.

21. Freeman, *Lee's Lieutenants,* 1:179–80; Sears, *To the Gates of Richmond,* 173–74; Newton, "Johnston," 353; *O.R.,* 11.1:536–37, 580, 602–3, 606–7.

22. Longstreet, *From Manassas to Appomattox,* 74; *O.R.,* 11.1:565, 602.

23. Sears, *To the Gates of Richmond,* 75–78; *O.R.,* 11.1:565, 577, 585–86, 588, 592–93, 595, 597, 599, 606.

24. Johnston, *Narrative,* 120.

25. *O.R.,* 11.1:275; Hamilton J. Eckenrode and Bryan Conrad, *James Longstreet: Lee's War Horse* (Chapel Hill, N.C., 1986), 52; *O.R.,* 11.1:933–46.

26. *O.R.,* 11.1:607.

27. Ibid.

28. Early asserted that the attack idea originated with Hill, but in this assertion he is alone and would appear to have been lying. In fact, no one was very anxious to claim responsibility for this affair after the fact. The situation described in the text—with Johnston, Longstreet, and Hill together when approached by Early—seems the most likely harmonization of the various participants' accounts. Longstreet, *From Manassas to Appomattox,* 77–78; Jeffry D. Wert, *General James Longstreet: The Confederacy's Most Controversial Solider—A Biography* (New York: Simon and Schuster, 1993), 104; *O.R.,* 11.1:565, 602–3, 607.

29. *O.R.,* 11.1:603, 607.

30. Ibid., 603.

31. Ibid., 607; Sears, *To the Gates of Richmond,* 79.

32. *O.R.,* 11.1:603.

33. Ibid.

34. Ibid., 606, 591, 580–81.

35. Freeman, *Lee's Lieutenants,* 1:177, 189, 192; Sears, *To the Gates of Richmond,* 73; Wirt, *Longstreet,* 107.

Chapter Four. Davis and Lee in the Seven Days

1. Davis, *Rise and Fall,* 2:130.

2. Ibid., 2:38, 32; William C. Davis, *Jefferson Davis,* 228–45.

3. Jefferson Davis to Varina Davis, June 23, 1862, Museum of the Confederacy, Richmond, Virginia; *O.R.,* 11.3:568–69.

4. Longstreet, *From Manassas to Appomattox,* 112. The quote from the *Examiner* is in Hudson Strode, *Jefferson Davis, Confederate President*

(New York: Harcourt Brace, 1959), 220; McClellan is quoted in Shelby Foote, *The Civil War,* 3 vols. (New York: Vintage, 1986), 1:465.

5. E. Porter Alexander, *Military Memoirs of a Confederate* (New York, 1912), 110–11.

6. *O.R.,* 11.3:569–70.

7. Douglas Southall Freeman, ed., *Lee's Dispatches* (New York, 1957), 3–5.

8. Davis, *Rise and Fall,* 2:130–31.

9. Clifford Dowdey and Louis H. Manarin, eds., *The Wartime Papers of R. E. Lee* (New York: Bramhall House, 1961), 183–84, 188, 193; *O.R.,* 11.3:572.

10. Quoted in William C. Davis, *Jefferson Davis,* 430–31.

11. Douglas Southall Freeman, *R. E. Lee* (New York: Scribners, 1936), 104–6.

12. Davis, *Rise and Fall,* 2:132.

13. Jefferson Davis to Varina Davis, June 23, 1862, Museum of the Confederacy, Richmond, Virginia.

14. Freeman, *Lee's Dispatches,* 12–13. Davis is quoted in William C. Davis, *Jefferson Davis,* 434.

15. Freeman, *Lee's Dispatches,* 15–17; *O.R.,* 11.3:617; Freeman, *R. E. Lee,* 2:129; Alexander, *Military Memoirs,* 118.

16. Robert Underwood Johnson and Clarence Clough Buel, eds., *Battles and Leaders of the Civil War* (New York, 1956), 2:352.

17. Freeman, *R. E. Lee,* 2:131–32.

18. Alexander, *Military Memoirs,* 119; Longstreet, *From Manassas to Appomattox,* 124; Freeman, *Lee's Lieutenants,* 1:515.

19. Freemen, *R. E. Lee,* 2:157; Davis, *Rise and Fall,* 2:132, 140; Freeman, *Lee's Dispatches,* 18–19.

20. Freeman, *Lee's Dispatches,* 19–22; Freeman, *R. E. Lee,* 2:172.

21. Longstreet, *From Manassas to Appomattox,* 134; Alexander, *Military Memoirs,* 140; Freeman, *R. E. Lee,* 2:181–82.

22. Davis, *Rise and Fall,* 2:143–44.

23. Freeman, *Lee's Lieutenants,* 1:617.

24. Jedediah Hotchkiss Papers, Library of Congress Manuscript Division, Washington, D.C., microfilm reel 34, frame 125.

CHAPTER FIVE. "DISMEMBERING THE CONFEDERACY": JEFFERSON DAVIS AND THE TRANS-MISSISSIPPI WEST

1. Joseph H. Parks, *General Edmund Kirby Smith, C.S.A.* (Baton Rouge: Louisiana State University Press, 1954), 427.

2. *Military Affairs* 34 (April 1970): 49–53.

3. *O.R.*, 13:914–15.

4. *O.R.*, 15:1005. For Smith's performance at First Manassas and the resulting accolades, see Parks, *General Edmund Kirby Smith*, 136–38; Davis, *Battle at Bull Run*, 133, 224–26; and Freeman, *Lee's Lieutenants*, 1:41, 71. For Smith's failure to cooperate with Bragg during the Kentucky campaign, see Gary Donaldson, "'Into Africa': Kirby Smith and Braxton Bragg's Invasion of Kentucky," *Filson Club Historical Quarterly* 61 (October 1987): 464; Woodworth, *Jefferson Davis and His Generals*, chap. 9.

5. Parks, *General Edmund Kirby Smith*, 255–56, 269–72.

6. *O.R.*, 52.2:115.

7. Davis, *Rise and Fall*, 1:309.

8. Horn, *The Army of Tennessee*, 58–59.

9. Chesnut, *A Diary from Dixie*, 84; Jones, *A Rebel War Clerk's Diary*, 21–41; Jefferson Davis to Leonidas Polk, September 2, 1861, Leonidas Polk Papers, Southern Historical Collection, University of North Carolina at Chapel Hill Library.

10. *O.R.*, 6:788–89.

11. Ibid., 797–98.

12. Ibid., 8:728–29.

13. Ibid., 7:826.

14. Ibid., 8:790.

15. Ibid., 10.2:354.

16. Connelly, *Army of the Heartland*, 60–142. Connelly is very critical of Johnston's qualities as a general, and others have followed his lead.

17. *O.R.*, 10.2:547.

18. Ibid., 15:773–75.

19. Ibid., 17.2:653; Freeman, *Lee's Lieutenants*, 1:145, 274, 582–84.

20. *O.R.*, 17.2:593; Hattaway and Jones, *How the North Won*, 22.

21. *O.R.*, 15:791, 795.

22. Ibid., 802, 817.

23. Ibid., 17.2:724.

24. Ibid., 728.

25. Ibid., 16.2:970.

26. Ibid., 13:889–90.

27. Dunbar Rowland, ed., *Jefferson Davis, Constitutionalist: His Letters, Papers, and Speeches*, 10 vols. (Jackson: Mississippi Department of Archives and History, 1923), 5:356–57.

28. *O.R.*, 17.2:737.

29. Ibid., 13:906–7.

30. Rowland, ed., *Jefferson Davis,* 5:356–57.

31. Jones, *Rebel War Clerk's Diary,* 118.

32. *O.R.,* 13:914–25.

33. Ibid., 13:906–7, 914–25.

34. Rowland, ed., *Jefferson Davis,* 5:371.

35. Ibid., 5:371, 374; Randolph to Davis, November 15, 1862, in Randolph Family Papers, Edgehill Randolph Collection, University of Virginia Library.

36. *O.R.,* 17.2:751, 753.

37. Ibid., 17.2:756, 762; 15:873; 17.2:763, 766.

38. Ibid., 17.2:757.

39. Ibid., 767.

40. Ibid., 765–66, 768.

41. Ibid., 777, 780–81.

42. Ibid., 17.2:783–84, 786; 20.2:444; 17.2:782–83, 787–88.

43. Rowland, ed., *Jefferson Davis,* 5:384; *O.R.,* 17.2:793.

44. Rowland, ed., *Jefferson Davis,* 5:387–88.

45. Theophilus H. Holmes to Jefferson Davis, December 29, 1862, Duke University Library.

CHAPTER SIX. SOLDIER WITH A BLUNTED SWORD: BRAXTON BRAGG AND HIS LIEUTENANTS IN THE CHICKAMAUGA CAMPAIGN

1. *O.R.,* 16.2:745–46, 748, 751–53, 766–67, 859, 866; 17.2:627–28, 654–55, 658, 667–68, 673; Donaldson, "'Into Africa,'" 464; Connelly, *Army of the Heartland,* 195.

2. See chapter 2.

3. Grady McWhiney, *Braxton Bragg and Confederate Defeat* (Tuscaloosa: 1991; originally published 1969), 328–29.

4. McWhiney, *Braxton Bragg and Confederate Defeat,* 328–29; Thomas Lawrence Connelly, *Autumn of Glory: The Army of Tennessee, 1862–1865* (Baton Rouge: Louisiana State University Press, 1971), 20–21.

5. Nathaniel C. Hughes, *General William J. Hardee: Old Reliable* (Baton Rouge: Louisiana State University Press, 1965), 3–85; Connelly, *Autumn of Glory,* 20–21, 90.

6. McWhiney, *Braxton Bragg and Confederate Defeat,* 329–33.

7. Woodworth, *Jefferson Davis and His Generals,* 187–98; McWhiney, *Braxton Bragg and Confederate Defeat;* Judith Lee Hallock, *Braxton Bragg*

and Confederate Defeat, vol. 2 (Tuscaloosa: University of Alabama Press, 1991).

8. Connelly, *Autumn of Glory,* 26–28, 123–29.

9. Quoted in Parks, *General Leonidas Polk,* 315.

10. Regarding the Tullahoma campaign, see Steven E. Woodworth, "Braxton Bragg and the Tullahoma Campaign," in *The Art of Command: Facets of Civil War Generalship* (Lincoln: University of Nebraska Press, 1998).

11. Parks, *General Leonidas Polk,* 321.

12. *O.R.,* 30.2: 22, 26–37.

13. On the Chickamauga campaign, see Steven E. Woodworth, *Six Armies in Tennessee: The Chickamauga and Chattanooga Campaigns* (Lincoln: University of Nebraska Press, 1998).

14. Freeman, *Lee's Lieutenants,* 1:19–22.

15. *O.R.,* 23.2:26–37; 23.4:634; Glen Tucker, *Chickamauga: Bloody Battle in the West* (Indianapolis: Bobbs-Merrill, 1961), 67–69.

16. *O.R.,* 30.4:636.

17. Ibid., 26–37, 49, 636.

CHAPTER SEVEN. THE PRESIDENT'S CHOICES: CONFEDERATE COMMAND OPTIONS ON THE EVE OF THE ATLANTA CAMPAIGN

1. Strode, *Jefferson Davis, Confederate President,* 479–80; Longstreet, *From Manassas to Appomattox,* 465–66; Connelly, *Autumn of Glory,* 241–45; Arndt M. Stickles, *Simon Bolivar Buckner: Borderland Knight* (Chapel Hill: University of North Carolina Press, 1940), 236.

2. Rowland, ed., *Jefferson Davis,* 6:93; Dowdey and Manarin, eds., *Wartime Papers,* 642; Woodworth, *Jefferson Davis and His Generals,* 162–99, 222–55.

3. Connelly, *Autumn of Glory,* 282–83; Dowdey and Manarin, eds., *Wartime Papers,* 642.

4. P. G. T. Beauregard to Thomas Jordan, July 12, 1862, in Beauregard papers, Duke University. Jefferson Davis to Varina Davis, June 13, 1862, Museum of the Confederacy.

5. James L. McDonough, *Shiloh: In Hell before Night* (Knoxville: University of Tennessee Press, 1977), 73–75; McWhiney, *Braxton Bragg and Confederate Defeat,* 243–45; Grady McWhiney, "General Beauregard's 'Complete Victory' at Shiloh: An Interpretation," *Journal of Southern History* 49 (August 1983): 421–34.

6. Craig Symonds, "No Margin for Error: Civil War in the Confederate Government," in *The Art of Command,* Woodworth, ed.; James R. Arnold, *Grant Wins the War: Decision at Vicksburg* (New York: John Wiley and Sons, 1997), 287–91. Jim Stanbery, *Civil War Regiments,* "A Failure of Command: The Confederate Loss of Vicksburg," 2.1:55–56.

7. *O.R.,* 38.5:988; Rowland, ed., *Jefferson Davis,* 6:132, 305, 334–35; Chesnut, *A Diary from Dixie,* 328; Hughes, *General William J. Hardee,* 186, 189; Thomas Robson Hay, "Pat Cleburne, Stonewall Jackson of the West," in Irving A. Buck, *Cleburne and His Command* (Jackson, Tenn.: McCowat-Mercer, 1959), 50–51.

8. Hughes, *General William J. Hardee.*

9. *O.R.,* 31.3:882.

10. Robert M. Epstein, *Napoleon's Last Victory and the Emergence of Modern War* (Lawrence: University Press of Kansas, 1994), 9–32.

11. *O.R.,* 32.2:561–62.

12. Steven E. Woodworth, *Davis and Lee at War* (Lawrence: University Press of Kansas, 1995), 25–26, 153–56.

13. Ibid., 82–84.

14. Jones, *A Rebel War Clerk's Diary,* 30–31; *O.R.,* 30.2:26–37, 55; 30.4:634; 32.2:561–62, 564; Ezra Warner, *Generals in Gray: Lives of the Confederate Commanders* (Baton Rouge: Louisiana State University Press, 1959), 137–38; Howell Purdue and Elizabeth Purdue, *Pat Cleburne, Confederate General* (Tuscaloosa, 1973), 27; Woodworth, *Six Armies in Tennessee,* 69–73.

15. Arthur W. Bergeron, Jr., "Mansfield Lovell," in *The Confederate General,* ed. William C. Davis (n.p.: National Historical Society, 1991), 5:173.

16. *O.R.,* 6:641–43, 657–58; 53:803; Joseph Davis to Jefferson Davis, June 18 and 22, 1862, Jeferson Davis papers, Transylvania University Library; Daniel E. Sutherland, "Mansfield Lovell's Quest for Justice: Another Look at the Fall of New Orleans," *Louisiana History* (1983): 233–59; Charles L. Dufour, *The Night the War Was Lost* (Garden City, N.Y.: Doubleday, 1960); Charles L. Dufour, "The Night the War Was Lost: The Fall of New Orelans: Causes, Consequences, Culpability," *Louisiana History* 2 (1961): 157–74; Davis, *Jefferson Davis,* 408; J. J. Pettus to Jefferson Davis, June 19, 1862, Dearborn Collection, Houghton Library, Harvard University; Jones, *Rebel War Clerk's Diary,* 330–31.

17. James Lee McDonough, *Chattanooga,* 206–19; Woodworth, *Six*

Armies in Tennessee; Woodworth, *Jefferson Davis and His Generals,* 144–99, 222–55.

18. Marshall Wingfield, *General A. P. Stewart: His Life and Letters* (Memphis: West Tennessee Historical Society, 1954), 9–95, 152–61; Warner, *Generals in Gray,* 53–54.

19. Jim Stanbery, "Confederate Loss of Vicksubrg," 58; Herman Hattaway, *General Stephen D. Lee* (Jackson: University Press of Mississippi, 1976), 123–225.

20. Richard M. McMurry, *John Bell Hood and the War for Southern Independence* (Lexington: University Press of Kentucky, 1982), 1–15; John B. Hood, *Advance and Retreat: Personal Experiences in the United States and Confederate States Armies* (Bloomington: University of Indiana Press, 1959), 5–8.

21. Richard M. McMurry, *The Road Past Kennesaw: The Atlanta Campaign of 1864* (Washington, D.C., 1972), 42.

22. Dowdy and Manarin, ed., *Wartime Papers,* 821–22; McMurry, *John Bell Hood,* 119; *O.R.,* 38.5: 879–80; Connelly, *Autumn of Glory,* 321–22, 417.

CHAPTER EIGHT. BEAUREGARD AT BERMUDA HUNDRED

1. *O.R.,* 46.1:19. The concept of Beauregard as an unused military asset crops up repeatedly in Civil War literature. See Bruce Catton, *Never Call Retreat* (New York: Doubleday, 1965), 333–34; Archer Jones, *Civil War Command and Strategy* (New York: Free Press, 1992), 121–22; Charles P. Roland, *An American Iliad: The Story of the Civil War* (Lexington: University Press of Kentucky, 1991), 112, 182.

2. Williams, *P. G. T. Beauregard,* 207; Roman, *Military Operations,* 2:193.

3. *O.R.,* 33:1283.

4. Williams, *P. G. T. Beauregard,* 208; Hallock, *Braxton Bragg and Confederate Defeat,* 182–83; *O.R.,* 33:1282–83; Dowdey and Manarin, eds., *Wartime Papers,* 699.

5. William G. Robertson, *Back Door to Richmond: The Bermuda Hundred Campaign, April–June, 1864* (Newark, N.J.: University of Delaware Press, 1987), 47–50; P. G. T. Beauregard, "The Defense of Drewry's Bluff," in Robert U. Johnson and Clarence C. Buel, eds., *Battles and Leaders of the Civil War,* 4 vols. (Secaucus, N.J.: Castle, 1987 [1884–1889]), 4:195.

6. Robertson, *Back Door to Richmond,* 53; *O.R.,* 51.2:886; Rowland, ed., *Jefferson Davis,* 6:246–47.

7. *O.R.*, 51.2:887; Douglas Southall Freeman and Grady McWhiney, eds., *Lee's Dispatches: Unpublished Letters of General Robert E. Lee, C.S.A., to Jefferson Davis and the War Department of the Confederate States of America, 1862–1865, from the Private Collection of Wymberley Jones De Renne, of Wormsloe, Georgia* (Baton Rouge: Louisiana State University Press, 1994 [1915]), 169–74.

8. *O.R.*, 51.2:887, 889; Rowland, ed., *Jefferson Davis*, 6:247.

9. Rowland, ed., *Jefferson Davis*, 6:247.

10. Robertson, *Back Door to Richmond*, 54; Rowland, ed., *Jefferson Davis*, 6:247–48; *O.R.*, 36.2:951.

11. Robertson, *Back Door to Richmond*, 66–69.

12. *O.R.*, 51.2:890–91; Robertson, *Back Door to Richmond*, 65–69; Beauregard, "Defense," 196.

13. Williams, *P. G. T. Beauregard*, 118; *O.R.*, 7:895–96; 10.2:297, 302, 327; McWhiney, *Braxton Bragg and Confederate Defeat*, 205; Jefferson Davis to Varina Davis, June 13, 1862, Museum of the Confederacy.

14. Rowland, *Jefferson Davis*, 6:248; *O.R.*, 36.2:964; 51.2:894; Robertson, *Back Door to Richmond*, 75–76.

15. Beauregard, "Defense," 196; Johnson Hagood, *Memoirs of the War of Secession* (Columbia, 1910), 219–22; Charles M. Cummings, *Yankee Quaker Confederate General: The Curious Career of Bushrod Rust Johnson* (Rutherford, N.J.: Fairleigh Dickinson University Press, 1971), 282–83; *O.R.*, 36.2:963–64; 51.2:902.

16. Dick Nolan, *Benjamin Franklin Butler: The Damnedest Yankee* (Novato, Calif., 1991), 223; *O.R.*, 51.2:902.

17. Evidence that Bragg forwarded Davis's recommended route to Beauregard is demonstrated by that general's reply, one of at least three dispatches he sent Bragg on May 8, in which he assured Bragg that he would leave that night by the first train, although he dismissed Davis's observation, claiming that the "Danville route [is] too long for troops." *O.R.*, 51.2:903–4. Beauregard, "Defense," 196.

18. Beauregard, "Defense," 196; *O.R.*, 51.2:906–15.

19. Robertson, *Back Door to Richmond*, 122–23, 128; *O.R.*, 51.2:915.

20. Rowland, *Jefferson Davis*, 6:249; *O.R.*, 36.2:986.

21. Noah Andre Trudeau, *Bloody Roads South: The Wilderness to Cold Harbor, May–June 1864* (Boston: Little Brown, 1989), 162–63; *O.R.*, 51.2:915–16; Roman, *Military Operations*, 2:554.

22. Robertson, *Back Door to Richmond*, 140–42; *O.R.*, 51.2:920.

23. *O.R.*, 51.2:921.

24. Ibid., 920.

25. Ibid., 919, 21.

26. Ibid., 36.2:991–92.

27. Ibid., 986; Roman, *Military Operations*, 2:554.

28. *O.R.*, 36.2:991–92.

29. Ibid., 991–92.

30. Rowland, *Jefferson Davis*, 6:250.

31. *O.R.*, 51.2:920.

32. Ibid., 920.

33. Robertson, *Back Door to Richmond*, 142; Hagood, *Memoirs*, 231–32; *O.R.*, 36.2:988.

34. *O.R.*, 51.2:927; Robertson, *Back Door to Richmond*, 142, 146–49; Hagood, *Memoirs*, 232.

35. Beauregard, "Defense," 198–99; Freeman, *Lee's Lieutenants*, 3:478–79; Robertson, *Back Door to Richmond*, 149–50; Henry A. Wise, "The Career of Wise's Brigade, 1861–5," *Southern Historical Society Papers* 25 (1897): 10.

36. Beauregard, "Defense," 197–98; Freeman, *Lee's Lieutenants*, 3:479–80.

37. *O.R.*, 36.2:1024.

38. Beauregard, "Defense," 199; Davis, *Rise and Fall*, 2:511–13.

39. Beauregard, "Defense," 200; Davis, *Rise and Fall*, 2:512–13.

40. Robertson, *Back Door to Richmond*, 153.

41. *O.R.*, 51.2:930, 934. The dispatch from Beauregard to Davis on page 930 is labeled as having been sent on May 14, but it is most likely misdated and was sent on the fifteenth.

42. Davis, *Rise and Fall*, 2:512–13; Beauregard, "Defense," 200.

43. *O.R.*, 51.2:934, 1077.

44. Charles T. Loehr, "Battle of Drewry's Bluff," *Southern Historical Society Papers* 19 (1891): 100–111.

45. Varina Howell Davis, *Jefferson Davis: Ex-President of the Confederate States of America, A Memoir by His Wife*, 2 vols. (New York: Appleton, 1890), 2:509–14. The intensity of the confusion on the field that morning is borne out by the fact that Johnson Hagood, commanding the left brigade of Hoke's division, later denied having received any help at all from Ransom. Hagood, *Memoirs*, 244–46. It is therefore reasonable to conclude that Ransom was fighting Federals on his right, where he presumed Hagood to be, while Hagood was fighting Federals on his left, where he presumed Ransom to be, with neither perceiving the actions

of the other. This would imply that the Federals had before them a gap that offered a remarkable opportunity to ruin Beauregard's army. That they did not exploit it is probably a factor both of poor visibility and a reflection of the timid mindset of Butler and his lieutenants.

46. *O.R.*, 36.2:236–38, 253–54; Cummings, *Yankee Quaker, Confederate General*, 285.

47. Robertson, *Back Door to Richmond*, 194.

48. *O.R.*, 36.2:196–97.

49. Ibid., 196–97; V. H. Davis, *Jefferson Davis*, 2:520.

50. *O.R.*, 36.2:198; Robertson, *Back Door to Richmond*, 206.

51. Robertson, *Back Door to Richmond*, 209–15; Freeman, *Lee's Lieutenants*, 3:492–93; Wise, "The Career of Wise's Brigade," 10–11; John H. Reagan, *Memoirs, with Special Reference to Secession and the Civil War*, Walter F. McCaleb, ed. (New York: Neale, 1906), 191.

CHAPTER NINE. HOOD, DAVIS AND THE ARMY OF TENNESSEE: ELEMENTS OF A CONFEDERATE DEBACLE

1. Wiley Sword, *Embrace an Angry Wind: The Confederacy's Last Hurrah—Spring Hill, Franklin, and Nashville* (New York: Harper Collins, 1992), 152–53, 263.

2. McMurry, *John Bell Hood*, 1–15; Hood, *Advance and Retreat*, 5–8; William C. Davis, *Breckinridge: Statesman, Soldier, Symbol* (Baton Rouge: Louisiana State University Press, 1974), 118–19.

3. McMurry, *John Bell Hood*.

4. Freeman, *Lee's Lieutenants*.

5. Perry D. Jamieson, *Death in September: The Antietam Campaign* (Abilene, Texas: Grady McWhiney Foundation Press, 1998).

6. Peter Cozzens, *This Terrible Sound: The Battle of Chickamauga* (Urbana: University of Illinois Press, 1991).

7. McMurry, *John Bell Hood*, 40, 83–86; Hood, *Advance and Retreat*, 67; Chesnut, *A Diary from Dixie*, 367.

8. See Woodworth, *Jefferson Davis and His Generals*, 125–99, 222–55.

9. Connelly, *Autumn of Glory*, 282–83.

10. *O.R.*, 38.5:988; Rowland, ed. *Jefferson Davis*, 6:132, 305, 334–35; Chesnut, *A Diary from Dixie*, 328; Strode, *Jefferson Davis, Confederate President*, 502–3; Hughes, *General William J. Hardee*, 184.

11. Dowdey and Manarin, eds., *Wartime Papers*, 821–22.

12. Rowland, ed., *Jefferson Davis*, 6:255; McMurry, *John Bell Hood*,

107–9; Connelly, *Autumn of Glory*, 352, 406; McMurry, *The Road past Kennesaw*, 16; *O.R.*, 38.4:728, 736.

13. McMurry, *John Bell Hood*, 89, 118–19; Connelly, *Autumn of Glory*, 22, 321–23, 417; Rowland, ed., *Jefferson Davis*, 6:286, 295–96; *O.R.*, 38.5:879–80, 885, 888–89; 52.2:708–9; Hood, *Advance and Retreat*, 128.

14. Rowland, ed., *Jefferson Davis*, 6:334–35; Connelly, *Autumn of Glory*, 419, 441; *O.R.*, 38.5:888–89, 892; Hattaway, *General Stephen D. Lee*, 123–26; McMurry, *John Bell Hood*, 84, 128–33; Hughes, *General William J. Hardee*, 225.

15. Rowland, ed., *Jefferson Davis*, 6:348; Jones, *A Rebel War Clerk's Diary*, 431; William J. Cooper, "A Reassessment of Jefferson Davis as War Leader: The Case from Atlanta to Nashville," *Journal of Southern History* 36 (1970): 199–201; McMurry, *John Bell Hood*, 158; Connelly, *Autumn of Glory*, 472.

16. McMurry, *John Bell Hood*, 163; Hood, *Advance and Retreat*, 274; *O.R.*, 45.1:1215, 1225.

17. McMurry, *John Bell Hood*, 169–76; Hood, *Advance and Retreat*, 278; Connelly, *Autumn of Glory*, 399–402, 490–92; 501–2; Hattaway, *General Stephen D. Lee*, 134–37; Hattaway and Jones, *How the North Won*, 646–47; Sword, *Embrace an Angry Wind*, 124–231.

CHAPTER TEN. HOMESPUN GENERALS: NONPROFESSIONAL OFFICERS IN THE CONFEDERATE ARMY

1. Ralph Lowell Eckert, *John Brown Gordon: Soldier, Southerner, American* (Baton Rouge: Louisiana State University Press, 1989), 110–11.

2. Warner, *Generals in Gray*, xx–xxi.

3. Parks, *General Leonidas Polk*, 153–386; Woodworth, *Jefferson Davis and His Generals*, 26–45, 156–60, 199, 239–41; Hattaway and Jones, *How the North Won*, 164.

4. Warner, *Generals in Gray*, 193; Michael B. Ballard, *Pemberton: A Biography* (Oxford: University of Mississippi Press, 1991), 133–34, 144–45, 154–55, 163.

5. Warner, *Generals in Gray*, xxiii, 102–3.

6. Davis to Polk, February 7, 1862, National Archives.

7. Harris to Davis, July 13, 1861, Isham G. Harris Papers, Tennessee State Library and Archives; *O.R.*, 4:365–66, 374–75; 51.2:180; Jones, *A Rebel War Clerk's Diary*, 41.

8. Warner, *Generals in Gray*, 89–90.

9. Ibid., 341–42.

10. *O.R.,* 7:130–31, 880; Charles P. Roland, *Albert Sidney Johnston: Soldier of Three Republics* (Austin: University of Texas Press, 1964), 295; Connelly, *Army of the Heartland,* 109–10.

11. Nathaniel Cheairs Hughes, Jr., and Roy P. Stonesifer, Jr., *The Life and Wars of Gideon J. Pillow* (Chapel Hill: University of North Carolina Press, 1993), 47–104; Milo Milton Quaife, ed., *The Diary of James K. Polk,* 4 vols. (Chicago: McClung, 1910), 4:5–9, 22.

12. Hughes and Stonesifer, *Pillow,* 213–37; *O.R.,* 7:255; Benjamin Franklin Cooling, *Forts Henry and Donelson: The Key to the Confederate Heartland* (Knoxville: University of Tennessee Press, 1987), 132–80; Horn, *The Army of Tennessee,* 93–98; Arndt M. Stickles, *Simon Bolivar Buckner: Borderland Knight* (Chapel Hill: University of North Carolina Press, 1940), 144.

13. Hughes and Stonesifer, *Pillow,* 254–55; Davis, *Breckinridge,* 343.

14. Davis, *Breckinridge,* 336–56; *O.R.,* 20.1:663–72, 789–90; Connelly, *Autumn of Glory,* 53, 56–60; James Lee McDonough, *Stones River— Bloody Winter in Tennessee* (Knoxville: University of Tennessee Press, 1980), 36, 148–49; McWhiney, *Braxton Bragg and Confederate Defeat,* 347–64.

15. Davis, *Breckinridge,* 58, 389–99; Cozzens, *This Terrible Sound,* 319–37; Bragg to Davis, November 30 and December 1, 1863, William P. Palmer Collection of Braxton Bragg Papers, Western Reserve Historical Society, Cleveland, Ohio; Connelly, *Autumn of Glory,* 273; James Lee McDonough, *Chattanooga—Death Grip on the Confederacy* (Knoxville: University of Tennessee Press, 1984), 227–28; Wiley Sword, *Mountains Touched with Fire: Chattanooga Besieged, 1863* (New York: St. Martin's, 1995), 235–36.

16. Davis, *Breckinridge,* 400–524.

17. Warner, *Generals in Gray,* xxi–xxii, 16, 19, 57, 171; T. Michael Parrish, *Richard Taylor: Soldier Prince of Dixie* (Chapel Hill: University of North Carolina Press, 1992), 125–28; Craig L. Symonds, *Stonewall of the West: Patrick Cleburne and the Civil War* (Lawrence: University Press of Kansas, 1997), 45; Eckert, *John Brown Gordon,* 16–26; Brian Steele Wills, *A Battle from the Start: The Life of Nathan Bedford Forrest* (New York: Harper Collins, 1992), 45.

18. Parrish, *Richard Taylor,* 68–125; Warner, *Generals in Gray,* 19, 171.

19. Warner, *Generals in Gray,* 16, 19, 171; Symonds, *Stonewall of the West,* 21–25.

20. Parrish, *Richard Taylor,* 128–37; Stephen Davis, "A Georgia Firebrand: Major General W. H. T. Walker." *Georgia Historical Quarterly* 64 (winter 1979): 447–60.

21. Parrish, *Richard Taylor,* 133–41.

22. Ibid., 152–53.

23. Ibid., 150–244; Freeman, *Lee's Lieutenants,* 1:366–487.

24. Parrish, *Richard Taylor,* 245–446.

25. *O.R.,* 11.1:970–71, 977, 979–80; Eckert, *John Brown Gordon,* 23–28; John B. Gordon, *Reminiscences of the Civil War* (Baton Rouge: Louisiana State University Press, 1993 [1903]), 58–59; Freeman, *Lee's Lieutenants,* 1:241–52.

26. *O.R.,* 11.2:628–29, 633–35, 637; Eckert, *John Brown Gordon,* 23–28; Gordon, *Reminiscences,* 70–79; Freeman, *Lee's Lieutenants,* 1:589–651.

27. Eckert, *John Brown Gordon,* 29–30; *O.R.,* 11.2:635; Freeman, *Lee's Lieutenants,* 1:240–48.

28. Eckert, *John Brown Gordon,* 30–36; *O.R.,* 19.1:1033–39; Freeman, *Lee's Lieutenants,* 2:211–12; Gordon, *Reminiscences,* 80–91.

29. *O.R.,* 19.1:1027, 1035; 27.2:445, 468–71, 481, 492, 93; Eckert, *John Brown Gordon,* 38–59; Freeman, *Lee's Lieutenants,* 3:21–100; Gordon, *Reminiscences,* 100–101, 151–57.

30. *O.R.,* 33:1124, 1321; Gordon, *Reminiscences,* 243–48; Eckert, *John Brown Gordon,* 63–72; Freeman, *Lee's Lieutenants,* 3:370, 443.

31. Gordon, *Reminiscences,* 314–74; Eckert, *John Brown Gordon,* 72–104; Freeman, *Lee's Lieutenants,* 3:557–612.

32. Eckert, *John Brown Gordon,* 104–14; Freeman, *Lee's Lieutenants,* 3:645–55; Gordon, *Reminiscences,* 395–413.

33. Gordon, *Reminiscences,* 429–38; Eckert, *John Brown Gordon,* 114–23; Freeman, *Lee's Lieutenants,* 3:726–39.

34. Warner, *Generals in Gray,* 307.

35. Wills, *A Battle from the Start,* 1–42.

36. Robert Selph Henry, *"First with the Most": Forrest* (Indianapolis: Bobbs-Merrill, 1944), 13–81.

37. Parker Hills, *A Study in Warfighting: Nathan Bedford Forrest and the Battle of Brice's Crossroads* (Danville, Va.: Blue and Gray Education Society, 1995), throughout.

38. Henry, *"First with the Most,"* 142–44; Wills, *Battle from the Start,* 102, 145–47.

39. Benjamin Franklin Cooling, *Fort Donelson's Legacy: War and Society in Kentucky and Tennessee, 1862–1863* (Knoxville: University of

Tennessee Press, 1997), 192–206; Wills, *Battle from the Start*, 89–102; Woodworth, *Six Armies in Tennessee.*

40. Woodworth, *Jefferson Davis and His Generals*, 265–66.

41. Symonds, *Stonewall of the West*, 1–177; Woodworth, *Six Armies in Tennessee.*

42. Symonds, *Stonewall of the West*, 181–260; Woodworth, *Jefferson Davis and His Generals*, 262–64; Buck, *Cleburne and His Command*, 187–200; Connelly, *Autumn of Glory*, 320.

Index